When Only God Can See

'This beautifully written and harrowing book does several things magisterially: it bears witness to the devastating experience of imprisonment in Egypt and the carceral houses-of-horror devised by the US in its War on Terror; it shows the centrality of faith in the lives of the Muslim prisoners whose stories are so sensitively rendered here; and tenderly details the dreams, prayers, communities and acts of resistance that sustained these prisoners when faced with forced disappearance, punishment, and torture.'

—Laleh Khalili, author of *Time in the Shadows*

'This is no easy read – but, for anyone who wants to understand the story of Muslim political prisoners in the twenty-first century and their unique connection to faith, it's essential reading. Quisay and Qureshi have welded together the experiences and reflections of prisoners held in torturous conditions across continents and given life to their inner strengths and sensitivities. In giving a substantive voice to Egyptian women prisoners as much as it does to Muslim men imprisoned in Bagram and Guantanamo, this book opens a holistic door into the very heart and soul of how we all survived some of the most brutal prisons in the world.'

—Moazzam Begg, former Guantanamo Bay detainee and author of *Enemy Combatant*

'After working for 30 years with survivors of brutal torture in Egyptian prisons and while watching with the rest of the world the horrors suffered by Palestinians in the war on the Gaza strip and the West Bank, *When Only God Can See* comes as a passionate revelation of the secret of endurance of people suffering extraordinary trauma. The secret is as simple as well as complicated as is Faith. A passionately written work which tenderly investigates the limitless resources of human beings who when subjected to horrors committed by other human beings, seek refuge and power in a realm that belongs to them alone, a conviction that comes as a rescue when all other forms of rescue are unattainable. A must-read to understand the limitless potential of a human spirit.'

—Aida Seif El-Dawla, psychiatrist and co-founder of El Nadeem Centre for Rehabilitation of Victims of Violence and Torture

'*When Only God Can See* presents the victims of a global "War on Terror" as protagonists in their own stories – despite suffering unspeakable traumas. In the midst of their incarceration, they turn back and speak to the One who created them with dignity. In examining the faith of Muslim political prisoners outside of a narrative of radicalisation, we not only see how powerful Islam is as a spiritual source of enlightenment, but how pervasive the cruel narrative surrounding Muslim political prisoners is.'
—Imam Omar Suleiman, author of *40 on Justice: The Prophetic Voice on Social Reform*

'Profoundly illuminating work that looks at how faith and prayer become acts of radical resistance. By bearing witness to the lives and stories of Muslim political prisoners at the putrefying heart of the American empire, this book is a record of both repression and resistance to it.'
—Suchitra Vijayan, co-author of *How Long Can the Moon Be Caged?: Voices of Indian Political Prisoners*

When Only God Can See

The Faith of Muslim Political Prisoners

Walaa Quisay and Asim Qureshi

Foreword by Omar Khadr and Layla al-Azhari

First published 2024 by Pluto Press
New Wing, Somerset House, Strand, London WC2R 1LA
and Pluto Press, Inc.
1930 Village Center Circle, 3-834, Las Vegas, NV 89134

www.plutobooks.com

British Library Cataloguing in Publication Data
A catalogue record for this book is available from the British Library

ISBN   978 0 7453 4895 7   Paperback
ISBN   978 0 7453 4897 1   PDF
ISBN   978 0 7453 4896 4   EPUB

This book is printed on paper suitable for recycling and made from fully
managed and sustained forest sources. Logging, pulping and manufacturing
processes are expected to conform to the environmental standards of the
country of origin.

Typeset by Stanford DTP Services, Northampton, England

Simultaneously printed in the United Kingdom and United States of America

Here, in this country, we are like God. We say Be! And it is {kun fa yakun}. Whatever we want we will get.

—[Senior Officer – Egypt]

Baby girl, we are not free. In Islam, people like us are called captives. There are different rulings for us.

—Auntie Magda to Asmaa – Qanater El Khayereya Women's Prison – Qalyubiyya, Egypt

I remember being in solitary confinement, when no one could see me except for Allah, I would cry so much when I recited the verse of Yaqub {I only complain of my grief and sorrow to Allah, and I know from Allah that which you know not}. When you are by yourself, all alone, this verse is such a strong reminder that Allah is always with you.

—Mansoor Adayfi – Guantánamo Bay

بِسْمِ ٱللَّهِ ٱلرَّحْمَٰنِ ٱلرَّحِيمِ

أَلَمْ يَعْلَم بِأَنَّ ٱللَّهَ يَرَىٰ

Does he not realise that God sees all?
(96:14)

Contents

Foreword

Omar Khadr and Layla al-Azhari

'What does it mean to come of age in confinement?' We, Omar and Layla, crossed the threshold of adulthood within the confining walls of the prison complexes in Guantanamo Bay and Egypt. Omar endured the distinction of being the youngest inmate in Guantanamo at just 15, and Layla, too was often the youngest in the cell, first being arrested in Egypt at 13, then again at 15 and 18. Asim and Walaa suggested we use this question as our starting point; but as we wield our pens our story feels less like the story of youth betrayed. Our story is one of finding freedom in God's power despite the control of the prison. Therefore, the question is not just what it means to come to age in confinement but to do so under His watchful Eye:

{Put him into a chest, then put it into the river. The river will wash it ashore, and he will be taken by 'Pharaoh,' an enemy of Mine and his.' And I endeared you with love from Me 'O Moses' so that you would be brought up under My 'watchful' Eye} (20:39).

At the age of 15 when I, Omar, was taken to Guantanamo everything physical was stripped away from me. I was lost in an ocean in every sense. I had to hold on to something that couldn't be taken away from me. My only hope; Islam. Holding on to Islam was pure survival. I still don't know why. It just was. As years passed, and I grew older, I started reflecting on what couldn't be taken away from me. What is this hope, why is it hope, and is it truly hope?

Before Guantánamo – this is an embarrassing admission – I had a bit of an inferiority complex as I desired a world that could be found in the West. Prison broke that inferiority complex towards the West and the white man. I was right there in prison – the core on which this society was built – a system of law but empty of morality. I could see that this elaborate system had a rotten core. For the longest time, the Qur'an was the only thing we had for comfort, that and each other as prisoners. I would read Surah Yusuf, and it was complete. Everything was laid out – from the start, the progression, and how it ended. I would read,

{And they cried, 'Could it be that you are Yusuf?' He said, 'I am Yusuf. This is my brother. God has been gracious to us: God does not deny anyone who is mindful of God and steadfast in adversity the rewards of those who do good'} (12:90).

The story is one hardship after another, but this verse is such a promise of hope. I found myself among the strongest men in Guantanamo's cages, but it was the humanity of Islam that struck me most. It was for this reason that I came to choose Islam. It does not criticise a person for being weak. It does not belittle someone for their brokenness. It was a strange conclusion to reach that it was okay to be human in the most dehumanising place. I do not know how I would have felt if I had been in Layla's place and was imprisoned by other Muslims.

While Omar had been captured unlawfully by America, my experience in Egypt has led me to the conclusion that even if there were no political prisoners, the injustice that even guilty people face in prison should be enough to collapse this institution. These are tyrants who administer oppression. I can never forget one of my cellmates, who killed her husband. She was beaten, stripped, and sexually assaulted in interrogation. The world needs to rethink the very notion of imprisonment, judgement, and punishment. Every time I was detained, I learned something new. I always found the psyche of soldiers and the guards to be an enigma. They had a warped view of God, women and law. The officer who electrocuted me and prevented me from praying believed he did this in the name of Islam. I was a threat to Islam. Some of them would apologise to us when they'd put us in handcuffs. They would say, 'I am sorry, my daughter, but I am only following orders.' My emotions would be a mix of anger and pity. My brother, submit your resignation. How can you sleep with this burden? Every night, you go home and lay your head on a pillow knowing that you locked innocent people in a cell. It was as if they were too afraid to listen to their own hearts, too afraid to carry the burden of their injustice.

Layla, you write of the apology of those who knew they oppressed you, and it takes me back to words used by the Pakistani officers, with beards down to their navels in open displays of piety, that would use the word *majburi* – that they wanted those of us who were sold to the Americans to grant them forgiveness because they were coerced. Perhaps they were asking for our forgiveness because they were fully aware God can see all they do – and they placed the burden of their guilt on us.

The title of this book *When Only God Can See* is fitting – it speaks to our collective experience as young people caught in a system of incarceration that were so far from one another geographically, but so intimately tied to a global malignancy of injustice. Prisons are terrible places. They serve little purpose other than to dehumanise and destroy, and were it not our certainty that God can see and control all that takes place, we would not have been able to take meaning from our experience in the way that we have. God's control of our affairs does not detract from the violence of these institutions, and so we must work together to end the daily indignities and torture that define modern day prisons.

(*Layla al-Azhari is a pseudonym*)

Acknowledgments

All praise and thanks are due to Allah, the final arbiter of all justice. We would like to begin by thanking the former prisoners who gave so much of themselves in the process of writing this book. We are honoured by the trust they placed in us to convey their stories of survival in the most difficult of circumstances. Although we were limited by our focus on those who were detained in the custody of Egypt and the US for the purposes of this book, we would like to acknowledge that there are Muslims who have been subject to carceral regimes across the world that have had their faith attacked in similar ways – far too many to list.

As we put the finishing touches to this book – we want to recognise the Palestinians who are fighting every single day to make known the settler colonial genocide that is taking place against the people of Gaza. Palestinian captives number in the thousands in Israeli custody – spanning decades – and yet, undeterred, they continue to remind the world of their right to a land that had been systemically stolen from them.

Our thanks to the whole team at Pluto Press for supporting this project and making it a reality. To our brilliant editor, Neda Tehrani, who believed in this book when it was simply an idea, but also to Sophie O'Reirdan, Patrick Hughes, James Kelly, Jonila Krasniqi, Robert Webb and Dave Stanford – we appreciate all your efforts. A special thanks to the anonymous reviewers, their comments, feedback, and encouragement was pivotal to the making of this book. Many thanks to Dr Laleh Khalili, Dr Aida Seif El Dawla, Moazzam Begg, Imam Omar Suleiman, and Dr Suchitra Vijayan. Also, to Safia Latif, whose stunning painting adorns the front cover of this book, you captured so much of what we were hoping to convey in a single image.

Walaa

To my father Hamed Quisay and my mother Eman Atuian, I am forever indebted wisdom, guidance, and endless encouragement.

Your stories, values, and faith are my anchor and guide. To my partner – Amr El Afifi – no one has supported me and inspired me in this path as much as you have. Thank you for standing by me, for your sacrifices, and for being my sounding board through the ups and downs of this journey. To my wonderful sisters, Gehad, Esteshhad, Eman and Baraa. Your strength and resilience inspire me every day. Your presence in my life has been one of my greatest blessings. A special thanks to Zainab Shah whose input was crucial to this project.

I owe a debt of gratitude to Mohamed Soltan, Abdullah El Shamy, Ola al-Qaradawi, Sami Alarian, Sara Mohammad, Halim Henish, Omar and Ammin Henish, Joshua Ralston, Shadaab Rahemtulla, Mina Ibrahim, Maysaa Alamoudi, Emad Shahin, Abdelrahman Ayyash, Mona Arafat, Deema Ayyash, Abdullah Alaoudh, Taghrid Al Sabeh, Tarek Younis, Khadijah El Shayyal, Basit Iqbal, Miray Philips, Hafsa Kanjwal, Sahar Ghumkhor, Muneeza Rizvi, Seif Al-Islam Eid, and many others who chose to remain anonymous. Your insights and wisdom have been a cornerstone in the crafting of this book. I am especially grateful to Ahmed and Selwan. Thank you for your constant support and guidance.

I would also like to express my deep appreciation to my colleagues at the School of Divinity at the University of Edinburgh for this constant support and encouragement. I am also thankful to the Leverhulme Trust for supporting this project.

Finally, I write this in memory of my beautiful revolutionary friend Roqiya Sabeg, who was always on the side of justice and on the side of the oppressed. This book is dedicated to my friend Suhaib Saad and 'amu Tawfik Ghanem. The prison walls will crumble and we will soon be reunited.

Asim

To my wife Samira, you have been so central to everything that I have undertaken – always willing to listen and provide your thoughts on the violence of a world that I am struggling to understand. To my sons Haytham, Aadam and Sulayman – as you come into your teenage years, I am increasingly proud of how much you centre the plight of the oppressed in your lives – always asking the

right questions about others, and always standing up for them as
you read, listen, learn, march and boycott. May Allah bless you all,
always, ameen.

To Abu and Ammi – for encouraging me to always centre *taqwa*
of Allah in every part of our lives. I am honoured to be your son
and to locate my love of Allah not only in your lessons, but also
in the way you live Islam. That has set the tone for a family that
has supported me through all my siblings; Usman, Imran, Sohaib
and Haaroon, their wives and all my nephews and nieces. Also,
to my other Ammi and my late father-in-law – in marrying your
daughter, I was granted a family that very much feels my own
because the values you have given your children, are ones that are
my own.

Many thanks to my CAGE family, without whom I would not
be able to have been able to do anything at all – you all are the
strength and backbone of my activism. I would never be able to
stand up without the support you give me. To the Muslim Aca-
demics group who always sharpen my thinking and provide the
necessary cathartic dose of dark humour that helps me survive the
daily aggressions and Islamophobia of this world. It has now been
fifteen years since I started working with the wonderful Team AH
– thank you for all you do. Last, but not least, to the scholars and
brothers of the Abu Bakr programme who have taught me how
to contemplate the Qur'an in ways that opened my heart to it –
studying with you and learning from you, has been one of the great
gifts that Allah blessed me with.

Introduction

When suspended in the air and in perfect sensory isolation, can the human person conceive of their being – or indeed their soul? This human exists in a void. They do not feel their fingers or toes. Their limbs do not touch. In fact, the mere notion of human touch or sensation is far beyond their possible worlds. They have no access to their laughter or screams. They exist beyond corporeality; they have no body to be violated or brutalised. They have no body that could be fatigued or feel pleasure. This human person cannot conceive of a brain to think or a heart to feel. Does this human exist?

This question haunted and permeated the work and life of tenth-century Muslim philosopher and polymath Ibn Sina. In the prisons of the castle of Fardajan near Hamadhan, Iran, where Ibn Sina languished; he wrote a short parable *Hayy ibn Yaqzan* (Alive the son of the Ever Wakeful) to illustrate this point through an allegory for the human soul.[1] According to Ibn Sina, this human does not need to refer to a body or senses to recognise that they exist. Amid his confinement, Ibn Sina argued that the human soul – separated and independent from the human body – is the means, 'by which God communicates His truth to the human mind, and indeed imparts all order and intelligibility to nature.'[2]

Abdelrahman ElGendy was 17 years old when he was snatched from the streets of Egypt and found himself in confinement for six years and four months. Years into his imprisonment, he began to feel distinctly separated from his body and senses – as though he were floating. The feeling of living beyond corporeality, a non-feeling of being disembodied was much more ominous for him. Speaking in the third person, Abdelrahman illustrates a truth very similar to the philosophical musings of Ibn Sina, albeit more disturbing:

1

He observes his life from afar ... He finds no response in his mind to any external stimuli, so he feels detached from his body and self. He always feels like he's in a dream or seeing the world through someone else's eyes. He halts in the middle of the street sometimes, uncomprehending that he is the protagonist of this scene. That these legs are his legs, and these steps are his steps, and that he is now returning home – the very scene which he had played repeatedly for years and years in the theatre of his imagination, imagining each time a new, wilder, more beautiful and passionate sensation. He stopped feeling when he was inside, because naturally, all the colorful sensations outside will make up for all those he lost. So the lack of feeling now must be evidence that he's still making it all up. That he's still inside.[3]

Abdelrahman was not necessarily looking for his soul. He knows he exists; although he may not know how. He is uncertain that his reality is the reality he finds himself. Was freedom a convoluted dream his mind had concocted? He had come to realise this disembodied state was a shared feature of depersonalisation – a disorder common to people who have undergone extreme trauma. Renowned psychiatrist Judith Herman clarified:

The psychological distress symptoms of traumatized people simultaneously call attention to the existence of an unspeakable secret and deflect attention from it. This is most apparent in the way traumatized people alternate between feeling numb and reliving the event. The dialectic of trauma gives rise to complicated, sometimes uncanny alterations of consciousness.[4]

Herman elaborated that unspeakable atrocities can illicit not just a sense of rage and pain, but also a sense of eerie calm and detachment. The meanings ordinarily attached to pain, dissolve and alter. The very notion of time changes. Slowly, the person may feel as though they are observing their reality as though it was someone else's reality. Their body ceases to be their own. They may know they are there – conceptually – but not feel it.

This often leads to what Herman calls a 'truncated memory'. In our interviews, many of the released prisoners would have significant memory lapses or lose a sense of chronology. They may feel an emotion related to memory but cannot remember it adequately, or it remains only as a sensory feeling. On other occasions, they would recall every small detail of a particular event, finding themselves at times, 'caught between the extremes of amnesia or of reliving the trauma, between floods of intense, overwhelming feeling and arid states of no feeling at all'.[5] Due to the prolonged and continuous state of traumatisation, prisoners often may consciously or subconsciously enter into altered 'trance states' – known as dissociation. This dissociation is a form of altered consciousness and awareness that induces deep numbing, time distortion and enhanced imagination, and can be associated with heightened deep spiritualisation.

What, then, becomes of the body, the soul, and the spiritual self, capable of recognising Truth and God in prison? The trauma of confinement seeks to violate the body and spirit. It could sever the prisoner's view of natural divine order or faith in humanity. Herman explains that in the aftermath of such violation, a new self is produced – one that projects not just the mundane reality of everyday life, but also views their body and soul as one that could be controlled and violated: 'Her image of herself in relation to others must include a person who can lose and be lost to others. And her moral ideals must coexist with knowledge of the capacity for evil, both within others and within herself'.[6] As the prison infrastructure seeks to sever or disrupt the prisoners' relationships with the divine – and with the world, body, soul, time, and community – religion becomes a significant shield. A porous cosmology engineered and regulated by God has the capacity to deride the buffered prison claim to omnipotence.

The prisoner, disembodied and cast outside of time, is reintegrated into the world through prayer. They seek the sun beyond bars, to identify the *qibla* (the direction of prayer towards Mecca), and reintegrate and mend the severed connection to the Muslim community – as well as situate their existence in a physical world, surrendering to the decree of God. Their hands are raised in prayer – *Allahu Akbar* – the first *takbir* – proclaiming Allah (God) is greater than anything – announcing prayer. Their bodies move in an organised, repetitive and meticulous manner.[7] They can feel their hands move, their fingers raise, their bodies bend, kneel and prostrate. Their bodies, for a few minutes, are rendered back into a full life – a spiritual one. They exist – not as a disembodied soul – but as their bodies move, they are a fully integrated soul and body. Time and time again, prisoners in this book relate intricate journeys of faith where deep spiritualisation is rendered into being. They affirm that the deification of the state or prison complex through its violence and control continues to be fickle in the face of God.

This book examines the unique ways in which Muslim political prisoners in both Egypt after the 2013 coup and under US custody after 2001 at Guantánamo Bay, in black sites, and on the US mainland experience their faith and its practices of ritual purity, prayer and modes of resistance in their daily lives in confinement. Based on interviews with former prisoners (24 in Egyptian custody and 12 in US custody), we sought to determine the role of faith in the lives of political prisoners – outside 'radicalisation' narratives that pathologise Islam and, indeed, prisoners. By examining the political detentions in Egypt, a predominantly Muslim country, and juxtaposing them with the experiences of those held in Guantánamo Bay, we aim to highlight the stark similarities of not just carceral control but *fiqhi* (jurisprudential) deliberations and practices. We also show the divergences of prisoner experiences all generally caged within the rubric of the global War on Terror. The experience of political prisoners is not entirely uniform, and so the book will also seek to understand the ways in which these prisoners experience hardship in their faith at various times in their journey – made stark by our choice of providing their experiences in a Muslim-majority country (Egypt) and a predominantly non-Muslim country (the US). Prisoner experiences vary due to generational divides, gender, political and religious outlooks, and often due to the very sites of detention themselves.

At the outset, religion in prison – as Rachel Ellis aptly notes – offers both freedom and constraint from within carceral control.[8] That is, religion can provide an alternative meaning-making schema that counters the totalising control of the prison and undermines its power. Furthermore, by affirming the moral worthiness of a believer, it repudiates state narratives of criminality and the inherent dangers of a prisoner.[9] At the same time, religious practices are directly shaped by the carceral condition and could potentially reinforce its control. In both Egypt and the US (including Guantánamo) – where much of this research is based – prison chaplains serve the role of inculcating the prison population with statist narratives that reinforce the all-encompassing power of prisons. Like prison doctors, prison chaplains serve an important role in the infrastructure of prisons. In our contexts, they do not just implicitly reinforce carceral ideologies, they are often actively involved in torturing prisoners, interrogating them, and even (in the case of the Grand Mufti of Egypt) authorising executions.

THE ISLAM OF MUSLIM POLITICAL PRISONERS

The Arabic word *din* is often translated as 'religion'; however, that does little to capture the holistic nature of what *din* is – much better described as the entire spiritual circulatory system of Muslim life – one that does not produce false dichotomies between the material world and the spiritual one. Muslim prisoners often embody this notion of *din*, as they are actively stripped of their ability to worship God freely – and more often than not – systematically denied the ability to worship, from the basics of ablution, to prayer and fasting.

The basic tenets of being a Muslim is a connection that runs between the heart and the limbs – in a flow that connects belief to its outward manifestation. Thus, to be a Muslim as described by the Prophet Muhammad to the angel Jibril, is the testifying of faith in one's heart alongside its outward declaration from the tongue. This is accompanied by four other acts that complete the basics of a Muslim life: prayer five times a day at least, the mandatory tax that is to be paid yearly to charitable causes, abstention from food, drink and sexual relations during Ramadan, and finally the performing of the pilgrimage to Mecca once in the Muslim's life. These five acts of worship are commonly known as the five pillars of Islam – the foundation of what it means to come into Islam as having fully submitted to God. Muslim prisoners have internalised a verse of the Qur'an that carries them through every single barrier placed in their path by their torturers – whether they be American or Egyptian: {be conscious of God as much as you are

5

able} (64:16). Through this verse, they navigate their restrictions in the knowledge of God's mercy – praying in their mind when their interrogators are beating them for physically praying, performing ablution with dust, or sharing food as a form of charity – even while their own stomachs ache from hunger.

The spiritual and ethical lives of Muslims are found to be in stations of belief – so Muslims are informed that they can rise in their station of belief from being a *muslim* (one who submits), to *mu'min* (one who believes), to the highest station of *muhsin* (the one who has constant awareness of Allah). Despite the severe restrictions on them, Muslims find ways to seek increasing their reward with God, by building community with one another through the teaching of the Qur'an (even if, like Uzair Paracha, it needed to be recited through the piping system between solitary confinement cells), or through building community with insects in the way Shaker Aamer did in Guantánamo Bay. Ultimately, Islamic ethics of justice permeates their carceral experiences. The seeking of justice is not just a matter of worldly restitution – but is connected directly to their afterlife. Thus, interrogators would regularly be frustrated in attempts to coerce political prisoners into becoming informants and collaborators – being routinely told that the price of freedom was not worth damnation in an afterlife.

BEARING WITNESS

Judith Herman begins her book *Trauma and Recovery* by making an acute statement that this book seeks to echo: 'The ordinary response to atrocities is to banish them from consciousness. Certain violations of the social compact are too terrible to utter out loud: this is the meaning of the word unspeakable. Atrocities, however, refuse to be buried.'[10] Herman identified the all-illusive bystander. This bystander is neither a perpetrator nor a victim. As they witness atrocities, they could be compelled by conscience to react or propelled by a sense of personal safety to retreat. The bystander – bearing witness to atrocity – must take a side. To compassionately listen to the survivor is to take their side. In contrast, to do nothing is also to take a side. Herman adds, 'It is very tempting to take the side of the perpetrator. All the perpetrator asks is that the bystander do nothing. He appeals to the universal desire to see, hear, and speak no evil. The victim, on the contrary, asks the bystander to share the burden of pain.'[11] The perpetrator thrives in a culture of forgetting and ambivalence. If forgetting is not possible, then they put the victim's integrity in question. If the victim still cannot be silenced, then the perpetrator makes sure that no one listens:

> After every atrocity one can expect to hear the same predictable apologies: it never happened; the victim lies; the victim exaggerates; the victim brought it upon herself; and in any case it is time to forget the past and move on. The more powerful the perpetrator, the greater is his prerogative to name and define reality, and the more completely his arguments prevail.[12]

From within the tradition of bearing witness, we write this book. We do not seek to make grand theoretical contributions. Rather, this book seeks to amplify prisoners' own voices in narrating their devotional practices, their commitments and struggles with God, their modes of resistance, and ultimately their pain and suffering. Although we are not discounting the importance of rigorous theoretical study of Islam in prison, it is our contention that any work that does not begin from the voices of the most aggrieved will ultimately have a skewed view. Furthermore, we are keenly aware of the possibility of research mimicking the very violence it seeks to study and thus pathologising and victimising our interlocutors further. As such, it was essential not to engage with the 'radicalisation' thesis at the heart of the War on Terror which posits religion and religious adherence suspect and potentially criminal. Instead, we engage the former prisoners we interviewed as human beings – not as extensions of criminalised identities or ideologies. In turn, our study of religion emphasises its centrality to their personhood, community-making, and prison life.

Violence can be enacted in the representation of the prisoners' narratives but ultimately it begins directly in the first encounter during the interview. One key issue we were concerned with was to avoid – as best we could – re-traumatisation. We utilised autobiographies and first- hand accounts – which were not sparse in the case of those held in US custody, but were less common in the Egyptian case. In both cases, we avoided asking in-depth questions about torture; however, in some interviews, former prisoners spoke of the horrific torture they endured. We allowed for space to share to the extent to which they were comfortable but consciously did not seek details that they did not choose to share. The accounts of torture documented here primarily come from second-hand reports from reputable organisations or from their own written accounts. We opted for pseudo-anonymisation in cases of former prisoners that are not as public about their experiences and are not easily identifiable from their stories – this is in the case of most of the Egyptians interviewed except a few well-known and public figures.

We write this book as believing Muslims – bearing witness not just to atrocity but to laughter and resilience. Joshua Ralston writes in his paper on the centrality of bearing witness to Muslim and Christian faith traditions: 'The primary criteria for becoming a Muslim is to recite the Shahada, a term that means testimony or witness and derives from the Arabic root for witness: sh-h-d ... For both Christians and Muslims, to bear witness is a key component of what it means to live in faithful submission to God.'[13] This article of faith intrinsically links the witness of God's oneness to justice: {Allah bears witness that there is no deity but God, and so do the angels and those with knowledge – that God is maintaining creation in justice. There is no deity except God, the Exalted in Might, the Wise} (3:18). Ralston states:

In Surat al-Nisa' (4:135), God implores those who believe to {be steadfast maintainers of justice, bearing witness for God, though it be against yourself, or your parents or kinsfolk, and whether it be someone rich or poor, for God is nearer unto both}. It is not enough, then, to bear witness to theological ideas. One is called to bear witness to a vision of God's rule or kingdom that combines truth and justice, what in Arabic is called *haqq* [truth].[14]

We thus invite you, also, to bear witness to the injustice and to share in the laughter as well as the pain of the former prisoners, as they reflect on their past and hope to build a future.

CARCERAL REGIMES AND THE GLOBAL WAR ON TERROR

Americans are asking, 'How will we fight and win this war?' ... Our response involves far more than instant retaliation and isolated strikes. Americans should not expect one battle, but a lengthy campaign unlike any other we have ever seen. It may include dramatic strikes visible on TV and covert operations secret even in success.

We will starve terrorists of funding, turn them one against another, drive them from place to place until there is no refuge or no rest. And we will pursue nations that provide aid or safe haven to terrorism.

Every nation in every region now has a decision to make: Either you are with us or you are with the terrorists.[15]

With these words, President George W. Bush on 20 September 2001 announced the commencement of the global War on Terror. Much critical research has since been produced on the subversion of legal norms to justify corrosive measures criminalising communities and waging war against nations. However, this book posits that the War on Terror was waged globally long before 9/11 and that the subversion of legal norms to criminalise 'suspect' populations, communities and identities is not new.[16] Thus we see George Bush's speech not as the beginning but rather as a significant point in a complex continuum. It is crucial to understand that the charge of terrorism is not regarded merely as a criminal act, but as an embodiment of a criminal identity capable of engaging in criminal acts. Sahar Aziz explains, 'Western countries considered terrorism a form of psychopathology that violated universal norms. In turn, terrorists were characterized as evil, irrational, pathological, and fundamentally different from the United States and its state allies whose violence was morally justified.'[17] Aziz points out that the Palestinian terrorist trope, particularly in the 1970s, was a significant precursor to the idea of the criminalised identity of the 'Muslim terrorist' as an allusive force of ideological violence. However, as Sylvia Chan-Malik notes, the Muslim terrorist trope did not just exist as a foreign identity, criminalising an external and allusive enemy. Islam signified a religious-racial archetype denoting the insurgency of Black Muslims and fuelling white anxieties. That is, 'the notion that Muslims are actively engaged in activities that rebel against and undermine Western "freedoms and democracy".'[18] She went on to explain that this 'laid out the ideological groundwork for how Islam and Muslims would exist within the nation's boundaries, as vehicles of harm to white Americans and U.S. liberal democracy.'[19]

While much can be said regarding the War on Terror waged globally – in Russia and former Soviet countries, in East Asia, Europe, South Asia, the Middle East, Africa, South America and the Caribbean – this book primarily focuses on Egypt and the United States. In his book *Counterterrorism Strategies in Egypt: Permanent Exceptions in the War on Terror*, Ahmed Abozaid points out that empirically the War on Terror waged by illiberal autocrats such as Bashar al-Assad or Hosni Mubarak is not significantly different from the War on Terror waged by democratically elected leaders like George Bush or Tony Blair.[20] He notes that a significant pitfall of dominant terrorism studies discourses is that they fail to engage with the long history of counterterrorism discourse – in autocracies as well as 'liberal democracies' – that intersect with 'war crimes, torture, mass killing, and even state terror'.[21]

In Egypt, Abozaid traces modern counterterrorism discourses of criminality to the British colonisation of Egypt. He explained, 'The official British occupation of Egypt in 1882 began, whereupon the occupation authorities adopted the same techniques and developed "modern" legal tools of torturing and the use of "legitimate" violence in dealing with Egyptian citizens and the opponents of the British presence and the occupation of Egypt.'[22] He identified three counterterrorism approaches which the British and subsequent regimes used as a mode of social control and discipline:

> The Egyptian authorities have strived for constructing a unified discourse that contributes to formulating a widely accepted

awareness about certain kinds of threats. This discourse aimed to normalise, institutionalise, and legitimise its practices and the way it deals with these threats and dangers. The first step is criminalising all forms of political opposition, and second is launching a wide range of legislations that systematically violate the rule of law and human rights. These steps allow the state's coercive apparatuses to distort all kind[s] of organisations, behaviours, and actions that contradict or oppose the authorities, thus facilitating the implementation of the third step that includes repressing and crushing the opposition, without any accountability or questioning of its violent, excessive, and unlawful practices against thousands of Egyptian citizens through the past century.[23]

The British colonising forces passed legislation against so-called 'subversive elements' and outlawed public demonstrations. The Egyptian regime at the behest of the British declared a state of emergency 'that obstructed the implementation of the penal code and relied on exceptional regulations'.[24] Subsequent regimes would utilise emergency law and governing by exception as a central counterterrorism strategy. This would not just include public efforts to quash dissent and political participation, but would also signify a massive expansion of the carceral state and intelligence apparatus (*mukhabarat*) to surveil, criminalise and detain those with the 'potential to dissent'. Hence, governing by exception allowed for the criminalisation not just of political dissidents but families, neighbours, and those in the 'wrong place at the wrong time'. Abozaid noted, 'Nasser's regime employed imprisonment, silencing, and narrowing the freedoms of expression, assembly, association, and movement to justify using torture against thousands of political dissenters (especially leftists and Islamists) who had been labelled and classified as "terrorists".'[25] Anwar El Sadat's era marked a short-lived hiatus on imprisonment (1973–77). In 1977, his free-market policies led to bread riots which he dubbed *intifadat al haramaya* (the uprising of the thieves). Sadat again announced emergency law and began a campaign of wholesale detention of leftwing political opponents.[26] After the ratification of the Camp David treaty with Israel in 1978 and the fear that the

Iranian Revolution of 1979 posed, the government arrested more than 1,500 opposition figures.[27] After the assassination of Sadat, Hosni Mubarak ascended to power and declared a 'state of emergency' that lasted throughout his 30-year reign.

Hosni Mubarak was overthrown on 11 February 2011. The protesters in the street raged against the nexus of state surveillance, torture, police brutality and poverty, while the military stepped in to oversee the 'transition' of power. This proved to be a violent battle between competing forces, with the military demanding compliance and complicity from civilian partisans. In late June 2012, Mohamed Morsi – a leading Muslim Brotherhood figure – would be elected as the first civilian president of Egypt. Less than a year later, Morsi would be overthrown, sent to prison where he would die and the Egyptian military would conduct the largest massacre in modern Egyptian history – the Rabaa massacre:

> The main narrative of the new regime was that Morsi, the [Muslim Brotherhood], and other Islamist movements were tyrant-terrorists. Between June 30 and August 14 of 2013, Egyptian police and military forces killed more than 1,000 pro-Morsi protesters and injured more than 4,000. Human Rights Watch (HRW) called what happened in Eastern Cairo's Rabaa Square a 'massacre' and 'a crime against humanity' (HRW, 2014). One year later, General Abdul Fatah El-Sisi (the minister of defence and the architect of the coup d'état) became President.[28]

Three weeks after General Sisi overthrew President Morsi, he called for mass protests that would give him a mandate to 'eradicate terrorism' – which then legitimised the subsequent massacre in Rabaa.[29] Human rights organisations estimate that there have been 60,000 political prisoners in Egypt since the military coup.[30]

Like in Egypt, the marker of the War on Terror in the US (and by extension the UK) was circumventing legal norms and governing by exception. The US mobilised networks of global security apparatuses to wage war on an unnamed enemy classified primarily through subversive identities. Fifty-four countries worldwide participated in the US's rendition programme.[31] Many of the Egyptian prisons cited in this book were also sites of US rendition, such as

State Security Intelligence National Headquarters in Nasr City, Abu Zabaal Prison, Damanhour Prison, Lazoghli Security Intelligence Headquarters, Mukhabarat al-Aama Headquarters and Tora Prison.[32] Furthermore, the US has exercised its rendition programmes in some of the most notorious prisons in the Middle East – in Syria, Iraq, the United Arab Emirates, and Jordan.[33] However, the first move internationally was waged in Bosnia. Bosnian citizens of Algerian origin or those connected somehow to Saudi Arabia through work were depicted as threats:

Two weeks after the 9/11 attacks two young men in Bosnia, Nihad Karsic and Almin Hardaus, were kidnapped by US military agents, subjected to sensory deprivation, beaten and finally held and interrogated in metal shipping containers. The same techniques would later be used on those captured in Afghanistan and placed on rendition flights to Guantánamo Bay and other secret prisons around the world.[34]

While enforced disappearance in secret detention facilities was a significant tool in keeping detainees outside legal protections (a tool used very frequently in Egypt), there were also other places where prisoners would be 'disappeared'. This included the use of black sites, rendition, proxy detention, military detention facilities and also civilian buildings.[35] In that period, the government of Pakistan was heavily involved in facilitating mass detentions by proxy. Around 85 per cent of those detained in Guantánamo, were individuals sold to the US by the Pakistani government for $5,000 each. Many were aid workers, business people, or ordinary civilians.[36] Pakistan also became a site of detention outside any form of legal protection, with sites established all over the country 'located from the south in the provinces of Sindh, through Balochistan, Punjab, and up to Kashmir and the North-West Frontier Province.'[37] Before being sent to Guantánamo Bay, many others would undergo proxy detention in the Middle East. These countries often subject suspects to extreme torture in cooperation with the United States – allowing the US to escape legal or moral culpability but still able to use confessions extracted under torture. The most infamous of cases include the Fara' Falastin prison in Syria –

a country that was ostensibly labelled as part of an 'axis of evil' by the US.[38] In theorising these relationships between carceral sites of torture, Darryl Li conjures the image of an archipelago of detention sites that flow from the carceral metropole of the US:

> ... if the image of an island prison is meant to convey Guantánamo's allegedly special status outside the law, one must also bear in mind that archipelagos are only the above-water aspects of larger interlinked, submerged formations. For each extraterritorial and extraordinary prison like gitmo, there are many more 'ordinary' prisons and detention sites run by other governments in their own territory. These act as sorting centers and dumping grounds for people detained at the behest of the United States.[39]

In his chapter 'From Exception to Empire', Li writes of the first weeks after 9/11 when groups of naturalised Bosnian men who had taken part in the *jihad* (struggle) in the early 1990s had their citizenships removed on the threat of repercussion by the US. Two separate jurisdictional issues arose for the Americans: they ultimately wanted these men to be removed to the custody of their countries of origin – Algeria refusing to take those who originated from their country, while Egypt was more than willing to take their own nationals. Egyptian diplomats met with Bosnian and US officials on the very day their national had his second Bosnian citizenship revoked – fast-tracking his rendition and disappearance into Egypt's carceral system. Close relations between the US and Egypt since Camp David in 1978 and the pumping of billions of dollars of military aid effectively placed Egypt in the position of an extension of the US carceral state – whereas Algeria felt no need to take any such position, resulting in its own nationals being sent to Guantánamo Bay.[40] Detention by the US authorities thus became less about crime and punishment, and became more a form of filtering through the US's geopolitical relations with other nations and a hierarchy of citizenship:

> When Guantánamo is viewed not as an aberration, but as the most visible node of a global network of formal and informal incarceration arrangements, citizenship's importance in deter-

mining where detainees are sent and how they are disposed of becomes visible. Rather than debating whether 'exceptional' sites are spaces for the absence of law or its excess, we can attend instead to how empire mobilizes multiple state sovereignties as a way of structuring and mediating unequal power relations. For example, the experiences of those captured in Afghanistan differed according to their citizenship. For Yaser Hamdi, U.S. citizenship meant rapid transfer from gitmo to a military brig in the continental U.S. and prompt review of his case by the Supreme Court. For British Muslims, the result was a relatively early return home thanks to pressure from a key U.S. ally. However, for Yemenis, citizenship from a 'weak state' condemned them to languish in prison, even when individually cleared for release, simply because their government was deemed incapable of controlling them.[41]

Before being sent to Guantánamo Bay, the prisoners were first detained in the Bagram or Kandahar Airbases in Afghanistan for processing. These were among the worst torture sites in the world.[42] Prisoners were subsequently transported to Guantánamo Bay, Cuba. Since Guantánamo was not situated on US soil, the US government argued that it was not under duty to uphold the Geneva Conventions or US constitutional obligations.[43] However, as mentioned by Darryl Li above, Yaser Hamdi and two others were detained on US soil as enemy combatants and remained for years in solitary confinement at the Charleston Naval Brig in South Carolina – unlike the Guantánamo Bay detainees, they were denied the US Constitution, despite being on US soil.

The existence of CIA black sites, proxy prisons and Guantánamo Bay in some ways mask how they operate as an extension of incarceration practices in the US domestically. Many of the standard operating procedures used against Muslim prisoners in international US custody found their genesis in a long history of 'Supermax' prisons that have warehoused disproportionally large numbers of Black men. The first real engagement that the US carceral system had with Muslims came in the 1960s as members of the Nation of Islam (NOI) were detained in large numbers due to the state's perception of them as politically seditious – heralding the increased use of solitary confinement to attempt to deter proselytising efforts by NOI prisoners to other Black prisoners. These restrictions were not simply accepted, as the NOI leadership supported the efforts of their prisoner population by funding legal challenges to their restrictive conditions:

> Prison officials sought to undermine NOI practice by splitting up adherents, placing them in solitary confinement, and denying them access to basic necessities like drinking water and adequate health care. In the years that followed, incarcerated devotees filed myriad grievances, and NOI leadership brought a case to the U.S. Supreme Court, *Cooper v. Pate*, arguing that incarcerated persons could sue state prisons for religious discrimination under the 1871 Civil Rights Act. The Supreme Court ruled in their favor, thereby supporting greater religious protection inside correctional facilities.[44]

The racist policymaking of the US carceral system consistently pathologised the beliefs and behaviours of NOI members as the FBI's counter-intelligence programme (COINTELPRO) framed their activism as a public danger. In perhaps the earliest example of the US attempting to dictate the form of Islam that its prisoner population could practice as a form of pacification, they would only permit NOI prisoners to have access to clergy from the Ahmadiyya community – one that was seen as more obsequious to US domestic policies. In 1957, the warden of Attica Prison wrote of four prisoners who had identified as Muslim, which he believed to be a gimmick:

> Muslim prisoners requested access to the Quran in Arabic, religious literature published in Black newspapers, and correspondence with ministers such as Malcolm X in Harlem and Robert X Williams in Buffalo. They challenged the lawfulness of punishing them for their religious beliefs with such measures as solitary confinement and loss of good time. In many of these cases, the state used the Ahmadiyya Movement in Islam (AMI) to undermine these claims, offering prisoners only English translations of the Quran and correspondence with Ahmadi religious

leaders. An early precursor to the contemporary 'good Muslim/ bad Muslim' dichotomy in the United States ... .[45]

The ill-treatment of NOI prisoners ended up exposing the US (in) justice system as described by SpearIt in his work on the treatment of Muslim prisoners in domestic US custody: 'For prison officials, Muslims in prison represented the ultimate intersectional identity: all at once, he was a criminal, prisoner, Black, poor, gangster, and a religious subversive.'[46] Carceral practices in the global War on Terror did not emerge as an anomaly; rather, they built on top of the pre-existing structures of oppression and repression that had played a significant role in resulting in a widespread system of mass incarceration. The framework that was used to target civil rights activists and those identified as 'Black nationalists' was re-purposed in counterterrorism efforts in order to present Muslims as being a special threat.[47] The well-established practice of solitary confinement was taken to a completely different level of repression, as Supermax facilities were re-engineered to include Communications Management Units (CMUs) that restrict, manage and monitor all of a prisoner's external communications. The CMUs have been used on 213 individuals; all but two of whom are Muslim.[48]

The reality of the US criminal justice system is that close to 98 per cent of all criminal convictions are secured through plea deals – largely due to the emphasis on harsh sentences for those who choose any attempt to defend themselves in the courts.[49] In the context of the global War on Terror, the sentencing regime is so extreme that most prisoners refuse to engage in the process of defending themselves for two reasons. The first is that after 11 September 2001, the creation of a new class of offence in the US, called 'material support for terrorism', made almost any activity by Muslims deemed to be an act of supporting terrorism, including the giving of charity.[50] The other is the extremity of the terrorism enhancement that is applied to cases involving Muslims, where any indication of terrorism involvement (even where the case is not about terrorism) can result in the addition of decades onto a sentence.[51] As with the prisoner accounts related in this book, we are less interested in notions of guilt and innocence, because the very nature of the legal regimes they have been forced to engage in are political.

The accounts of the political prisoners detained on the US mainland, which include Yahia Lindh, Uzair Paracha, Babar Ahmad, Adel Abdel Bary and Sami al-Arian, represent just some of the severe conditions that Muslims are forced to endure in their daily lives. Their experience is not just connected to the NOI inmates of the 1960s, but rather their experience sits on a continuity that began with the transatlantic slave trade. Uzair Paracha couldn't help but make these connections as he considered the history of the US in light of his own detention experience:

> There was a book I read in prison by Sylviane Diouf called *Servants of Allah* about the experience of Black Muslims in the transatlantic slave trade. I used to tell brothers that I've read so many books on Islamic history from the time of the Prophet through to the time of Salahuddin Ayyubi and many others, but I could not relate to anyone as much as the brothers and sisters who were sold into the slave trade. I am not saying that I went through what they went through. They were maimed, beaten and raped, they went through so many hardships, but at the same time there were so many things like the issue of no respect for their clothing, their need to cover themselves. There were so many things that I could really relate to. Ayuba Suleiman Diallo was in Maryland, and I knew brothers who were being held in Maryland, you feel that they were on [the] land we are on. They obviously went through something much worse than us, and I'm not trying to make that claim we are on the same level, but I feel that I could relate to that.

The global War on Terror is simply the latest in a series of oppressions that the US has never come to terms with; rather, like a shape-shifter, it has morphed into another iteration of its oppression, claiming new public panics as it evades scrutiny over its previous ill practices. Right now, it is Muslim political prisoners that are placed through a largely exceptional form of control through the exercise of repressing every part of the belief system – except this is the one area that is almost impossible to control, as these Muslims continually find ways to be faithful. As the system shifts to find new ways to be violent, Muslims pivot, secure in the knowledge of God's ultimate mercy. In this book, we examine the myriad of ways Muslims practice their faith in different moments of confinement. From the first moment of capture and throughout the life cycle of detention, we examine how they worship and maintain ritual purity, how they forge community and study together, their distinct relationships with the supernatural, the torture they endure and how they resist it.

1
Custody

CIA Black Site
Bagram Airbase – Parvan, Afghanistan

Waiting to be executed by his captors, Mansoor Adayfi prayed to Allah as he sat kneeling in the bitter cold of Afghanistan. Echoing around him, he could hear the shuffling of men, women and children as the physical darkness they were forced to endure only served to reflect the darkness of their situation. There was a constant stream of crying, punctuated by the crunch of a soldier's boot breaking through their bitterly cold bones, leading to wails that would go through them even deeper than the cold that had set in. Mansoor knew nothing of his fate, but despite his young age of 18, his Afghan captors believed him to be a middle-aged Egyptian man – a man they believed to be a senior member of al-Qaeda. These militias had spoken of the bounties they would receive from the American soldiers for handing over such a prized suspect, and yet this mistake in identity did little to assuage Mansoor's belief that he would be killed:

> Waiting on my knees to be executed, I wished that I could see my mother one last time to say goodbye. I regretted my sins and the mistakes I'd made, and I prayed to Allah to forgive me, wishing that I was closer to Him and had done more good deeds in my life. One day, we all will stand before Him. He knows I haven't wronged these people who tortured me. He knows I have caused harm to no one.[1]

As a whipsmart young man, Mansoor had left his family and rural life in Yemen at the age of 14 to seek his fortune elsewhere. A series of opportunities opened for him, resulting in his arrival in Afghanistan prior to the al-Qaeda attack on the US on 11 September 2001. Instead of finding work, he found himself caught in the maelstrom of international events, becoming a victim of an American collective punishment on anyone who might be in any way connected to al-Qaeda – even if all they shared was their faith.

A teenager, Mansoor found himself hanging from his wrists from the ceiling of a room he couldn't quite make out – the plastic wire cuffs cutting into his skin as the CIA interrogated him about his 'true' identity. They kept him hanging naked in this position while they electrocuted him over his body, being dissatisfied with the answers he gave until they got what they wanted – a confession that he was Adel – an Egyptian man double his age. He would be their Adel, providing the intense pain would stop. For Mansoor, this would only be the beginning of his torture, resulting in the one litany that he would recite millions of times over the following 14 years of detention, 'Allah, oh Allah', the only sanctuary and succour he could find. They would be the same words that taxi driver Dilawar would repeat every single time he was struck by US soldiers at Bagram, each invocation resulting in mocking and further blows until they murdered him.

Mansoor sought solace from his torture by turning to Allah, placing his difficulties within a larger metaphysics. This re-situating of what he considered necessary in those moments was a shift that many other prisoners also experienced. Rather than resigning himself, he thought of his own life and his ultimate resurrection before Allah. For many of those captured, the seemingly inescapable moment of capture and detention could only be resolved through justice in an afterlife.

Like many others who had been sent to Guantánamo, Mansoor had been sold for bounties to US military forces by those unscrupulous enough to take advantage of the suspect identity of being a foreigner in Afghanistan or Pakistan. Although the direct target of the US principal attack was Afghanistan, it only later emerged that the vast majority of those detained had been captured outside of Afghan borders, with over two-thirds from inside neighbouring Pakistan. Nearly the entire population of those who would go on to be eventually detained had nothing to do with al-Qaeda, but found themselves in custody due to US bounties of between $5,000 to $5 million being offered for the capture of foreign nationals based in Pakistan or Afghanistan. As Pakistan's former President Pervez Musharraf wrote in his autobiography, 'We have captured 672 and handed over 369 to the United States. We have earned bounties totalling millions of dollars [2] ... .'

For those captured in Afghanistan and Pakistan due to the bounties on offer, there was a sense of deep betrayal by their fellow co-religionists. Many of these Muslims had assumed that their sharing of faith with other Muslims would afford them some degree of protection over their rights, treatment and the sanctity of their lives. This erroneous belief was brought into stark contrast for the captured by the acknowledgement of their guards. The Pakistani soldiers and policemen, in particular, made explicit apologies to those they were handing over to the Americans. There is an expression of helplessness, of compulsion, that was being expressed by the Pakistani officials as they sold those under their charge: 'majburi', the call of those dispossessed of any agency when faced with the violence of a larger force.

The Sudanese Al Jazeera cameraman, Sami Elhaj, was taken by Pakistani officers and held at the instruction of the US in December 2001. Despite Sami's status as a journalist, this offered him little protection: the US officials determined to hold him for information Sami might have about Al Jazeera. Sami's conversation with his Pakistani guards turned on matters of theology, in relation to the possibility of harm that might come to him after he was handed over to the Americans. His captors believed there was a possibility that Sami might be executed by the Americans. Much in the same vein as Mansoor Adayfi, Sami expressed how death was something he did not fear, as he believed in the justice of an afterlife, but he did question why his Muslim brothers would sell him:

'What's the story here? Why are we being sold to the Americans?'
'We are forced to do this,' [the guard] replied, with flimsy excuses that they were following orders.
'We will not forgive you,' I said, 'in front of God Almighty. We will claim our rights from you there.'[3]

From the very beginning of the detention experience, many Muslim men who were detained by the US through the role played by partners in Pakistan and Afghanistan situated their difficulties within a larger metaphysics – choosing to understand their plight as a difficulty that they would have to accept in their present moment, but that would ultimately be recompensed in an afterlife. The men turned to praying to Allah, but also maintained a sense of personal accountability by refusing to simply accept that their detention was the very end of their story. Ultimately, they would all be placed on rendition flights to Guantánamo Bay, having first been processed through the airbases at Bagram and Kandahar in Afghanistan. As Mansoor Adayfi describes, this was never without holding on to some semblance of faith:

> Allah, oh Allah. I bear witness that there is no deity but Allah, I bear witness that Muhammad is the messenger of Allah. Allah, oh Allah.
> I told myself that I would be strong when they came for me. I'll make them work. I won't walk. So they dragged me, my toes digging into the dirt. Allah, oh Allah. They threw me to the ground and tore off my clothes and stripped me naked. They searched me in the worst way, and what did they think they would find after I had been tortured and left naked for months? They pulled a hood over my head, put me into a burlap sack, and taped me up. But they didn't shoot me. They threw me into what I imagined was a truck and tied me to the floor. At least the floor was warm. Engines rumbled to life and shook my entire body. I wasn't in a truck; I was in an airplane.[4]

Tora Prison Complex – Cairo, Egypt
HMP Long Lartin – South Littleton, United Kingdom
Metropolitan Correctional Center (MCC) – New York
ADX Florence – Colorado

Adel Abdel Bary closed his eyes as he thought of his torture in Egypt during the 1980s. He had been in and out of the prisons of Hosni Mubarak twelve times in the space of ten years, with torture being a frequent part of his detention experience. When he was first arrested, in 1982, he was a student at 'Ain Shams University, intent on reading law to combat the injustices he had witnessed in society – convinced that Islam had solutions to the endemic corruption that had plagued Egyptian society from the colonial period, through the reigns of Gamal Abdel Nasser, Anwar Sadat, and then Mubarak. In his mind, the path he had embarked on carried the risk of detention without charge – he was convinced that the work of seeking justice for the dispossessed could not be done without challenging the state.

That first arrest has never left Adel – detention at the infamous Tora political prison – located on the banks of the Nile as you follow it south, close to the Pharaonic relics at Giza. It is branded into his memory, because the brutality of his treatment only reinforced for him the pressing need for change in Egypt. He was beaten beyond any recognition, until the lead interrogators were unable to identify him by his face any longer. He turned his attention to Allah during this period, the only One who could provide a balm to his difficulties:

> I am going to tell you that during this time, that when you pray, you wish something, you ask Allah for something small. My ask, to Allah, was not to go home or to be released, it was just that the door of the cell not to be opened anymore. Every time the cell of the door would open, I knew I was going to be tortured. I asked Allah just that the door not be opened anymore. That was the maximum. Sometimes I prayed, but I had no idea how many *rakat*s I had prayed, just that I had prayed. In my cell, I would pray and sometimes I would fall asleep during my *salat*; I would just collapse and not know which prayers I had performed fully or at all.

During the periodic moments of freedom he was permitted over the following ten years, Adel somehow managed to complete his law degree and establish a law practice, one that would provide support to those who were detained without charge or trial. He would always remember, though, that it was *Muslim* interrogators in Egypt that would treat him so awfully, that they would tell him that they were Muslim, but would then tell him that his prayers, his cries and his invocations could not be heard, that 'Allah cannot hear you here.' Despite the years in detention, Adel was never once convicted of a crime.

In 1992, Adel finally decided that the long-term future of his family could not be secured in Egypt, and so he travelled to the UK where he felt that at least he would be able to continue with his political activities free of government intrusion. For seven years, he finally felt the safety of a regular family life, even openly carrying out his political campaigning against the Mubarak regime. That would all change in 1999, when the US government would seek Adel's extradition from the UK, resulting in a period of detention that would last for 13 years, without charge or trial. Adel spent those years attempting to gain the ability to even see the evidence against him, let alone actually being able to challenge it from the UK.

Adel ended up spending the next eight years in maximum security prisons in the US, where he took a plea deal because of the oppressive conditions that make the criminal justice system frightening, but also the risk of living the rest of your life in a 'Supermax' – a system of incarceration that has become more akin to warehousing of human beings, rather than a prison system that considers how to help those in its custody:

> One thing you have to understand when you arrive in the US system, is that you cannot even think of having any other choice other than taking a plea deal … The plea deal was going to be a potential range between eight years left, or the prospect of life without parole. The other aspect was the conditions of the Supermax – which are the worst prisons in the world. I was facing the prospect of solitary confinement; you can't even see your doctor in person, it is only through a camera. You can only see your family through glass and you have one 15-minute phone call a month which they can take away from you, so you have to wait a full whole month. You can't talk to or see anyone.

It was only at the end of his entire time in prison in the UK and US that evidence emerged that would have vindicated Adel, evidence that the British had in their possession all along. By the time of its revelation, already 21 years of his life had been taken away from him and his family.

Rabaa Al Adawia Square – Cairo
Cairo Stadium – Nasr City, Cairo, Egypt

In Egypt, 14 August 2013 was the day it all began – the day of the Rabaa massacre. Al Jazeera journalist Abdullah El Shamy was detained by plain-clothed police officers. The stench of blood and indignation suffocated the Nasr City streets. Abdullah was not scared. He was angry.

For the last 24 hours, he had witnessed the streets flow with the blood of the thousand souls lost that day. The mosques were turned into morgues. The makeshift field hospital was crammed with the bodies of the silent dead and the piercing wails of the injured. As horrifying as the screams were, the silence was even more terrifying. Abdullah pondered how this snapshot, in one day, was enough blood for a lifetime. As he was being taken away, he looked up to the sky. There was smoke everywhere, but the screams had stopped. All that was left was the eerie quiet. Soldiers crowded the streets and people were looking out from their balconies:

> For a moment, I started thinking. Why is everyone just watching us? Is that it? A few hours ago, almost one thousand people were just killed – just like that. People are just going about their life like nothing happened ... And then the moment you leave the square, people are fine. Cafes are open. You would think as someone who has just witnessed what you've witnessed, that people might be angry that people are being killed just a few kilometres away but that just didn't happen.

First, he was taken to a station by the airport and put in a cell with 29 other people detained from Rabaa. The detainees were being moved in a frenzy; no one knew or understood what was happening. The officers moved them at 4 a.m. the following day. They were then transported to the stadium. The stadium was packed – about 900 prisoners were being moved in crowds. And from the stadium, they were split up into groups. His group was the first to arrive at the stadium. They were told to squat in lines and the officers watched them closely. Out of nowhere, the officers would strike the prisoners with a belt to their faces and back or stomp on them with their military boots: 'This was not sporadic or random. It is on purpose. And the purpose is to make you rethink your dignity. It is an intentional act that aims to make you as a prisoner less willing to resist.'

They were moved into the conscripts' quarters, which were filthy with garbage, and food and human waste. The prisoners were made to clean the quarters. The officers used a welder to break down the metal bed frames to allow for maximum space to fit as many detainees as possible. At one point, someone rushed in and called for the welder. Prisoners outside were dying:

We were hearing loud screams from one of the trucks loaded with prisoners coming in. But the thing is throughout these hours of waiting, it was normal to hear people screaming. See, the ventilation in these trucks is more than inhumane. Actually, there isn't any kind of ventilation at all. The material these trucks are made of means that in the winter it is extremely cold and in the summer it is scorching hot. The prisoners were kept in [the trucks] for a very long time. You can imagine forty people packed in a boiling metal vehicle less than two metres long. They were screaming and begging for water. Of course, as is common for Egyptian police officers, they started making fun of them. The prisoners started shouting back at them: 'We are dying!' The police replied: 'Well, we want you to die!' Eventually, the voices started to fade. The people started dying from thirst and from heat. [The police] couldn't even open the door because the door swung inward and the people by the door were already dead. They had to call the welder to break it open.

From 14 August 2013 onwards, the military orchestrated concurrent massacres against Egyptians who opposed the coup – in Rabaa, Nahda and then the truck (actually a metal shipping container) massacre. For those later detained, this meant that the moment of capture did not signal a break into a new reality of incarceration and prisons, but rather a continuation of a very bloody one.

It was not until a week later, in a holding cell where Abdullah was crammed in with 86 other detainees that a different reality set in. The metal doors were shut and he began to realise he was likely going to languish in prison for a long time.

Amn al-Watani – Cairo
Qanater El Khayereya Women's Prison – Qalyubiyya, Egypt

Unlike Abdullah, Asmaa was not particularly political, or religious for that matter. She was a new mother of a small baby boy. After his birth, she experienced serious mental health issues including suffering from severe post-partum depression, and she was further diagnosed with borderline personality disorder. Her psychiatrist prescribed strong anti-psychotic medication to reduce the intensity of her emotions and manage her symptoms.

One day, Asmaa had to go to the bank due to a fault with her card, and on her way was sexually harassed by a taxi driver in front of an old man, a bystander to her abuse. Asmaa was incensed that the old man stood there and did nothing:

By the time I realised what was going on, I began to feel a burst of anger. The medication causes a delay in my response; so I had this anger inside me but I didn't know why. I went into the bank and when my card still didn't work, this anger was mixed with that anger and I started screaming hysterically. I was disoriented and escorted out. A police officer started following me. I was walking on a side street. He unzipped his trousers and took out his penis. Then I realised that he was starting to pin me down and forcing me onto the hood of a car. As soon as my mind could actually gather what was happening – I started to scream.

By then, the officer had zipped his trousers back up, as people started to gather. This was when she began to feel his blows as he beat her, words spraying as he continually shouted at her. She fought back though, and shouted – how could she be seen as the one in the wrong? The bystanders began to hush her, in an attempt to calm her down, even yelling, 'You're going to get yourself in trouble; just be quiet', while others shouted that she was not raised right:

I went home in a state of complete anger. Why am I being touched? Why couldn't I defend myself? Why am I feeling this delay in reaction? Why can't I get my rights? Why are the police treating me this way? Why am I ill? I was angry. I was angry at everyone. I was angry at myself and those that stood by and watch him beat me; they were normal people. This was the reaction of normal people.

Asmaa's sense of helplessness drove her to post a video on her private Facebook account. She was angry at the world, at herself, and at the country. Most of all – she was broken.

Someone leaked her video and it became a matter of public debate. A few days later, her husband called her in a panic. The video blew up. She knew that it was only a matter of days before she would be arrested, but despite this, she felt a strange sense of apathy. There was no fear, just anger. She did not want to run or hide. She wanted them to come and take her from her home:

I thought I knew what the consequences of what I did were. But I had no idea that I would face two separate criminal charges. I thought I would spend a few nights in jail and pay a fine. I discovered that the criminal charges I faced were spreading false news, indecent exposure, attempting to overthrow the government, and joining a terrorist organisation.

The officer asked, 'Do you know the consequences of your action? This is a clear attempt to overthrow the government.'

Asmaa chuckled. 'Yes, I put my foot out and the government tripped, right?'

The officer then asked, 'What were you wearing?'

Asmaa responded, 'A bikini. I was wearing a bikini in the middle of the day in downtown Cairo. What else would I be wearing but a bikini? Of course, a loose woman like me who entraps men. What else would she be wearing?'

Then, they started asking her about Giulio Regeni, the Italian leftist student killed by Egyptian police. She responded that she did not know him:

He started banging on the desk. 'Tell me the truth!' It was so dramatic. I asked him, 'Are you just bored, bro? What are you even doing?' I was so cold with them. To the point that one of them put a gun to my head and said, 'I'm going to kill you.' I said, 'Okay. If you gotta do it, do it.' Then he said, 'We are going to set you on fire. We will burn down your house and kill your husband and your son.' I said, 'Sir, just do what you're ordered to do.'

It was as if God held my heart; kept me calm and safe to the extent that one officer said, 'I want to know where you get your cool from?' I said, 'From the supermarket.'

Asmaa was then moved to the women's prison, with prisoners incarcerated for financial crimes. It was there she began to change:

My relationship with Allah and my worldview changed completely in prison. Who taught me what I now know to be the truth? I don't know. I came to certainty in my heart. Maybe it's maturity; maybe it is inspiration; maybe it is divine guidance. I don't know.

Before going to prison, Asmaa did not pray, and in her first week of Ramadan in prison she did not fast:

I started to heal when I began to cry; I used to never cry. [After I spent months in prison] I lost all sense of emotions – no anger, no sadness, no feelings at all. Once I cried, I felt like I needed to cry to someone. I looked up, and there was a woman praying. By the way, I used to pray incorrectly at first. I used to pray wrong because no one had taught me to pray before. No one in my home growing up prayed. With every prostration, I would cry and supplicate. I used my normal words. From that point onwards, I did not stop praying.

Asmaa's story is not unique. The charge of subversion and indeed terrorism is not weaponised just against political or ideological foes; at its heart, it is a matter of authoritarian self-preservation. On a more fundamental level, while prisons can often be saturated with religious expression, for Asmaa her sense of spiritual longing translated into an inquiry into proper and consistent ritual practices.

CONDITIONS OF CONFINEMENT

CIA Black Site – Jordan
Bagram Air Base – Parvan, Afghanistan
JTF-GTMO – Guantánamo Bay, Cuba

Even prior to the start of the global War on Terror, Mohamedou Ould Slahi had been drawn into the dragnet of investigations relating to terrorism after he was detained and questioned in Senegal, then Mauritania, about being involved in the Millennium bomb plot.[5] He had hoped that the worst was behind him, and that he could carry on with his life, free of being associated with violent acts of which he knew nothing about. When the FBI came to him in Mauritania in September 2001, he felt that he would simply have to comply a little before being released back to his family; he never envisaged that two months later he would be on a CIA rendition flight to a black site in Amman, Jordan, where he would be tortured for over seven months. He would have two more rendition flights; the first was to Bagram Airbase in Afghanistan, where detainees were processed before many were eventually sent to Guantánamo Bay.

Bagram was akin to a warehousing of prisoners, treated as if they were battery-farmed chicken – they were forced to live, sleep, defecate and eat in the place that they were caged. The guards laid out a set of rules that Mohemadou and other prisoners had to adhere to: 'no speaking, no praying loudly, no washing for prayer, and a bunch of other no's in that direction.'[6] Female guards processing him could barely speak Arabic, and yet had the authority to deny him his basic rights to practise his faith. Hopeful of being clean for a moment, he accepted these female guards' offer of the chance to use a bathroom, except what was presented was a barrel filled with faeces – a double humiliation as the guards looked on as he released his waste.[7] The conditions in Bagram were hot and disgusting; there was no sanctuary from the smells that would emanate from the buckets full of faeces, exponentially made worse by the summer heat – all the detainees felt nauseous constantly. As for praying, it became an exercise of fulfilling the basics, without any of the rituals, without any of the togetherness that the prisoners were used to in the real world. Rendition to Guantánamo Bay – Mohamedou's second rendition flight – did not provide any relief for those who had been housed at US military or CIA sites across the world; it became a concentration of all that had already taken place. Small box cages had been erected in an open space – what came to be known as 'Camp X-Ray'. Detainees were housed in their own individual wire-mesh cages, exposed to Cuba's summer climate.

It was almost a year later that Mohamedou found himself in a physical cell, one that had some protection from the elements, except now he faced sensory isolation – he didn't know what time of the day it was nor was he able to tell the direction of the *qibla* by tracking the direction of the sun:

> In the block the recipe [i.e., routine] started. I was deprived of my comfort items, except for a thin iso-mat and a very thin, small, worn-out blanket. I was deprived of my books, which I owned, I was deprived of my Qur'an, I was deprived of my soap. I was deprived of my toothpaste and of the roll of toilet paper I had. The cell – better, the box – was cooled down to the point that I was shaking most of the time. I was forbidden from seeing the light of the day; every once in a while they gave me a rec-time at night to keep me from seeing or interacting with any detainees. I was living literally in terror. For the next seventy days I wouldn't know the sweetness of sleeping: interrogation 24 hours a day, three and sometimes four shifts a day. I rarely got a day off I don't remember sleeping one night quietly. 'If you start to cooperate you'll have some sleep and hot meals.'[8]

The conditions in the cell blocks were a barrier for Mohamedou from gaining what information he could about the days and times of the week – however, he found small ways to try and mitigate the sensory deprivation. Being kept in the dark on the passing of time, he managed to glimpse the watch of a guard that informed him of both the date and time, and crucially, that it was a Friday. Having already figured out how to tell day from night due to the guard shifts, he developed a method of counting the days through the Qur'an, by reciting ten pages in a day, allowing him to know that every sixty days he would finish and thus keep a track of the months as they were passing.[9]

The contestation between those detained in the camps and those responsible for their incarceration oscillated in power, primarily over the ability of the detained men to practise their religious duties. The US interrogators understood this and attempted to use the men's religion against them, while for the men, the conditions of their religious practice became the one ground that they would not be willing to make any concession – this would remain an issue throughout their period of detention.

MCC – New York
Charleston Naval Brig – South Carolina

During the same period that detainees were being rounded up across the world and sold to the US military to be held as enemy combatants, Ali Saleh Kahlah al-Marri was being investigated by the FBI. He came to the US for work on behalf of Qatar National Bank on 10 September 2001, and within that month had received his first visit by FBI agents on the pretext of a passenger suspecting Ali's luggage. He understood that after the attacks, the ordinary American citizen had now become the eyes and ears of the government: anyone who looked out of place would be immediately reported to the authorities. The FBI would visit him again in October, this time claiming he was using the Social Security number of another person. Finally, they came to him on 10 December 2001, this time to arrest him for allegedly funding al-Qaeda through credit cards.

Initially, Ali was taken to the Metropolitan Correctional Center (MCC) in New York as one of thousands of Arab and South Asian Muslim men who were detained by the authorities for the most spurious reasons in the months after 9/11. He had been ripped away from his family but he had an enduring trust in God. This would not be his life forever. The conditions at the MCC were horrific, as the detained men were not permitted any change of clothes, bedding, or underwear for months on end. Ali felt the unease of a person who could not wash, his body and clothes sticky and greasy due to the denial of water, compounding his discomfort at being ritually impure, as he was forced to await a decision on how his case would proceed. If nothing else, he was desperate to feel clean to carry out his prayers.

Ali's case went from initially being about credit card fraud, to shifting to material support for terrorism. He was placed in a Segregated Housing Unit (SHU) under a legal regime called Special Administrative Measures (SAMs) – a system that was put in place to deny prisoners any meaningful access to the outside world. Ali understood that they were trying to force him into a box through severe restrictions, and so he directed his lawyers to not sign the SAMs conditions which would allow them to represent him; he refused to be complicit in his own abuse. As the charges against him were changed and then eventually dropped, the Bush administration changed track entirely: after almost 18 months in detention, Ali al-Marri found himself re-classified an enemy combatant – on US soil.

With his new status being akin to those detained at Bagram, Kandahar and Guantánamo Bay, on 23 June 2003, Ali endured a rendition flight to the Charleston Naval Brig in South Carolina. His faith in God provided him a degree of calm during the transportation, one that permitted submission to his destiny – that this was part of a plan laid out by God, one which Ali had little control over.

He was detained at the Naval Brig alongside two others who were also declared enemy combatants. The three men were monitored and controlled closely by a variety of interrogators that included psychologists, military interrogators and the FBI. Ali's cell was small, measuring 2 x 3 metres, with only a metal toilet, no sink and a metal bed that was perforated with holes. They did not allow him a mattress or blanket for his bed. Ali slept on the metal rack, until the pain of the holes digging into his sides was too much to bear. To ease the pain, he would position himself below the rack and sleep on the concrete floor. In total isolation, he could not communicate with his family, his lawyers, or other detainees during the initial and harshest period of his interrogations. Even the guards would refuse to talk to him, even if it were to simply answer questions about the weather. Ali al-Marri was all of a sudden completely alone. However, his was an isolation that was closely monitored and documented.

From 17 December 2003, Ali was subjected to three months of intense interrogations by agents of the Department of Defense (DoD) and the FBI. Their own documentation highlighted the extent to which their standard operating procedures (SOPs) were taken directly from Guantánamo Bay. Prior to any interrogation, Ali would be subjected to a denial of any form of basic comfort items to force his compliance. This included hygiene products, but most importantly for him, access to a copy of the Qur'an:

> The guy's name was Ramos, and I believe at the time he was a lieutenant colonel, he was with the DoD. He said, 'My name is Ramos and I've given you a chance to meet with us.' I said to him simply, that over the last five months, they had deprived me of a mattress and a pillow, of a blanket, of a Qur'an and *sajjadah* [prayer rug] and these things are essential for every prisoner in the United States who is a Muslim. I had been deprived of these things, so once I had received them, they were welcome to come back after another five months to talk. As they had deprived me of my things, I would deprive them of talking to me. Then we will talk. He said, 'Who do you think we are, we are America and this is an American jail, you have no rights now.' I said, 'You want me to talk to you right?' I asked, 'Can you force me to move my lips and my tongue to talk?' I said that you will come back again after five months, but then at that time it will be ten months you will need to make up to me of denied items. I said the same thing, 'I don't care. I can go back to my cell, I don't need you.'

The US government had been at pains to claim that abuse of detainees was largely restricted to the actions of lower-level soldiers and interrogators who had not operated according to their SOPs. According to the Defence Intelligence Agency, however, everything that was done to Ali had the specific purpose of coercing him into cooperating with interrogations:

> Because Al-Marri had never been interviewed in a controlled environment, it was also necessary to extinguish his expectations

of due process and entitlements in order to induce compliance. This was accomplished by removing all privilege items, such as his mattress and copy of the Qur'an ... Al-Marri's hair and beard were shaved off the day he arrived at the brig. This was due to severe head lice, but it served the purpose of impacting on his self-image. In addition, brig personnel removed the mirror in Al-Marri's cell.[10]

Ali had no idea the extent to which the interrogators were going in their attempts to control his body. Still, he could feel that they were consciously trying to stop him from practising Islam. For him, this made little difference. The interrogators created an environment where Ali's religion was attacked as a way of forcing him to comply with them. This was not out of a sense of ignorance, but rather that the prison environment was explicitly designed to hurt him, one that Ali refused to submit to – whether it was being able to receive water to clean himself if he had a wet dream, or being given food at the start and end times of his fasting during Ramadan. Denied a razor, Ali winced hundreds of times, as he decided to ritually cleanse himself of his pubic hair – a requirement for Muslim men and women. A notation from the guards acknowledges they watched him do this, '#2 [Ali] sat on toilette and started plucking out his pubic + underarm hair,'[11] yet he cared little for the pain he endured; the conditions designed to attack the faith of Ali al-Marri were met with his unwavering ability to always find ways to subvert these attempts and find a sense of contentment with his own beliefs.

Enforced Disappearance, Transitory Cell
Tora Prison – Cairo, Egypt

The methods and conditions of confinement in Egypt are subsumed within wider rituals of subjugation and humiliation. These rituals differ from prison to prison and from time to time and therefore the experiences of prisoners can differ dramatically. However, common to many prisoners is the *tashrifa* – what is known as the 'welcoming party' – the beatings, torture and sexual humiliation prisoners habitually encounter when they are first detained. Likewise, many prisoners are forcibly 'disappeared' into clandestine places for a period that can be as short as two days or can extend to five, six, or even ten years. Political prisoners are also moved to transitory cells before being sent to prison. These transitory cells can be crowded – with over eighty people in one small cell and limited access to a toilet – or in a solitary cell with even fewer amenities.

The *tashrifa* begins with the metal shipping containers. Mohamed Soltan was being transported with 50 other inmates in a vehicle made for no more than 15 people. By the time the inmates were able to leave these vehicles, gasping for air, they were made to stand in queues as the officers took turns beating them. Mohamed was injured at the time, and all the while he was handcuffed to other inmates, making it difficult for any of them to escape the beating:

> The adrenaline was just so high. You're only trying to survive. There was a Sudanese guy that was handcuffed with us and they beat him up so badly all because of the colour of his skin. They broke his foot. It was crazy. My arms were in a cast and they started targeting my arm on purpose. So the other prisoners – some were political and others were not – would try to manoeuvre in front of me just so they can take the beatings instead of my arm. I don't think I would have had a functioning arm still if it wasn't for them. I felt like what the hell is this? Like why so much brutality? Where is God's help? It has to be coming!

The precarity of his life struck Mohamed, particularly as he was forced to witness a prisoner die that day from the beatings. As the prisoners were moved back, some were crying with horror and others were in shock, but everyone was supplicating and begging God for help. They did not know this murdered man, but they had lived his last moments with him.

The cruelty of early detention for many is debilitating. When Mustafa was first detained, he was disappeared to a place more clandestine than other locations of enforced disappearances. For the first four days, he was in a state of shock. He couldn't pray; he couldn't think. His mind could not compute what was happening.

He was placed in solitary confinement and for the first forty days, he was tortured without pause or break:

> I was always the type of person on top of my prayers but in the first four days I was in a state of shock that I didn't move at all. I didn't know where I was.

He was blindfolded the whole time and relied purely on sound to gauge what was happening around him – the sounds of the prison, the keys of guards opening and closing doors – they became the minute-by-minute terror of what he was forced to endure. Outside, he would recall, the officers turned on loud, grainy Qur'an recitations from the radio to cover up the faint screams of the prisoners being tortured. Still, he would hear the screams blurred in with the verses of the Qur'an.

Enforced Disappearance, Police Station
Enforced Disappearance, Amn al-Watani – Cairo, Egypt

Layla, much younger than Mustafa and Mohamed, experienced prison on three separate occasions. First, when she was 13 years old, then when she was 15, and finally, when she was 18. It was her participation at protests alongside her schoolmates that prompted the first two arrests. Layla did not know what to expect, particularly due to her young age. It was gruesome and would forever damage her relationship with her body. The detaining officers would often use older inmates incarcerated for criminal offences to partake in hazing rituals for the newly arrived. Layla recalls a female inmate – whom she later befriended – was ordered to inspect her:

> I was 13, and I was on my period at the time. She stripped me naked and started to search me. One of my friends was there with me – a guy I went to school with since kindergarten. They made him stand behind me while they were searching me. The woman saw my pad and said, 'What is this?' I told her I was on my period. She said, 'Show me.' I looked at the officer in terror. I asked her 'What exactly do you want to see?' The officer looked at me and smirked. He said to me, 'She has to see every bit of

you!' I was so scared but I just said, 'What do you want me to do?' The woman then asked me how old I was. I told her that I was only 13. She said, 'Oh my God, you're just a baby. Just go to the toilet and show me there.' There were about twenty girls in the toilet. I took off my pad and showed it to her. She then went to the officer and said, 'She is okay, Pasha.'

These rituals of humiliation appear in most prisoners' narratives. They are moments of exerting sexual and physical domination, with the aim of leaving the prisoners in a state of panic and subjugation. For Layla, she was insistent each time she was imprisoned not to give the guards the satisfaction that they sought through their exertion of power and domination. When she was 18, the officers came to her home to take her. By then she knew what the rituals of detention looked like. She took a change of clothes, hijab, and her inhaler with her. First, she was forcibly disappeared into a police station; later, she was taken to the Amn al-Watani state security compound:

It was the most bizarre enforced disappearance. I was sleeping on a bench outside their office to the point that I was like a part of the furniture. I was so bored, so to beat the boredom I would mess with the officers. They started bringing up stupid *fiqhi* debates: like why do I have to eat with my right hand? Will I go to hell if I eat with my left? I'd roll my eyes and say no you won't go to hell. He would be like: how can you say that? It is *sunnah* [Prophetic tradition]; it is very important by the way.

As soon as the officers knew she was a student at Al Azhar, they began religious posturing. She pointed out that the same officers who would exploit the female inmates sexually would insist it was forbidden for her to pray in front of them because she was a woman. In Amn al-Watani, she could not pray at all:

In Amn al-Watani, I didn't even bother to ask them if I could pray. You know, on the basis of {And do not abuse the ones whom they invoke apart from Allah, [or] then they would abuse Allah aggressively without knowledge} (6:108). I was blindfolded and made to stand for over seven hours. He was electrocuting me and torturing me that whole time. I did not ask him to sit down, to pray, eat, or go to the toilet. I made the intention of prayer, and prayed in my mind. Surely, I was not going to say, 'Uncle, can you stop torturing me for five minutes just so I can pray?' That would have been stupid.

At one point, while he was torturing me he said, 'So you people say we break girls' hymens? That's fine; I'll show you. Maybe I'll get someone to take your virginity.' Inside I was dying of fear and terror, but *Subhan Allah*, God gave me a sense of extreme forbearance. I was ice cold. All I said to him was, 'Eww ... you're very gross by the way.' He got angry and responded, 'You have no sense of shame.'

I had the sniffles and so he asked, 'Are you crying?' I said, 'Nope ... just a cold.' He responded, 'What was I thinking? God forbid you have any feelings.'

Layla was fully aware of the impact that her responses had on shocking the guards – who were conditioned to expect weakness. The significant determinant in how a prisoner deals with capture, interrogation, and the first period of detention appears to be whether or not they expected to ever be detained and their knowledge of detention procedures. The stronger the familiarity with the process and tactics employed, the more intentional detainees are with their responses. However, the paradox of forbearance, spiritual resilience, reliance on God, and physical helplessness and vulnerability is amplified in their experiences. Layla's own experience was not archetypal, but rather was just one in a constellation of responses by prisoners throughout the varying stages of their detention.

Marwa was 20 years old when she was forcibly disappeared, a fact made more difficult she was in a wheelchair due to previous injuries. The first four days were terrible; she could find no way to sleep and instead cried the entire time. They would wheel her into interrogation and wheel her out – always alone in a male prison facility: enforced disappearance for 16 days. Amidst the fear and terror of interrogation and disappearance, she faced one big problem. The day she was disappeared was the last day of her period:

I thought, how the hell am I going to pray? I'm in this disaster but I can't pray. There is no place to shower or make *ghusl*! But can I even pray in front of them? These people are calling me Muslim Brotherhood; if I show them I pray they might use that to convict me. The full 16 days I couldn't make *ghusl*.*

Marwa decided to pray in the safest place she could find – her mind. She began with the first *takbir* – conjured through her thoughts – and signalled the commencement of each prayer during her enforced disappearance. She would recite the *fatiha* (the first chapter of the Qur'an), bow, prostate, recite *tashahhud* in her mind out of sight from the interrogators and guards.** When she was finally sent to her cell in the evening after long periods of interrogation, it would be the only time she would feel safe to pray two *rak'at*s and would collapse in tears. She did so with the intention that if she was killed or somehow died, she would have at least prayed something. On the sixth day, a kind officer took pity on her and asked her if she needed anything. She asked for some food and a copy of the Qur'an, which he proceeded to bring along with yoghurt and a packet of crisps:

I collapsed crying. I needed very badly to read Surah Yusuf. Afterwards, every time they would send me back to the cell I would only read Surah Yusuf. I so very much needed to be found. With the story of Yusuf, there is this feeling. I don't know. It is just that he goes back to his dad. His family finds him in the end. There was a point I was really upset, Walaa. I thought, is really no one looking for me? I then thought why can't Baba and Mama find me? I then thought of *Finding Nemo*. Do you know the animation? Nemo also thought that his dad stopped looking for him but really his dad was looking all over the ocean for him. These stories helped me a lot.

---

* *Ghusl* is the ritual washing of the whole body, as prescribed by Islamic law to be performed in preparation for prayer and worship, and after sexual activity, childbirth, menstruation, etc.
** *Tashahhud* (lit., testimony [of faith]) is supplication while sitting in prayer, of Allah's One-ness and the finality of the Prophet Muhammad.

In fact, although Marwa did not explicitly know or cite this, the manner in which she prayed had long been a matter of debate in the books of *fiqh* and the practice is extrapolated from the principle of *salat al-khawf* (prayer during a period of fear). This manner (or manners) of prayer is traced from the prayer of the Prophet during the campaigns against Quraysh; whereby Muslims would seek protection, all the while maintaining their prayers.

2

The Prayers of Prisoners

ABLUTION

Kandahar International Airbase – Kandahar
Bagram Airbase – Parvan, Afghanistan
JTF-GTMO – Guantánamo Bay, Cuba

Bagram Airbase was often the second of two airbases that housed and processed detainees before they were sent to Guantánamo Bay; many were first held at Kandahar. The cold Kandahari climate in the winter could see minus zero temperatures, and the winter of 2002 was bitterly cold. Those detained by the US in cages were actively denied any sanitary items, warm clothes, or religious items that would provide them some degree of respect and dignity. The cages held twenty prisoners each, with one bucket provided between them and a single roll of toilet paper per day. Once the buckets were full, a prisoner would be required to throw out the excrement under guard supervision.

The bucket had been an improvement. Prisoners initially were not provided any form of utensil to release themselves, and so despite cries to use the toilet, would find ways to come close to the edge of the fence as far away from others as possible, and relieve themselves. Clothing came as a one-piece red-orange overall that itched and provided next to no protection from the cold weather conditions. It was in the moment of relieving their bowels that the prisoners found the greatest difficulty in relation to the overalls – defecation required removing the entirety of the overall because there was no physical way to remain clothed while relieving themselves. It was in these moments that they would see fingers pointing at them, female guards pointing directly at their members and making jokes about them. The American soldiers had never seen Muslim men naked before, and as the removal of the overall exposed their private area, the soldiers saw the prisoners' shaved pubic areas in compliance with Islamic ritual purity – a point of great amusement for the soldiers, and intense humiliation for the prisoners.

Among those who arrived at the camps in Kandahar was the Al Jazeera cameraman Sami Elhaj. By the time he was four months into his detention, dirt that had accumulated and travelled with him from Pakistan, now merged on his body with the dirt of Afghanistan until it had all baked into his skin. He thought of the Prophet's statement, that cleanliness was half of faith, and then thought of the literal filth he was forced to endure. He had not been permitted any water for general washing, or even for ritual purity for his prayers, and his clothes, hair and body were infested with lice; he thought to himself, 'I will never forget the suffering, degradation and humiliation they put us through.'[1]

By the time the prisoners were finally able to take a shower, after five months, it was only under extreme circumstances. Seven prisoners were first stripped naked, tied to one another, and provided with a bucket of water and some soap to wash with – being forced to shower in front of one another. Until that point, had they attempted to wash with the bottles of drinking water that came from Kuwait, they would be severely punished – and so their desperation for cleanliness led them to manage the situation they were confronted with. Speaking in hushed tones, they kindly encouraged one another to bathe, reassuring the one washing that at the very least the others would avert their gaze to offer some degree of privacy.

After months in Kandahar, many of the men were transported to Bagram where they would remain for many more months before their transfer to Guantánamo Bay. Again, they found similar conditions, with no facilities to wash themselves or defecate. Ahmed Errachidi, a British resident of Moroccan origin, had been sold to the Americans by unscrupulous Afghan militias and warlords, looking to make some quick money. He would later come to be known as 'The General' while in Guantánamo Bay, due to his defiant attitude and constant attempts at trying to win rights for the other prisoners. On his arrival at Bagram, Ahmed exuded an

indomitable spirit that would not permit him to accept the horrifying conditions, to defecate in front of others without any cover. He
complained incessantly until he won a small victory – being able to
hold up a towel while using the bucket, but only up to waist height
– and only if their hands were visible.[2]

Ritual ablution was always on his mind; for months he had been
denied his right to be clean, but the soldiers had been ordered to
maintain that water could only ever be used for drinking. Ahmed
recalled one female soldier who went out of her way to try and
dominate the prisoners, always shouting at them not to use their
water for ablution. He tried to reason with her, explaining that
stopping them from using the water, was effectively stopping them
from praying, to which she would respond, 'Then don't pray.'[3]

Sami had the same experience in Bagram; he wondered why
such a strong emphasis was being placed on denying the prisoners
any right to use their bottled water to perform ablutions, and could
only reason that it was because the soldiers wanted to torture them
by attacking their faith:

At dawn, I wanted to pray the *fajr* [pre-sunrise] prayers. I
couldn't see the sun, but I reckoned it was seven or eight in the
morning since there was some light. When I wanted to stand up,
a soldier ordered me to sit back down.

'Standing is forbidden,' he said, 'the same goes for looking up
or down, or talking to the other prisoners.' He continued reading
me the rules: If I wanted anything, I had to raise my hand for permission to speak, and I had to obey all orders from the soldiers.
After he was done reading, I said, 'I would like some water for
wudu [ritual purification before prayer].'

'You are only allowed one bottle per day,' he said. 'And don't let
me catch you washing with it! You are only allowed to use it for
drinking. If not, you'll be punished'"

The soldiers wore helmets and carried M16 rifles, handguns
and backpacks. They had rods in their hands that they would
beat on the ground when they talked. They threatened us, cursed
us, hurled obscene and lewd words at us – words that I cannot
bear to repeat here.

I saw a prisoner rubbing the ground with his hands, he was doing *tayamum* [ritual purification with dust, when water is not accessible] and praying while seated, so I did the same. After finishing my prayer, I asked for water, and they gave me a small bottle and I took two mouthfuls, then sat, looking around me.

Our hands and legs were in restraints the whole time. We were allowed to use the toilets in the early morning, at midday and in the evening. After our midday meal, they started taking us to do that, but when my turn to stand came, my legs betrayed me and couldn't carry me. I managed to stand, and was told to step forward, raise my hands and turn while looking back.

They opened a door in the barbed wire and grabbed my arms while my hands and legs were restrained, then brought me out and closed the gate quickly. Again, they ordered me to look down and not to move except with their permission. They walked me a few metres to the building's door, which had a pit directly in front of it. "Do your business here," they said.

I asked them to remove my handcuffs, which they did, but when I waited for them to leave, they didn't go.

'Do it!' they told me.

'You can either wait for a short time or go away,' I said.

'No,' they said. 'We won't go. We'll stay here, and if you don't use the toilet in two minutes, we'll bring you back another time. You only have three opportunities a day, and this is your second. You only have one other chance, at the end of the day.'

I retreated into my thoughts, but they jolted me out of them: 'Just look straight ahead. There's no time to delay.'

I heard a woman laughing and raised my head. A female soldier stood with her automatic weapon pointed at me. She moved her finger, indicating that I should hurry up, while she laughed with the other soldiers in mockery. I managed to use the toilet quickly, but they didn't give me anything to clean myself. No water, no paper, nothing. So I stood up.[4]

By the time the men arrived at Guantánamo Bay, access to water became slightly more relaxed after the initial few months, with the men even going as far as to describe their happiness at being able to perform *wudu* for the first time. For some, denial of water for

THE PRAYERS OF PRISONERS

wudu had been so prolonged, that they had forgotten the correct sequence for ablution. Showering was still an issue for the men, as they became used to showering escorted, monitored and provided with only 120 seconds from start to end to have a full shower, as recalled by Mansoor Adayfi: 'We trained hard at showering and could strip, wash, and rinse in 90 seconds and then have a few moments to enjoy the cold water before the guards started the countdown.'[5]

Over the years in Guantánamo Bay, as his confrontations with the guards had lessened, and as the conditions were relaxed somewhat, Sami Elhaj came to understand that while individual guards could eventually be reasoned with, ultimately the policy decision of how Muslims should be managed, was coming from much further up.

Charleston Naval Brig – South Carolina, United States of America

During his period of military detention at the Charleston Naval Brig in South Carolina, Ali al-Marri was forced to contend with the times when he would be denied water for *wudu*. Usually, this had not been an issue for him, but due to the complicated ways that prisoners were moved in the US, being taken to court for a hearing would often result in him not being able to correctly estimate the time from one prayer to the next. In those circumstances, he would delay the prayer as long as he could in order to see if there was any opportunity to make *wudu*, and if not, he would put his hands below the shackles on his feet, touch the ground and perform *tayamum*, a way of ritually purifying yourself through dust. Ali's knowledge of Islam had made him aware of the dispensations that exist within the religion – when a situation was outside of his control, God's mercy would always prevail:

One of the beautiful things about Islam, is that whenever the situation gets harder or tighter, the rules become easier and more lenient, *Subhan Allah* [glory be to Allah]. Allah does not burden the believer with more than he can bear. This is why the Prophet Muhammad (peace and blessings be upon him) said, that whatever I ask you not to do, don't do it, whatever I ask you to do, do what you can. The wording is important: the prohibition does not necessitate any action from you, you are not required to do anything; whatever you are asked to do, then you need to do an action, so you do what you can. So *wudu* or *ghusl*, I never had any problem with it because I am aware, I am comfortable.

Access to water was one of the ways Ali's interrogators attempted to control him. There was a buzzer Ali would press to request water, having an 8-ounce cup deposited through his bean hole. The one cup was insufficient to perform the full *wudu*, so he became accustomed to performing the *arkaan* (obligatory act), which was to repeat each part of the ritual ablution once, rather than three times. This way he knew that with careful application of his one cup, he would be able to complete his purification for prayer. He would then request another water to drink, which he had come to understand from the SOPs they could not decline. Before long, Ali understood the extent to which they wanted to deprive him of purifying himself, when they would only give him half a cup when he would request it, a way of sending a message that the water was only for drinking.

When Ali, like many men, would have a wet dream that would result in a state of *janaba* (ritual impurity due to semen discharge), the guards would actively prevent him from ritually purifying himself. Unlike breaking one's *wudu*, either through using the toilet or sleep, a wet dream requires a full shower in order to come into a state where you are permitted to pray again. The guards closely monitored these moments and were aware of Ali's need for a shower, but they refused to provide him access to one. Instead, they would note his need in their guard logs. Ali could neither pray nor touch the Qur'an – in the brief periods he had access to it – because he was not ritually pure. Out of desperation, he would first try to use the small sink to wash. When the guards found out, they decided to further punish him and switched off his water supply completely. Ultimately, Ali had no other option but to perform *tayamum*.

While Ali was constantly aware of Allah's mercy throughout his detention, this did not quell his own anxiety. Ali is a Muslim man raised in Qatar. He was not used to being touched by women that were not closely related to him, to those whom he was *mahram*.* There is jurisprudential debate as to whether touching a non-*mahram* would invalidate one's *wudu*, but for Ali it was much more than that. He knew it was about maintaining his own religious convictions and self-respect. Thus, if female guards ever came to cuff him while he was in his cell, he would refuse to place his hands through the bean hole, but he knew he was powerless to stop them once he was out of his cell. He knew full well that preserving his life and protecting the body that had been given to him by God was more important than receiving a beating for non-compliance, so when outside of his cell, he would comply out of coercion.

Burj al-Arab Prison – Alexandria, Egypt
Damanhour Prison – Buhayrah, Egypt
Qanater El Khayereya Women's Prison, Qalyubiyya, Egypt

Ali Hashem recalled *gina'i* inmates (those incarcerated for criminal offences) staring at him as if he lost his mind, when he was tapping his hands on the ground for *tayamum*.[6] He was a young student activist imprisoned for joining university protests after the 2013 coup. Inside prison, he continued to organise both political and *gina'i* prisoners in small acts of resistance. The *gina'i* inmates all knew how to do their ablution but the idea of *tayamum* was foreign to them. The prison infrastructure was old, and, in many prisons, water was limited. This very limitation opened prisoners to a plethora of questions on ritual purity, ablution and prayer.

Abbas, like Ali, was a student activist when he was first detained. In prison, the limited access to water quickly became a major concern and an issue he constantly debated with other prisoners. They had access to water for only two hours a day and that water caused scabies and other skin diseases. At first, Abbas and the other prisoners used it to make *wudu* but then they started developing severe skin diseases from the water. The question that first arose in his mind and that of other prisoners, was whether the water

---

* *Mahram* – a person with whom marriage is prohibited because of their close blood relationship, because of *radaa'ah* (breastfeeding) by the same mother, or because of being related by marriage.

was pure or impure. The Azharis – who lived locally and knew the source of the water – said it was not impure. They had lived with this contaminated water in their villages and so they were able to withstand it better. Abbas's skin could not bear it and so he stopped making *wudu* with it. This then led to another question: with the availability of limited clean drinking water, should prisoners prioritise *wudu* or drinking? This split the prison population into three groups: some made *wudu* with the contaminated tap water, others made it with the drinking water, and the last group, in which Abbas found himself, opted for *tayamum* instead.

Mona, too, was detained for participating in a student protest. Soon after her detention by the authorities, her image was disseminated among activist groups, who saw her as a symbol of resilience and demanded her release. This angered the authorities and they decided to punish her. In solitary confinement, where Mona spent the first weeks of her prison sentence, the issue of ritual purity was even more complicated. She was allowed to use the toilet once a day in the morning; however, she would have to pay the guards money if she wanted to be let out to use the toilet throughout the day:

> I tried not to pee throughout the day so I could at least keep my *wudu*. I am directionally challenged in normal times, so trying to guess the *qibla* was just hard. I was also very scared so I always prayed facing the door. Even when we were moved to a bigger cell, we didn't feel safe and we had no way of knowing the *qibla*. So we prayed facing the wall.

The worst thing for her was not knowing whether it was day or night. Slowly, however, she began to gauge time through the prison routine. The guards would wake the prisoners at 7 a.m. to clean: that indicated the morning. Visitations began at 6 p.m. and so *maghrib* (post-sunset prayer) was guessed to be around 6:30. Visitations ended at 9 p.m. and that is when *isha* approximately was.

For prisoners who could see the sun, gauging the place of the *qibla* and the approximate timing of prayer was not as difficult a task. After leaving the transitory cell, Layla asked the officer if he knew where the *qibla* was so she could pray. He said he did not know:

I knew it was sunset and I knew how to figure out the *qibla* from the sun. Baba taught me. And so I did. He was like, 'How the hell did you figure out the *qibla*?' I said, 'From the sun.' He panicked and said, 'And you're telling me you're not Ikhwan!'

Often, in larger cells, organic modes of mentorship emerged. This occurs especially when a senior inmate is present with some knowledge of religious sciences and particularly *fiqh*.[7] For Asmaa, this guide was an older auntie called Auntie Magda who had been in prison for 25 years. She acted as a guarantor for someone who ended up running away with the money he borrowed. So she went to prison instead of him. Asmaa welled up with pride as she spoke about Auntie Magda:

> She had this amazing sense of contentment. Maybe, I was impacted by her internal state. I asked her all the *fiqh* questions. I asked her which blood counts as menstrual blood. She taught me what was required for *ghusl* and what is recommended. Once, I found blood after making *ghusl* and she explained that if the blood is brown, I don't have to repeat the *ghusl* and I could pray. If it is red blood, then I have to repeat the *ghusl* again when it stops. She told me that in Islam we had different schools of law and they each have different opinions. Follow whichever you find easiest. I told her that when I have a court session, I end up missing *asr* on my way to the courthouse and they don't let me pray in court. She told me to combine *dhuhr* and *asr* before I leave for court. I told her sometimes when I'm in the toilet, they rush me and I can't complete my *wudu*. She explained that I can wipe on my socks if I made *wudu* earlier that day. If there is no water at all, I can make *tayamum*.

Asmaa was emotional when she spoke of Auntie Magda as she was a young woman when she was first detained – a memory that hurt even more knowing that Auntie Magda died in prison only one year before her name appeared on the list of presidential pardons. What Asmaa and other female prisoners faced, was something that the minutiae of Islamic law, or the kindness of elders, could not protect them from. It was the darker side to the large female prison wards – that when they would go to perform *ghusl* to become ritually pure, the younger females would relate that they were sexually assaulted by older prisoners. Life in prison for Asmaa and others was precarious.

PRAYER

Enforced Disappearance – Islamabad, Pakistan
Kandahar International Airport – Kandahar and Bagram
Airbase – Parvan, Afghanistan
JTF-GTMO – Guantánamo Bay, Cuba

It was the Pakistani authorities who raided the Islamabad home of Moazzam Begg, ripping him from his pregnant wife and three children as they were roused from sleep in the early hours. For a short while, he was held by the Pakistanis, before eventually being handed over to Americans. All the while his Pakistani captors tried to apologise to him for the role they were playing, the last of them telling him, 'Moazzam … you know, my friend, I have sold both this life and the next for what I am about to do.'[8] These words were received as platitudes by Moazzam, as his reality was not changed by the sorrow expressed by these complicit Pakistani agents. Moazzam had been living with his family in Afghanistan, having relocated to establish a girls' school after deciding to leave the UK. He fled from Afghanistan as the US invaded in 2001, seeking to make a new home for himself in Pakistan; after all, he originally came from there.

The weather in Islamabad was warm. He had not anticipated that he would be thrown in the freezing Kandahar prison, where he was unlawfully transferred from one state to another – euphemistically known as a 'rendition'. Moazzam was detained by the Pakistani authorities, who had handed him over to US agents at Islamabad airport. He had no coat; he was taken on to the plane wearing only a shirt, trousers and socks, and forced to sit directly on the floor of the plane with shackles on his ankles and his hands strapped and cuffed behind his back. It was difficult for him to see anything because of the darkness under the hood that had been forced over his head – in some ways, the hood compounded the sounds of the plane engine and rattled the vibrations of the plane around his head. While terrified over what the future was going to hold for him, he heard a voice beside him saying, 'Shall we pray, brother?'

Almost immediately a soldier screamed at them, 'Shut up, motherfucker, if you speak again I'll kill you.' Although Moazzam heard the soldier's words, he was in a state of disbelief that in this circumstance of intense fear and uncertainty, one of the men he was being kidnapped with had thought to recite the morning prayer. Quietly, Moazzam whispered to him to lead them both in prayer as he was seated to the right of the man who had caught his attention. It was in this circumstance he would pray his very first prayer in the custody of the US, with the threat of being murdered hanging over his hooded head.

Moazzam was not among the first prisoners to have been transferred from Islamabad to Kandahar. Already Abdul Salam Zaaef, the Taliban's ambassador to Pakistan, had been unlawfully arrested in contravention of the Vienna Convention on Diplomatic Relations, and placed in the hands of the US. From the very beginning of Kandahar's operation as a detention site, interrogators and guards were angry, terrified and hostile to any form of communication between the prisoners. They would threaten to shoot anyone caught attempting to pray in *jama'ah* (congregational prayer), regularly beating those they suspected of having done so. Eventually, high-ranking officers began to permit congregational prayer, but only because they realised it was becoming a security risk to deny it – the prisoners had come to the stage where they were willing to die in order to express their beliefs. Abdul Salam, who had more knowledge of Islam, often led the prayers, yet felt helpless as he was forced to watch the desecration of his faith, as a prisoner who was praying behind him was dragged away to an interrogation in the middle of their *fajr* prayer. This resulted in the men breaking their prayer and crying for the one who had been stripped from them – they were forced to repeat the prayer after they had composed themselves.[9]

After he had been placed on a rendition flight to Guantánamo Bay, Abdul Salam woke to a new environment; there was even a change in the climate. Those who had been transported found themselves in a completely different set-up than the one they had experienced in Afghanistan. At the naval base in Cuba, there were no large cells that kept twenty men together – instead, they were kept in individual cages, making impossible the communal prayer that they had always practised throughout their lives – now it would take other forms. The US soldiers found it difficult to police the praying of the prisoners, but as a general rule in the early days of Camp X-Ray, it was forbidden. On their knees and with their faces pressed to the ground for between two to four hours at a stretch, the punishment for even the most silent of prayers forced them into this stress position by their guards.[10]

The Arab men who had been sent to Guantánamo Bay alongside him, could not countenance that they had flown as far as Cuba, and so were convinced that they were somewhere in the Middle East. Abdul Salam had been explicitly told by his captors the place of their destination, and so understood that they were much further west than the location of their departure. For that reason, Abdul Salam witnessed the Arabs turn their faces towards the west at prayer times, thinking that they were still east of the Grand Mosque in Mecca. Abdul Salam, the Afghans, and those of the many other nationalities they were with chose instead to face eastwards, understanding that the *qibla* was in that direction.

A unique situation emerged for Abdul Salam and his fellow prisoners. For the most part, they had been praying in their own individual cells, until one of the scholars among them mooted the idea that they could pray communally from their individual cages. The scholar suggested that the person at the front cage when facing in the direction of the *qibla* should be the one to lead the prayer with the others following from their own individual positions. Mansoor Adayfi described how the prison authorities took issue with this practice, but eventually the prisoners paid no attention to the commands of the guards, as they instituted the importance of praying communally:

I wanted to offer my morning prayers. Just seeing the light gave me a sense of comfort, knowing I could do something I had done all my life. I have been praying five times a day since I was in my mother's womb. I was born knowing the rhythms and sounds of each of the day's prayers. Praying was like the breath of life to me that connected me to Allah. I hadn't heard a call to prayer in days – we weren't allowed to call out – and I was surprised when I heard the familiar sound of a man singing the *adhan* [call to prayer] several cages away. The men around me stirred and we all began the same movements we had been doing all our lives. I used water from the bucket for my ablutions. I washed my face, hands, head, my ears, my feet ... 'NO WASHING!' The soldiers went crazy. They went from cage to cage banging the fences as we prepared for our prayers. 'SIT THE FUCK DOWN!'

We all assumed the *takbir*, standing straight as we faced what we believed was Mecca, preparing to enter the state of prayer. 'NO STANDING!'

We raised our hands just above our shoulders and made our offering to Allah. *'Allahu Akbar!'* we called out together, as if we were one. 'SHUT THE FUCK UP!'

We did this, all of us, not thinking, our bodies going through the movements of the *qiyaam, ruku', sujud,* and *tashahhud* [stages of prayer – standing, bending, prostrating, sitting], guided by a higher power.

The soldiers seemed more afraid than angry. 'SIT DOWN!' they screamed. Guards in armour came running as if preparing to battle. 'NO STANDING!' What were we to do – stop our prayers? No, it was the morning prayer and we finished just as we have done since we were children. We prayed together as one of the men led the prayer. If they knew anything about Islam, they would know that we pray together five times a day. We weren't preparing for battle. We weren't being defiant or ignoring their orders. We were praying the way we had prayed all our lives because prayer was as much a part of us as our skin and bones.

When we had finished, soldiers stormed the cage of the man who led the prayer and took him away.[11]

Despite these moments of resistance, the guards would take every opportunity to mock the *adhan* and the *salat* whenever they could. In the hours-long interrogations that would take place, prayer became a contested issue for all the prisoners. Some would attempt to pray in the middle of an interrogation, only to be shouted at, beaten, and on occasions have female soldiers seductively position themselves in front of them, blowing smoke in their faces while doing so. Ahmed Errachidi took every opportunity to pray, but would experience every form of disruption his interrogators could conceive. Reciting verses of the Qur'an in his mind, he attempted to push past the loud decibels of Drowning Pool's 'Let the Bodies Hit the Floor' being blasted into his ears.[12] These tactics were used specifically to harm the prisoners, with their interrogators knowing full well the importance of the prayer to them.

Northern Correctional Institution Supermax – Connecticut, United States of America

Babar Ahmad found himself detained in solitary confinement at the Northern Correctional Institution Supermax, based in Connecticut. Like Adel Abdel Bary, Babar Ahmad had been on an extradition warrant to the US, although he had never visited the country, and the crimes he had been alleged to commit took place in the UK (even though the UK did not consider he had committed any crime). Despite his nine-year challenge in detention without charge in the UK, he was ultimately extradited to the US. The Northern Supermax was designed to be as 'disorientating as possible',[13] with seemingly endless aluminium and glass walls and corridors that conveyed a sense of inescapability. In the US's system of mass incarceration, there is very little in the way of humanity in a place like Northern; it is a hellscape of solitary confinement with the glass and metal echoing with the screams and wails of those who have been condemned to be there.

Fataqullah mastat'atum – be mindful of God, as much as you are able. This was the part of the Qur'an that aided Babar in navigating his religious duties throughout the time of his detention. Like so many other prisoners around the world who had studied Islam to some extent, he was aware of the flexibility that Islam gave someone, but still wanted to try his best to perform his prayers. From the beginning of his extradition from the UK to the US, Babar was forced to think of his prayers as he was brought onto a private jet. He was shackled to his chair and could not move, so pressed his fingers to the floor to perform *tayamum* and prayed in his seat.

He recalled how being transferred in the US from one prison to the next was akin to being a DHL parcel: it could take days because of a system of hubs from which you would be transferred during the day or night – during those transfers, he prayed on many occasions fastened to his seat. There were others he would come across, who took a much more literal approach to their practice and would make life hard for other Muslim prisoners:

There was a tension between that fact that we are Muslims who have rules and regulations to follow in relation to our *salat*, hygiene, etc., in how things are meant to be, and on the other hand, we had the circumstances we were in. I remember in the UK, of all people, Sajid Badat was leading us in prayer once and we were praying in one brother's cell and on his desk there was a letter that someone had sent him with a postage stamp on it, with the outline of the Queen and he told someone to cover it – I mean *really* strict. You had brothers who were obsessed with these rulings, not understanding the circumstances that we were in. I always tried my best and knew that I would not try to take liberties with Allah, that I could do whatever I like, but on the other side you had brothers who would insist that you have to do it like this, or that you have to do it like that. It reminded me of the *hadith* where the *sahabi* (Prophet's companion) was coming back from battle and he was in an injured state and needed to make *ghusl*, saying that he could not make it, and a *sahaba* insisted that he do it, and then when he did it, he died. Then the Prophet was so angry at this that he said, 'they killed him so may Allah kill them' as an expression of how angry he was. The Prophet said that if you didn't know, why didn't you ask? So I knew that I was in prison for Allah's sake, I knew that, and I knew that Allah knows my circumstances, and supposing he were to ask me on the Day of Judgement, why did you do x, y or z, I would say that I was in prison and was not in control of my circumstances, and that I tried my best and that Allah would say it's not acceptable? That's not Allah. You are already away from your family for His sake, already in prison, your every breath, your every living moment of existence in this place was for the sake of Allah, and to think He is going to catch you out because of an outline on a postage stamp in the room, and that while you are doing that – like Sajid – you are making up hundreds of lies about other people to destroy them, then that's not Islam. It's easy to control the external, that the brothers who were the most strict in prison when it came to these external manifestations of the religion, they were the easiest to crack, they were the easiest ones to fall to pieces, or they were the ones who would turn into informants. It's easy to control the external, but harder to control the internal.

There were other more practical problems that Babar would encounter. Throughout the day, he would have a clock that he could see, and so he was able to look at the time and know when exactly the time for prayer came. The issue was always *fajr*, as there was no alarm to wake him before sunrise. In the UK, he had help – another prisoner who was in the cell next to him, used to stay up all night, and so offered to attach a string to an empty bottle of vitamins which he would tug through the window of his own cell, making it fall on the floor and thus waking Babar up at the time he had requested. In solitary confinement in the US, the isolation was complete – there was no prospect of getting assistance from another prisoner:

At a time when I did not have anyone, I didn't have another Muslim brother in the cell, and I didn't have someone near me – and of course we couldn't give *adhan* out loud as it would be disrespectful to the other prisoners who were non-Muslim – so I would use the water trick. The water trick is basically you drink like half a litre of water and then you need to get up. Say half a litre makes you need to go to the toilet in around four hours, so you're bursting to go. Going to the toilet isn't a problem because you are living in a toilet, there is one in your cell. So the water trick, it would be a matter of calculation, so now it's like I'm trying to go to sleep at 10 p.m. and *fajr* is at 6 a.m., so basically you practise until you get an idea of how much water you need to drink in order to wake up in six hours. Initially, you'd have to get up a couple of times in the night and then you'd drink more water to see what time you'd then wake up, but you get it eventually.

Transitory Cell, Damanhour – Buhayrah, Egypt
Scorpion Prison – Cairo, Egypt
Qanater El Khayereya Women's Prison – Qalyubiyya, Egypt

The room was 4 x 6 metres and had a little over thirty inmates. Everyone was naked and they were all smoking. The prison authorities wouldn't allow them food, but they would get cigarettes. They would give a group of inmates cigarettes and wouldn't give the other group so they would kill each other. We were the only political prisoners there. 23 August 2014 – that was one of the worst nights of my life.

Abbas was sent to a transitory cell for disciplining after he had an altercation with the guards. This was not the first time he was disciplined. He had already spent many nights in solitary confinement, to the point that he thought he would lose his mind, but this was different. The cell he found himself in for punishment was crowded, scorching hot, and dark. He struggled as the guards stripped him naked. It was only once his eyes had a chance to settle in the cell that he noticed all the other prisoners too were without their clothes. There was no light and an overwhelming stench of urine. The other inmates knew he was a political prisoner and so they asked, 'Shaykh, can you give us a lesson?' Abbas spoke to them of the importance of prayer, but understood why they had so many dilemmas. As he looked on, he could see the state they were in, their *awrah* (nakedness, i.e., parts of the body that are not permitted to be exposed to others) was exposed, and the very floor upon which they sat, slept and ate was impure, so they were unsure about how they could even pray in such a situation. 'In *fiqh*,' Abbas explained, 'there is a dispensation that allows for those who cannot cover their nakedness to pray, with the caveat that they must avert their gaze from each other.' He then led a congregation of prisoners, standing naked before their Lord. Later that evening, what was the worst night of his life developed into something different. After they prayed together, a prisoner asked him if God could ever forgive him. Abbas told him the story of the man who killed 99 souls, took a path to repentance, and God still forgave him. They then asked if he could relay the story of Yusuf; and ended up discussing the stories of Prophets Yusuf, Yunus and Ibrahim. These prophets had been, like the prisoners, outcasts from societies – some endured confinement and imprisonment – yet they found solace in the intimate dialogue with their Lord. Something the prisoners, stripped naked and in the midst of their vulnerability, so very much craved.

Abbas keenly remembers the solace that being around other people brought in one of his lowest moments in prison. It was a far cry from the time he spent in solitary confinement. There he was alone with his thoughts:

> Solitary was like being buried alive in a grave. It was dark. The person before me set fire to his blankets so he could kill himself. There were the remains of a burning corpse and I could smell burning flesh. I thought this was it; I was going to die here.

Abbas had no way of knowing whether it was day or night. He had no access to clean water. He was stuck: 'I would wake up and pray. I didn't know if it was right. I would do *tayamum* and pray wherever. I had no way of knowing where the *qibla* was. I just followed my heart.'

Ola al-Qaradawi, the daughter of the late Shaykh Yusuf al-Qaradawi, spent three years in solitary confinement before being moved to a cell with other people, where she spent another year and a half. She was in a state of complete shock and denial for the first two months:

> I remember when I first went to the interrogation room I asked the prosecutor, 'Does this mean I am in prison now? Am I really a prisoner?' He looked confused and said, 'Didn't you just come from your cell?' I said, 'But did you actually really imprison me? Why would you do that?' He just looked at me very confused.

Ola was in complete isolation. She was allowed to use the toilet once a day at 8 a.m. She then tried to gauge prayer time through the prison routine:

First day, I did not know where the *qibla* was. I had to guess. I had a deposition early that morning. I woke up and saw the female guard standing over me. I was in shock! 'Where am I?' She said, 'You have a deposition. Get up. Get dressed.' I went to go to the toilet but there was no toilet. Just a hole in the ground. There was no sink but jars of dirty water on the ground. I told myself, I'll wait for the deposition and I could use the toilet there. I hadn't eaten or drank anything for three days; so I was fine. I asked her how can I make *wudu*; the sink wasn't working. She pointed to a small tap on the floor. I made *wudu* and I prayed in the car in whatever direction.

In solitary, she would only know it was time for noon prayer if they opened the gates for visitation, but most of the time she did not know:

If I slept and woke up, I wouldn't know when I slept or when I woke up. I wouldn't know if I slept a little or slept a lot. So whenever I woke up, I would just make *wudu* and pray. I would use the bucket they kept in my room as a toilet and kept a bottle of water for *wudu*.

In early days of confinement and when they are being transported, prisoners are often restrained and held in stress positions as a form of punishment. Mohamed Soltan, during his initial period of enforced disappearance, was put in a transitory cell nicknamed the *talaga* (the fridge). It was called the fridge because it was where they kept prisoners before they could cook up a case for them. All of the inmates were handcuffed to each other and they were not allowed food. Mohamed's arm was broken and so he was bound with one arm. This made performing even *tayamum* difficult for him, but he would do so either way and then would pray while he was sitting – a reconciled form of prayer that many others would also perform.

Omar too spent the first days of incarceration bound. He was alone and blindfolded in his cell. Denied the key sense of sight, he managed to fumble his restraints so that they loosened, and reached around for the small bottle of what he was provided in order to make ablution. The restraints, however, were still too restrictive to pray in any other way than in his seated position. The sensory deprivation, coupled with not knowing his fate, meant that he would choose to combine his prayers, in order to ensure he could pray as much as possible.

In the particular prison complex that Hamza and Omar found themselves, all the cells were designated for solitary confinement, and they were placed next to one another in rows. Despite the solitary nature of their captivity, it was still possible for them to speak through the walls to one another, which is how they decided to organise themselves in a way that would permit congregational prayer. The call for prayer would be recited by the inmates for everyone to hear. Like the prisoners detained in Guantánamo, the inmate in the solitary cell at the furthest end of the ward would lead the prayer. Prisoners would stand closest to the wall to ensure there is a semblance of symmetry and line. They would then pray in congregation. However, there were voices who disagreed with this, citing that the imam must be visible for the congregation to be valid. In fact, two prominent scholars imprisoned in the same ward were involved in this *fiqh* debate and the prisoners followed whichever opinion they found most convincing.

The space of the prison is ripe with *fiqhi* pluralism. In cells where prisoners share an overarching religious orientation, the disagreements would typically be amicable. This is not true for political disagreements which could sometimes lead to altercations among the prisoners. The chances for physical disagreements increase in particular when the prisons have inmates with *takfiri* orientations,* or when ISIS affiliates are put in the same ward with other prisoners. The question then becomes which orientation dominates the ward. Abbas, for example, noted that one of his cellmates would always feign a stomach-ache when they got up to pray in congregation, or when they sat together to eat. They later found out that it was because he did not consider them Muslim. That said, the most significant point of contention was the very basis of *fiqhi* principles by which rulings on their acts of worship could be derived.

---

* *Takfiri* – a Muslim who claims other Muslims have disassociated themselves from Islam.

Still, conducting communal prayer is very central to prison life. When someone dies inside or outside prison, they pray *Salat al-Gha'ib* (absentee funeral prayer). Abbas recalled:

We would pray *Salat al-Gha'ib* for those that died from medical neglect. We considered them martyrs. They died in captivity. We would even pray for those that died on the outside. Our cell-mate's brother was killed in government extrajudicial killings. We prayed for him and had a funeral.

The rituals and customs of life and death would continue on the inside as best they could. The giving of condolences on the passing of a loved one in freedom is considered such an important part of communal Muslim life, that prisoners would do their utmost to carry on this practice. During the yard time, when three cells would be opened, the brother of the deceased would stand by his cell window and each person in the neighbouring cells would pass to give their condolences.

Tora Prison – Cairo, Egypt
Qanater El Khayereya Women's Prison – Qalyubiyya, Egypt

'*La jummah li-asir*': Friday prayer is not incumbent on the captive. The very notion of captivity becomes central to how prisoners theorise their own incarceration, since the *fiqh* for captivity allows for certain dispensations. Abdullah El Shamy explained he encountered this debate when he was first sent to the large holding cell with older inmates:

We prayed every prayer congregation; ironically, except Friday prayers. The inmates said '*La jummah li-asir*' (Friday prayer is not incumbent on the captive). They said that the primary purpose of Friday prayers is that it is a willing congregation of free Muslims. Prison life contradicts that. This always steered debate among people and it was an opinion I found convincing. Still, some people continued to say Friday prayers and that was okay.

Layla, too, found this argument convincing. She pointed out that the conditions for Friday and Eid prayers in prison cannot be fulfilled according to the four *madhhab*s (jurisridential schools). To illustrate her point, she added that no one from outside the prison could just join the prison congregation if they so chose. This contradicts the primary purpose of a Friday congregation.

That said, Friday prayers were frequently held by prisoners, even in female prisons. Both Ola al-Qaradawi and Munira noted that Friday prayers were typically always held in the prison ward. There were no debates as far as they were aware on the permissibility of Friday prayers being held in prison, and indeed, none of the female inmates questioned the permissibility of a woman leading Friday prayers. In the cell where Ola was detained, an older and learned woman would typically lead them in prayer. In Munira's ward, the inmates would take turns leading Friday prayers and giving the *khutba* (sermon). Munira recalled this proudly: 'We weren't trying to do anything different. We just wanted life to continue as it had outside prison. But one Ramadan, I gave a very heavy *khutba* on Friday. Next day *amn al-dawla* [state security] called. It really scared them.'

In Asmaa's case, they also said Friday prayers, but it was different. There was an old television in the ward. On Fridays, they would turn on the television channel streaming the prayers, and they would congregate and follow the imam on television. Things were different for *gina'i* prisoners – in both the female and male prisons. The prison authorities were always cautious and would not allow them to pray. They would be beaten by the prison authorities if they prayed.

The other concern – pertaining the *fiqh* of captivity – that prisoners debated is shortening and combining prayers – a dispensation that the captives took advantage of when need be. Ali explained: '*Fiqh al-Asir* made rulings easier for captives. There were those who insisted they would pray normally and others who maintained that throughout their captivity that they would combine and shorten prayers.'

The majority, however, took a dispensation where they combined prayers but did not shorten them. Ali explained how some of this was down to the practicality of being in prison and not having free access to a toilet and water:

> We had thirty people and one toilet. The older inmates who had diabetes would have to use the toilet more often. Imagine if it took each of us two minutes to use the toilet for *wudu*, it would be impossible to pray. Not to mention those that might need to do *ghusl* or those that will need to use the toilet. This would likely last an hour and half ... actually more likely it will be two hours.

Another issue arose particularly for those detained in prisons further away from their hometowns. Are they considered travellers, and does that require they follow the dispensations allowed for a traveller vis-à-vis combining and shortening prayers? What about those that are enforced disappeared? The state does not recognise their very existence. They do not know for how long they will stay in any particular prison complex. They could be in the place of enforced disappearance for two days or two years. Does this lack of certainty in residence make them a traveller? Do all of these questions also apply to someone who has not yet been sentenced? As these questions arose for prisoners, more *fiqhi* conundrums had to be tackled. For example, can the person detained in their hometown lead a person detained outside of their hometown in prayer? This was a dilemma, given the non-traveller must pray the complete four *raka'a*s (units of prayer) and the traveller only prays two, and since it is impermissible for someone in the congregation to end their prayer before the imam.

So often, just the physical constraint of the spaces in which prisoners found themselves required a degree of flexibility in the rules of Islam. The overcrowded prison cell dictated in many ways how they would perform their prayers. Space was something hard to come by for Abbas and the other prisoners. Trapped alongside one another in a 1.8 x 2.5 metre cell with 23 other inmates meant that there was almost no room for manoeuvre. The toilet they had to share was simply a hole in the ground, on top of which they had to contend with how to pray since there was no space for prostration (*sujud*). Making the best of the limited space they had, they would move into the position of prostration, using the back of the one in front of them as the place to make *sujud*. Unlike in the male prison cells, female prisoners had beds, and so while they were given this one amenity, it reduced the available space to pray, so when it was overcrowded they would pray sitting on their beds.

3
The *Ummah* of Prisoners

COMMUNITY

Kandahar International Airport – Kandahar, Afghanistan
Bagram Airbase – Parvan, Afghanistan
JTF-GTMO – Guantánamo Bay, Cuba

If it were not for the squalid conditions of the camps, the sounds of
torture, and the cries of the men being abused of their rights, the
detention camps in Afghanistan could be confused for a gathering
of the *ummah* (the global Muslim community of Muslims). There
were representations across all the continental regions that Muslims
inhabit, from the American John Walker Lindh to the Australian
Mamdouh Habib, almost every time zone was represented by the
diverse nationalities that were detained. Even in the conditions he
found himself, the British national Moazzam Begg warmed to the
loud *As-salaamu alaikum* he received on entering the cage he was
to be held in at Bagram, along with 19 other men. He described his
cage as containing Egyptians, Turks, Chechens, Afghans, Pakistanis,
Uzbeks and even Uyghur Muslims from China.[1] Never having
met before, the men greeted him with the *salaam* that the Prophet
Muhammad (peace and blessings upon him) had described as
being among the best deeds that a Muslim could perform, embrac-
ing him warmly as if they had always been friends.

There was not much to occupy the men he was with; they were
mostly living with the fear of being taken for interrogations, which
were brutal. Moazzam had been harmed by his interrogators both
physically and psychologically – at one point even being made
to mistakenly believe that the sounds of a woman he could hear
screaming were that of his wife being abused in the interrogation
room next to his. Learning of the lives of one another through a

mixture of speaking Urdu, Arabic and English; prayer and the recitation of the Qur'an became ways of them managing their time together between being dragged off for interrogations. Moazzam would learn about the men he was with, and not forget about them or their stories, even once he was released from Guantánamo Bay.

The International Committee of the Red Cross (ICRC) eventually brought a chessboard for the men, to help relieve some of the monotony of their time in detention. Moazzam was amused by the controversy and debates that began murmuring at the presence of the game in the cells. Eventually, there were animated conversations taking place on whether or not the playing of chess was considered *haram* (i.e., prohibited, according to Islamic law) within the traditions of the Prophet Muhammad. There were a number of scholars who claimed that it was prohibited; however, a senior Islamic scholar who was with them explained that it was in fact backgammon that was prohibited due to the element of chance that exists within the game, whereas chess was much more of a game of skill.[2] Abdul Salam Zaeef explained this permissibility down to the scholar issuing the *fatwa* (Islamic legal opinion) being a *shafi'i* (a follower of the shafi'i jurisprudential school), and thus permissible for those who followed that *madhhab*.[3]

On their arrival at Guantánamo Bay, the prisoners greeted one another with the *salaam* again for each new arrival, with the new addition of '*marhaba, marhaba*', 'welcome, welcome', resonating around the camps, alongside the singing of Islamic devotional songs, providing the newcomers with the atmosphere of a party to ease their anxiety. Ahmed Errachidi became tearful at this welcome, feeling the warmth that was being extended to a stranger by the men dressed in orange jumpsuits with no certainty as to what their own futures might hold.[4] The emotional solidarity that was being extended at Guantánamo Bay soon became more practical as the prisoners began to witness the very first abuses of their fellow cellmates and specifically over the desecration of the Qur'an. For Mansoor Adayfi, 'when one of us was hurt, we all hurt', indicating how the prisoners began to build a culture of solidarity with one another, but one that was heightened at moments of egregious violence. Mansoor described the way they witnessed a man named Al Qurashi be abused, and have his Qur'an stamped on –

the response of the other prisoners was to shout '*Allahu Akbar*' and shout at the guards – it did not matter to them whether the man was a schoolteacher or Taliban, they felt compelled to assist him.[5]

It was those early incidents of abuse that forced the prisoners to organise themselves better, so that they could meet the challenges of prison life collectively. Murat Kurnaz, a German national of Turkish origin, had been captured in Pakistan and sold to the Americans like many others. He had gone through Kandahar before arriving at Guantánamo Bay and had already experienced a great deal of torture and humiliation at the hands of his captors before he was brought to his final destination. Murat held the Qur'an close to his heart and felt that collective action was the only way in which to respond to the transgressions against their persons as well as their faith:

After the incident with the Qur'an, we went ahead and elected a leader. All of the prisoners were allowed to nominate a candidate. It was a secret vote – the Americans knew nothing about it. It took several weeks because the vote was strictly oral, the preliminary results passed from cage to cage. Out of five hundred prisoners, ten men were chosen, and suggestions were collected and evaluated. Those ten men chose three other men, who in turn elected our leader. We called him the emir. No one but the three men who had elected him knew who he was. Officially, this man was not our leader. He chose a spokesperson to deal with the Americans and to appear as our leader. In that way, the real emir could remain in the background, undetected. We strung the Americans along. We acted as though we had elected an emir, the spokesperson, and let his name be known. Before long, the spokesperson disappeared for months. The Americans thought they had broken our resistance, and there wouldn't be any more hunger strikes. But the real emir was still making the decisions behind the scenes. He collected opinions from all the prisoners' representatives and decided what the figurehead emir would tell the Americans. We wanted to put an end to the defilements of the Koran. We wanted the Americans to respect our faith and stop playing the U.S. national anthem during *dhuhr* [midday] prayers. We wanted to restrict the level of torture and get medicine for some of the wounded prisoners.[6]

Murat would later take on the role of being a leader for one of the blocks he was moved to – this was largely due to his ability to speak a number of languages, including English. As English was the only language the guards could communicate with the prisoners, those prisoners who could speak English would become conduits for those who were not able to communicate directly. This would only last for so long, as before long the soldiers would transfer prisoners from one block to another as a strategy to disrupt prisoner organising. However, this resulted in a flow of information that came to become known as the Detainee News Network (DNN) – an informal system of exchanging information, tactics and advice that was unknowingly facilitated by the guards.

These informal systems of communication were not unique to life in Guantánamo, but had developed in one form or another in different carceral settings. Throughout his detention, Sami Al-Arian was moved around to 14 different prisons. He recalled, 'The day I went to federal prison, I had no idea how hard solitary confinement would be.' At the time, a group of Muslim prisoners were being disciplined in adjacent solitary cells:

They called out through the wall, 'What is going on, brother?' I said, 'They are preventing me from calling my family.' They all began banging on their cell doors. Whenever something like that happens, the prison authorities are required to videotape it. They kept shouting 'Give him his phone call!' So, they had to give me my phone call. The solidarity was so beautiful. In the cell above me, there was this Hispanic guy. He was very strong. He had become Muslim in prison. We started talking through the pipes. I started teaching him more about Islam. He took the name Abu Dujana because I had told him about the bravery of Abu Dujana. I was always safe when he was around. He had all kinds of questions and I would answer him. We were together for a year and a half but I had never seen him. One day, we were transferred together in a bus and I thought, 'Oh my god! His hands are the size of my thighs!'

Sami Al-Arian spent his time outside of solitary confinement teaching Arabic, maths and Islam to his fellow inmates. He helped them study for tests to get their degrees. He would fast – as recommended by the *sunnah* – every Monday and Thursday but because it was prohibited to eat outside of the cafeteria, Rastafarian inmates would hide his food in their Rastacaps so he could break his fast later.

Although the experiences of those in Guantánamo Bay were predominantly positive in terms of the relationships that developed between the prisoners, suspicion did creep in due to the way interrogators would ease the conditions of some prisoners over others. As Abdul Salam Zaeef recognised:

> It is understandable that under such intense confinement and scrutiny human beings become victims of their own suspicions. Prisoners began to blame one another for spreading intelligence and spying on their fellow detainees. Suspicion became rife and soon prisoners were identifying brothers whom they suspected of betraying them.[7]

While this was not common, it could lead to a prisoner becoming isolated due to the suspicion of him having renounced Islam or having collaborated with the interrogators, leading to them being spat at and even blamed for the actions of the soldiers. According to Zaeef, some of these prisoners would end up in the psychiatric wing of the detention camp. There were others who spoke out against abusing those who had publicly renounced the faith, however, urging their fellow prisoners to think of the pressure of being in a prison environment and how it could impact on a person's mental health. This approach was adopted among the prisoner population and a more charitable view was taken towards those who were seen as having separated themselves from the rest.

Al-Qal'a – Cairo, Egypt
HMP Long Lartin – South Littleton, United Kingdom
Federal Correctional Institution (FCI) Fairton – New Jersey, United States of America

Adel Abdel Bary always attempted to build a community for himself whenever he found himself imprisoned, from his time in the prisons of Egypt, the UK and the US. He understood the fundamental importance of building and maintaining a community, particularly because of the emphasis that Islam places on the congregation and communal activities. During his time at the Qal'a prison in Cairo – a repurposed citadel from the time of Salahuddin in the twelfth century – providing he was not detained in a solitary confinement cell, he would ensure that he would be praying in *jama'ah* with four, five, or six men. Night-time would bring different forms of entertainment for the prisoners as they would sing *anasheed* – devotional songs – or recite poems to one another, and at times even huddle around a radio they might have smuggled into the prison.

Adel's decade of detention in Egypt was never linear; he was constantly in and out as he completed his legal studies and qualified as a lawyer. He started a practice with his friend Muntasser al-Zayat – who would become one of the most prominent human rights lawyers in Egypt – and they would regularly represent political prisoners. Part of the role they would play during hearings, would be to provide prisoners with material support by bringing family members to pass on comfort items, whether it be clothes, religious items such as the Qur'an, or food. Adel recalled how one day he saw a prisoner who he was not representing:

When I went to the cage, I saw the brothers and saw that one of them was not like the others, he was very smart with a suit and tie and looked very good. He was a young man with black hair that was neatly combed. I went to him and asked him how he was doing, giving him *salaam*. I asked him if he knew me, and he said, 'You are *Ustadh* [a title for lawyers] Adel Abdul Majeed.' I asked if he had a lawyer and he said he did but that the lawyer didn't come. I asked if he needed any assistance at all to tell the judge something, I told him not to be shy and that it wasn't a big deal. He asked that I help to adjourn the case to another time. I said this is easy and it was no problem at all. I went to the judge and made this request and it was granted, giving a delay to another time which I told the young man. I said to the young man, 'Can I ask you a question?' He said, 'Of course.' I asked, 'When you went to my home, did you find any explosives or weapon in my home?' He said, 'No, you know we just signed the paper, we didn't write anything.' I told him, 'I would like to advise you as a Muslim, whatever happened, but you can make your repentance to Allah and make your time to be with Him and that I am not happy to see you in this place.' This was the police officer who [had] raided my home, and he was the officer who tortured me. Me and Muntasser, when we saw him, we were shocked. His name is Muhammad Osama Kamal, and he was *muqaddam*, the lieutenant colonel of the police. He had been in prison for 14 months over an allegation that he shot his wife. Sometimes when you see such things in your life, we don't let it affect us because we are Muslims and we have a heart. When we deal with people, it is not about it being a battlefield. We don't revel in the misery of others. I believe that some of them are not even Muslim, saying that not even Allah can hear us, but when you are in a different position, you don't want to show happiness that someone is in difficulty.

Community for the prisoners was something that was built both inside and outside of the prison. During his detention in the UK for over a decade – at the request of the US – Adel experienced the system's racism in different ways, which impacted his ability to maintain his relationships with family and friends. He once went through a lengthy process of complaining through the prison ombudsman over the denial of his ability to say *Assalaamualaykum* to his family over the phone, as the guards claimed he was speaking in Arabic to them – despite the mundanity of the greeting. This was compounded when the guards also barred him from saying the names Muhammad and Abdul Majeed (his sons), as they claimed that again by using these names, he was speaking in Arabic, which was prohibited as part of his prison conditions. As soon as the guards would hear these names, they would cut the phone line.

In the US, Adel found it much more difficult to build community for other reasons, largely to do with the types of Islam that were practised once he was transferred out of solitary confinement. He would come into confrontation with Muslims who believed in a particularly obsequious understanding of Islam, that privileged the authority of the state over any other consideration, including the fulfilment of Islamic duties and rituals:

> One of the most difficult Muslims I found in the US prisons were the Madkhali drug dealers – these were the most idiotic people I ever encountered on this earth. Being detained along-side them was like being in hell, I've never come across people who are more idiotic in my life. They have no knowledge them-selves and they just repeat what they hear from someone whose name is Hassan al-Somali. They don't know anything about Rabee' al-Madkhali.[8] They would sit alongside me in the kitchen and ask me again and again, 'What do you think of Shaykh Rabee' al-Madkhali?' They would sit with me in Fairton Prison in New Jersey, they would constantly ask me this question. I asked them 'Which Shaykh are you speaking about? The Shaykh Muqbil I know is from Yemen', and he said 'No, Shaykh Rabee' al-Madkhali'. I said, 'Oh him, he's a *shaytaan*.' The guy stood up and said '*A'oodhubillah, La hawla wala quwwata illah billah*.' [I seek refuge in Allah. There is no might and no power except by Allah.] These guys have their girlfriends coming to the prison, have children with them from inside the prison, they are drug dealers and yet are obsessed with Rabee'. Some of them are serious and they did study very hard while in prison, and they became strong in their memorisation and learnt *sarf* and *nahu* [forms of Arabic grammar] very well.

Although Adel would pray with the men and have theological debates with them, he realised that some of the systems of cor-ruption that plagued American prisons, had found their way into the way that Muslims would organise themselves – thus at times replicating the logic of a gang in order to survive the harsh prison environment. There would be cooperating witnesses among them, those that were given special privileges by the prison authorities, and those who were running hustles within the prison with the guards which included the transfer of drugs. Adel was surprised by these actions, but understood that the way US prisons were con-structed meant that it was almost impossible to behave outside of an economy that has long been established.

Burj al-Arab Prison – Alexandria, Egypt
Tora Prison – Cairo, Egypt

Ali arrived at a cell that had 34 other inmates after being placed under solitary confinement for eight days as a form of *ta'dib* (disciplining). He was separated from most of his comrades and sent to a cell with prisoners incarcerated for criminal offences (*gina'i*). He had been severely beaten by officers and arrived at the cell barefoot; his clothes were torn, and his face was bloody. He had not eaten for eight days. Sending him to this cell proved not to be the punishment the prison authorities had intended:

> They welcomed me with a hero's welcome. They brought me a blanket, a fresh change of clothes and some food to eat. I had gone in without a thing, but they welcomed me. They said, 'You stood up to the guards!' At first, they were very scared of the officers, so they would do these nice things in secret. Slowly, they got braver and braver.

Officers often move political prisoners to *gina'i* cells as a form of punishment. Even though they are all in a small, enclosed space, the *gina'i* inmates are forbidden from interacting or talking to the political prisoners. Most cells have informants – either older prisoners tasked with maintaining discipline in the cell, or low-ranking officers who spend the night shift in the cell alongside other prisoners. The *gina'i* prisoners found ways of navigating the limited space of the cell. They would break down the food baskets they received during visitation and turn them into tight ropes. They would then weave the ropes together tightly to make impromptu hammocks to allow for more space for people to sleep. Ali noted it was not perfect, but it worked.

During the first few days in this cell, Ali prayed with three or four of his comrades in congregation and it was not long after that half of the inmates joined them regularly. Ali came to the realisation that many young political prisoners often reach, that these *gina'i* inmates never had a chance. Out of 34 inmates, only one was literate. Many did not know the details of their sentences and almost all had no real legal representation. Ali and other political prisoners would help teach them to read and write, including writing letters to their families:

> They came up to me one Thursday and said we are going to pray *Jummah* tomorrow. The previous Friday, they wanted to but I told them it wasn't really a good idea. That day, they insisted and said I was going to lead the prayers and be the one to say the Friday *khutba* (sermon). On that Friday, they all woke up very early. They went to shower and wore their best and cleanest prison uniforms. Whoever had a prayer mat brought it along; whoever had *tasbih* (prayer beads) also brought it along. It was really one of the best days in prison. I remember feeling an opening from God. I usually don't know how to do sermons, but this one was very good. It was about forgiveness. As soon as I finished they yelled, 'Allah! Allah bless you, Shaykh!' It was funny, I was this 21-year-old kid but truly it was beautiful. One of the happiest days in prison.

However, as Ali had suspected, the informants – or 'birdies' as they are called in prison lingo – informed the prison authorities of the *gina'i* prisoners praying, and he was moved to a different cell the following day and the remaining prisoners were punished. While the prison authorities anticipated that political prisoners – many of whom were deeply religious – to continue religious practices in prison, they would come to see *gina'i* developing religious practices or widening their intellectual scopes to be incredibly subversive – in many, albeit not all – prison complexes. They would almost always be punished for praying or (if caught) learning to read or write.

Mixed cells – with both *gina'i* and political prisoners – are spaces that can become embattled, as social class, prison formation, and practice of religion can come into acute confrontation. When Mohamed Soltan was moved to a mixed cell with Abdullah El Shamy, he was put in a small room with 80 other inmates who were both political and *gina'i*. The inmates needed to sleep in shifts due to the small space. Typically, one of the problems political prisoners – particularly those with health issues – face in these cells is the amount of smoking. This was always a point of contention between political prisoners and *gina'i* prisoners.

At the beginning of his time in the cell, Soltan recalls that the *gina'i* prisoners would not pray with them but would get out of the way to allow them room to pray – despite this being very difficult as the cell being extremely small:

I remember the *qibla* was directly facing the bathroom. It was disgusting. The toilet was a hole in the ground and a shower that would only work for two hours a day. Remember there were 80 people in that room. But we would pray. One day, we were praying but all the other inmates were just talking very loudly. One of the powerful inmates was taking a shower. He came out of the shower in his little underwear and screamed, 'Shut the hell up; people are praying!' They didn't listen and we were trying very hard not to crack up. Then he shouted again, 'You stupid motherfuckers shut up, can't you see people are praying!' He was so high. We couldn't keep it in. We just burst out laughing. He was high as a kite but he was still trying to do good. He then started to join us in prayer and the people followed him.

Enforced Disappearance, Police Station – Cairo, Egypt
Qanater El Khayereya Women's Prison – Qalyubiyya, Egypt
Wadi al-Natrun Prison – Buhayra, Egypt

The anecdotes female political prisoners shared from their interactions with *gina'i* inmates do not significantly diverge from the experiences of their male counterparts. Unlike male prisons, female prisons were larger in size, had more prisoners, and had beds. Most of the female political prisoners were sent either to Qanater Prison or to Wadi al-Natrun. However, before being moved to prison, prisoners first get sent to transitory cells. These cells are always mixed – including both political and *gina'i* inmates.

Denied any form of due process during her enforced disappearance, Marwa was sent to a transitory cell that was 3 x 4 metres and had small three-storey bunk beds. Marwa had arrived at the prison with an injury, so the other inmates allowed her to sleep on one of the beds, except that Marwa found that these beds were occupied by three women per bunk. The two women she was bunked with were in prison for very different reasons; they told her that they had been detained on prostitution charges. As Marwa started to recite *dhikr* (remembrance of Allah and supplications) on her prayer beads, they asked if they could join in and one would later ask if she could borrow the beads, so she could make her own *dhikr*:

> For some reason, they thought I was especially religious. An older *gina'i* auntie came up to me and asked if I could read her some Qur'an. She could not read or write and she really wanted to hear the Qur'an. And afterwards, the woman who borrowed my prayer beads was just sentenced to three months. She came back from the court ecstatic and said 'I will name my first daughter after you!'

Layla found herself navigating more peculiar circumstances. Unlike Marwa, Layla was never moved to a political cell, and she spent the entirety of her prison term in a mixed prison with both political and *gina'i* prisoners. Like Marwa, however, she spent the first days after her enforced disappearance in the transitory cell in circumstances that she could only describe as horrific. The sight before her was of 88 women, cramped together as they slept in a 4 x 4 metre cell – there was no room to move between the bodies, and every step, every move, resulted in a body being elbowed, pushed, or stepped on. As with Marwa's transitory cell, the sleeping arrangements were identical. Two senior *gina'i* inmates were in charge of the prison ward, and one had spent years in an execution ward which Layla described as a grave for the living – and the other was imprisoned on prostitution charges. These two women controlled the prison population closely:

> I supplicated to Allah so He could protect me. I was physically very ill. We were treated monstrously. I spent Eid there. I heard the *takbir*s from the mosques around the prison. So I started reciting '*Allahu Akbar, Allahu Akbar Wa Lillahil Hamd*' under my breath. They threatened us that whoever got up to pray *fajr* would be reported. We did all of our prayers sitting down because standing up was impermissible.

A few days into her detention, Layla got her period. Once it finished, she asked the head inmate if she was allowed to shower, as she was desperate to make *ghusl* in order to pray:

> She said, 'You can't make *ghusl* after your period and wear the same clothes you had on. Your prayer won't be valid.' I told her I didn't mind; just let me shower. She said, 'I can't let you pray while you're impure.' The reason of course I did not have a clean change of clothes was that she had stolen my clothes when I first went in. For two weeks, I could not shower and I was not allowed to pray because she insisted that my prayer would be invalid.

Layla was always the youngest in the cells. She recalled that when the police chief came to the cell, all the inmates stood up for him – Layla didn't. A junior officer reprimanded her: 'How dare you not stand up for the Pasha?'

'And what? What are you going to do? Will you electrocute me like he electrocuted me?'

The *gina'i* prisoners responded with a mixture of fear and pity. Why was this 18-year-old being electrocuted? An older woman, who was caught on bizarre sex crime charges, felt extreme pity towards her and started treating her like a daughter. She protected her from other inmates and the officers. In the transitory cell, Layla befriended another woman. She was an older woman who was a Sufi from Halayeb and Shalateen. Layla recalls that she was incredibly knowledgeable in *fiqh*. Together, they decided to learn Surah al-Baqarah – the longest chapter of the Qur'an.

After the transitory cell, Layla was moved to the Qanater Women's Prison. This prison complex was a behemoth, with one cell split into two wings. The first wing was where poorer inmates were placed and was nicknamed after one of the poorest and down-trodden neighbourhoods in Cairo – Duwiqa. The second wing was nicknamed Zamalek – after an upper-middle-class neighbour-hood. Layla was first placed in Duwiqa. Despite the wings being in the same cell, the living conditions reflected the class disparity that their names indicated.

The inmates watched closely as Layla began to pray. One inmate – nicknamed Honey – approached Layla after prayer. Honey had been caught in a prostitution ring and had been in prison for a long time:

> In the beginning, she asked me, 'Am I allowed to pray?' I really did not understand the question. She said, 'Can someone like me pray?' I said, 'Yeah, nothing is stopping you.' She said she didn't know how to make ablution, so we showed her. Then she started to pray with us. I cannot tell you how much the other inmates made fun of her. They would say, 'Look, Honey the *nijsa* [impure] is praying.' She stopped praying afterwards.

Another inmate came up to Layla after seeing Honey pray and asked if she, too, could pray:

> Again, I didn't understand the question. I said, 'What is prevent- ing you from praying?' She said, 'Well, I drink.' I asked her if she was drunk right now. She responded, 'Of course not!' I said, 'Yeah, there is no connection between the fact that you drink with your praying. They are two separate things.' She was like, 'I always heard that you can't be a drinker and pray.' Others got involved in the cell. An older inmate said, 'So you're saying God accepts the prayers of a drinker? My husband used to come at dawn drunk, and then he would sober up and go to *fajr* prayers at the mosque every day.'

What struck Layla the most was the way inmates spoke about and viewed themselves. Society treated them as untouchables, and that is how they saw themselves:

> They thought that they were born worthless, and will die worth- less and even in the afterlife, they were worthless. It was as though some people were born into piety and God's good grace and everyone else is stuck on the bottom of the piety pyramid. I came in and observed with no judgement, only questions. What the hell have these Islamists in charge of charities been doing all these years? They feed people, okay but without bringing them in or making them feel like they have value or worth.

After a few weeks in the Duwiqa wing, which had become over-crowded, the officers moved Layla to the Zamalek wing. The Zamalek wing was a mixed bag of people detained for protesting, white-collar crimes, murder felonies and sex crimes. Very quickly, and despite the range of life experiences among them, Layla made friends with her cellmates. Her closest friend in the cell was a woman named Hannah, who was a Christian woman accused of adultery by her husband. She had fallen in love with a Muslim man and told her husband that she wanted a civil divorce. To retali-ate, her husband reported her to the police on adultery and drug charges. Her boyfriend was also arrested. He could have gone free the very first day he was detained if he denied ever knowing her, but he did not. He said he loved her and wanted to marry her, and so they were both sentenced on adultery charges. They would sometimes see each other in court and it was only when they were both released that they married. Hannah was a unique individual. She came from a highly intellectual background. Her father was a voracious reader and loved poetry, philosophy and Arabic. He had encouraged her to read and learn about different religions and cultures while still remaining faithful to her Christian beliefs.

Among the inmates in the cell were a group of Qur'anists – a modern movement that rejects the validity of the Prophetic tradi-tion (*Hadith*) corpus. As an Azhari student, Layla found herself in constant conflict with the Qur'anists:

There was this one girl – she was forty-something – she was a lawyer who rejected the *Sunnah*. Every night she would take Hannah's Bible and try to pick out what she saw were flaws or inconsistencies. She would insist on debating Hannah and trying to convert her to Islam. This girl was not sure of Islam as a religion, yet she was sure she wanted to convert Hannah. It was very stupid. I hated mindless debates; but this woman would force me to respond to her questions. She would say, 'You rep-resent the institution of Al Azhar; why is polygyny allowed in Islam?' I never would respond directly to her question. I would try to nudge her to think about methodology and how we know what we know.

Layla found solace in her friendship with Hannah. Hannah would help her revise the chapters of the Qur'an she tried to memorise. Despite Hannah's strong sense of faith, one question haunted her:

> The one question she could not reconcile: if God is love, how can He do this to us? How can he allow for all this death and destruction? How can He let the innocent get hurt? I told her that there is nothing incumbent upon Allah. Good and evil are characteristics human beings invented to understand their lived realities. They are not applicable to God. If God can be benefited or harmed, then we can say He can do good or He can do bad. But Allah is beyond that, and we are His creation. He does with us as He pleases. If He had created us for eternity in hell, it would still not be good nor bad.

This was an enshrined belief in Layla's heart that never wavered – she did not blame God for her suffering; rather, she focused on what she could do to worship Him in the circumstances He had chosen to test her with. She started Qur'an recitation (*tajwid*) study circles that everyone joined – even the Qur'anists. With the *gina'i* prisoners, however, she would do one-on-one sessions. By the end of her time in prison, the difficult environment resulted in her relationship with God deteriorating. She did not have a crisis of faith, but she was just tired. In the beginning, she would pray to God to hasten her release, then she began to pray that if there was a benefit in her release for God to hasten it. By the end, she only prayed not to lose her mind:

> It was the first time meeting women who killed their children and women who killed their parents. At the same time, I was taught the true meaning of *tawba* and that sometimes things are not black and white. One woman killed her husband after 14 years of marriage. She told us how he used to hurt her. She fell in love with someone else and when she asked for a divorce, there was a physical altercation between them. She hit him on the head, and he died. I cried the day she was sent to execution. What's ironic was both a Qur'anist and an ISIS-affiliated inmate asked me how I could mourn someone like her.

Layla built strong relations with many of her cellmates. She would dance and sing with the *gina'i* prisoners whenever someone was set to be released or have something to celebrate. Some of the older female political prisoners looked down on her for it. In one instance, a prisoner incarcerated for drug offences was visited by her small son. He had been sent to an orphanage by the state, but was allowed to visit his mother from time to time:

He was so small when he came in but her eyes were beaming with pride. She yelled, 'Come, come *ya siyasyin* [political prisoners]. Come see my son; he memorised the Qur'an.' The little boy started reciting the small *surah*s. She was so proud. Then he started singing *Qamarun* (a song in praise of the Prophet). One of the older inmates said very sternly: 'This song is *haram*!' I told her to leave us alone and said to him, 'Don't worry about her; sing Habibi, sing.'

COMMUNAL ISLAM

Bagram Airbase – Parvan, Afghanistan

Not all prisoners detained in Afghanistan and Pakistan were eventually sent on to Guantánamo Bay. Afghanistan became a long-term detention site for thousands of detainees caught up in the global War on Terror. Abdul Basit Zadran had been captured in a joint operation between the US and Afghan forces; he was tortured severely by the CIA for 45 days at the Dark Prison before being sent to Bagram where he would be held for five years. The vast majority of prisoners detained for lengthy periods at Bagram Airbase were Afghan nationals, resulting in its own largely Afghan culture and religious practice being consistent within the camps. Unlike in other prisons where prisoners had slightly more flexibility on being transported by female soldiers, in Bagram, there was a regular cycle of riots and punishment over US personnel refusing to respect the prisoners' beliefs regarding direct contact with the opposite sex. Abdul Basit explained that this was largely due to Afghan culture much more than anything to do with Islam explicitly:

In Afghan society, and the majority of those detained at Bagram were Afghan, there was a general feeling of discomfort around the presence of female guards. In Islam, we are taught to respect women. Islam taught us not to look at women, to lower our eyesight when we see one out of respect. As for being touched by a woman, for our society, this was too far for us. I'll be honest and say that Afghan culture is probably even more strict in this regard than Islam itself; we have made it more difficult and more prohibited, even more than Islam – this is our culture.

Abdul Basit was somewhat of an outlier among his fellow prisoners. Mostly, whether they knew it or not, they culturally and religiously adopted the *hanafi* school of thought, and thus many of their practices reflected the positions of that school. They had come to understand their place of detention, even outside of their home city, as the place where they were now *muqeem* (inhabiting) and so would deem that they should pray all their required prayers on time and without shortening them. All the schools of thought provide some degree of *rukhsa* (leniency), where an individual is travelling or outside of their city by being able to shorten their prayers, and to even combine them. For Abdul Basit, who was one of the few prisoners studied in the *hanbali madhhab*, refusing the status of being *muqeem* was a both a religious and political act – for five years he prayed by shortening his prayers to send the message he was *musafir* – a traveller who had been removed from his home. His very prayer indicated his refusal to accept his imprisonment as his new normal – a defiant rejection. This would at times lead to difficulties with the other prisoners, who would encourage him to pray with them in *jama'ah*, which he would do on occasion in order to maintain some sense of unity.

The differences in the schools would come to a head during Ramadan, when they would want to pray the night prayers together, and Abdul Basit would excuse himself:

In Ramadan, we always had a bit of a problem because many of the brothers were from South Asia, and they would pray their *tarawih* very fast,* to the extent that you would not be able to hear anything of what the imam was saying. I would say to the brothers, that first understand what *tarawih* means, and then try and practise it properly. Go to the *sahih sitta*,** and see how the Prophet (peace and blessings be upon him) did this. One day I said to them ok, I will do *tarawih* with you, and the imam made the initial *takbir* to start the prayer. I got as far as al-Rahman al-Raheem in my Fatiha, before he went into *ruku'*. I said to myself 'What is this?' The shortest twenty *rakats* and *witr* [the final unit of night prayer] I saw them pray, was between 15 to 18 minutes – this is impossible! It was even worse for me, because the cages were having competitions to see who could finish the *tarawih* the fastest. I would get annoyed with them and so would pray by myself or with another small group who would agree with me. The others would get upset and ask why I was boycotting them, and I explained that I would pray the *fard* [obligatory] prayers with them, but I wanted to spend my *tarwih* in contemplation of the Qur'an, rather than rushing through it. I said this is *sunnah*, so it doesn't matter if I prayed on my own. We would have these arguments, but in the end it was ok.

Regardless of their differences, there were ways in which Abdul Basit would be able to share Islam with his fellow prisoners, and his favourite part of the day was the twice-daily classes that they had self-organised on the explanation of the Qur'an. He did not miss a single class the entire five years he was detained, because he found learning from others and learning from their own reflections of the Qur'an provided him a great deal of solace.

What really impacted the Bagram prisoners, however, was the level of hunger they all experienced during their detention. The food rations they were given could not even be considered to reach the levels of sustenance. They were given a handful of rice, a piece of stale bread and some kidney beans – this would be their food on

---

* *Tarawih* – evening prayers during Ramadan, completed alone and in congregation.
** *Sahih sitta* are the six collections of Prophetic traditions considered to be the most authentic.

a regular basis, and sometimes a morsel of tough meat. The intensity of the hunger was difficult for Abdul Basit to describe, that between 15 people a crumb on the floor was the most coveted possession. Once, he was sitting in a group, and a few of them noticed there was a crumb on the floor, but no one had moved for it. After a short while, Abdul Basit rose and pretended to stretch his legs and speak to a couple of the prisoners, but then sat by the crumb and popped it in his mouth. The other prisoners began to laugh at him saying that he was cleverer than they were, but ultimately, this crumb dissolved the moment it reached his tongue – it was so insubstantial. Yet, despite this hunger, the prisoners found ways of gifting one another food as *sadaqah* (charity), when for him a single bite was equated in his mind to a kilogram of gold.

Being confined with 15 to 20 other people had its own problems though; joint isolation can result in its own form of madness, as living in such close quarters will inevitably lead to problems between those detained. Abdul Basit was very aware of this and did his utmost in order to not let problems emerge:

> Generally, our brotherhood was very sweet. Sometimes you would have detainees who would fight one another, because you are together in a small space all the time. You are with each other 24 hours a day, week by week and year by year; where we don't see anything else except the faces of one another, it will eventually lead to some small problems between brothers. Even if you were to put Romeo and Juliet into a room together, they would end up fighting with one another after such a long period of time. In that time, I was giving the example to brothers of Layla and Majnun.[9] Otherwise, we were one voice, we loved one another. For me, over the five years, I never fought once with the other brothers.

This brotherhood described by Abdul Basit was a friendship and comradeship that developed in different ways, as there were moments of joviality between them too. Abdul Basit smiled as he thought of Bakh Muhammad, a shepherd from Uruzgan, who had almost no contact with the modern world. His entire life had been lived around his close family and livestock. Bakh had been detained for no reason except American anger at all Afghans who were not in their employ. Abdul Basit regretted his behaviour, but explained that being in such close quarters, the prisoners felt like they would need to do something different. Abdul Basit claimed to Bakh that everyone knew that the difference between men and animals is that men had three testicles while animals had two, and that someone had noticed Bakh only had two. Bakh immediately began to claim *wallahi* (by Allah), he had three as well, trying to convince all in their cage that he was like them – leading to all the others in the cage rolling around laughing endlessly. The teasing forced Abdul Basit to apologise to Bakh, the former using this story later during an interrogation to explain to his captors how they had detained those who were *miskeen* (unfortunate), *fakir* (a poor person) and completely innocent.

HMP Long Lartin – South Littleton, United Kingdom
Northern Correctional Institution Supermax – Connecticut, United States of America

Every *Eid al-Fitr*, Babar Ahmad knew that his parents would pay the yearly obligatory alms that were due to be given to the poor. Among Pakistanis, a culture had developed that the head of a household would take responsibility for paying the *zakat al-fitr** for all those under their care, except Babar had no savings, and no means to pay – he became reliant on his parents to ensure that the four or five pounds reached a destination that was in need of help. During his time in detention in the UK, a period of detention without charge due to an extradition demand from the US, he still felt compelled to give charity in any way that he could, to perform deeds that might benefit his afterlife and be of assistance to those he felt were in need:

> In the UK [prisons], you have a cash account, there is no physical cash you deal with. So if your family sends you money, or if you earn money as a cleaner or in the workshop, it goes into

---

* *Zakat al-fitr* – the obligatory tax to be paid or distributed before the Eid prayer after Ramadan ends.

your account. I remember in 2006, there was an earthquake in Balokot [northern Pakistan], and the imams were doing a collection for a registered charity to send to the earthquake victims. There were around 120 Muslim brothers at Long Lartin Prison, and they collectively raised around £2,000 which they donated from their own prisoner spend money to the victims of the earthquake. These are prisoners, some of whom had family that would send them, and some of them would earn £15 a week from cleaning prison toilets or showers, or working in the workshop. My *sadaqah*, which I'm mindful is not just financial but can be through other means, I would try and buy extra things from the commissary and give it to other prisoners who didn't have anyone. Some of them were mentally ill or some of them didn't have families who could help. I'd buy extra food or crisps and just give it to them, and that would be like my *sadaqah*. Obviously, you try and uplift people and I would try and do that wherever I was in America, in the Supermax, I would shout and talk to other prisoners. There were a lot of people with mental health problems, suffering, lots of different difficulties and my *sadaqah* would be talking to them, and not just the prisoners, but the officers as well.

Highly educated and with a great deal of worldly experience, Babar's natural kind disposition meant that even while prosecutors and the media were attempting to present him as a terrorist, the guards in the UK and US who would directly interact with him would see in him someone to whom they could bring their problems, to really confide in the hope they could benefit from his wisdom. This increased in the US, where those who had previously been soldiers in Afghanistan and Iraq, sometimes members of US special forces had now become prison guards, would turn to him in desperate need for a charitable ear that would help them through their daily anxieties. Babar understood the role he was playing and explained, 'Part of my *sadaqah* was just by talking, talking to other prisoners and guards and trying to help them, uplifting them when they were feeling down or feeling suicidal.'

Ramadan in the UK had not been a problem for Babar as the prison authorities would make provision for their unit of Muslim-only prisoners in joint isolation at HMP Long Lartin. In the Supermax in the US, the situation changed dramatically as there was no accommodation at all for his needs. Babar would have to estimate the start date of Ramadan because the prison imam would only come once a week, but he would also have to estimate the start and end times of each fasting day due to the lack of any clock. He did not worry though; he knew his efforts to estimate would be accepted by God, providing he did his best:

I knew that the evening meal would be brought around 4:30 p.m., and that sunset was around 8:30 p.m., so things were an estimate. Things that are associated with Ramadan are community, *tarawih*, communal gatherings and *iftar* [breaking of the fast during Ramadan]. There is a community aspect to it, but also there is the food aspect, Ramadan is also about food for many people rightly or wrongly. In the Supermax, you had an option of going on the Ramadan menu, and so I signed up for it. What would happen is that at the time of *suhoor* [the pre-*fajr* meal before beginning the fast], an officer would come and give me a bag of food which had milk, bread, and it had a piece of fruit and two packets of sugar-frosted cornflakes. Now apparently the diet in the Supermax prison was designed by nutritionists, but I do not know what nutritionist designed that, or if it was done on purpose, or that they couldn't care less. Even if I was to be given what the other prisoners had, the meal of porridge, that would be more nutritious than this. I mean, cornflakes, at the best of times, if I had a bowl I would be hungry again in 30 minutes. Sugar-frosted cornflakes, which I don't eat, but if you eat that you'll be hungry again in 15 minutes, like you haven't eaten at all. So I would supplement my *suhoor* with other things I had from my savings like fish, porridge, etc., and just try to eat that.

I didn't have a kettle for those two years, so how do you eat noodles? You press the warm water button in your sink, and it comes out for 60 seconds, and then you wait for five minutes, then you press it again and wait for five minutes again, then you press it again. If you do this six or seven times, the water will be warmish, and with that you would put your noodles, porridge, or tea into it. For two years, I required that hot water for the food.

In the evening, for *iftar* time, they would come just before sunset, and the officer would open the flap and give you a meal, which was the normal meal that other prisoners were having that day, but there would be an extra fish patty on top of it. By fish patty, I mean that little square that you get in a McDonalds fillet-o-fish. Imagine you had three fish fingers stuck together side by side, you'd just get one of those on top of what the other prisoners received. That whole meal was not enough, let alone if you had been fasting. I tried to supplement myself. I'd buy fish pouches, anything that was nutritious, to bulk up my Ramadan diet.

In the second year, I decided to do away with the Ramadan diet and just do the normal food. So most of the time I was in legal visits all day, eight hours from Monday to Friday, sometimes ten hours. The officers would open my cell and put the food on my table. In the morning, you'd get some porridge or semolina or this thing they call 'grits' and a piece of cake, and they'd leave that on my table. At lunchtime, they'd put my food there again and then the evening meal at 4:30 p.m. dinner would be served, and they would come again. The fast doesn't open until 8:30 p.m., so by the time the fast is opened, on my table I have a polystyrene box which has a porridge that has been there for 13 hours, I've got lunch, whatever it was (a salad, fish, etc.) and has been there for about nine hours, and in the evening, there was the dinner meal which has been there since 4:30 p.m., so been there for about four hours. I would open my fast, and then I would eat this food, freezing cold. But you know what, it was the most delicious food that I ever ate. Whatever it was. When you are fasting, everything is delicious. They would give this pot of maple syrup for dessert with a piece of French toast, I would keep it and use it instead of honey. I would open my fast, pray *maghrib*, eat and then pray *tarawih*. That was a really nice memory, a good memory. Once I opened my fast, I'd just be there after having had 8–10 hours of legal visits all day, and now I've just opened my fast with some Hershey's chocolate. One of the hardest things about being in prison in America was that the only chocolate available was Hershey's. The best way to describe it is a mixture of gone-off sour milk and vomit, and I don't know where the chocolate flavour comes from, but that's what I had –

that would be my dessert. The sad thing is, that after two years of having this, I actually began to like it and that's when I thought I need to head home.

Leeman Prison – Minya, Egypt
Damanhour Prison – Buhayra, Egypt
Scorpion Prison – Cairo, Egypt
Tora Prison – Cairo, Egypt
Qanater El Khayereya Women's Prison – Qalyubiyya, Egypt

Prison life does not just engender transformations in relationships with the unfamiliar, it also recalibrates relationships of the familiar. Mohamed spent years being moved from prison to prison. He encountered situations that were physically, spiritually and emotionally trying – especially after he spent more than a year on hunger strike. In prison, he was also reacquainted with his father, who became a mentor to many young people struggling to survive prison life. But also, this was the closest Mohamed ever felt to his father:

Me and baba spent eight months in a solitary cell together. He got to really know me. I think this was the longest time we ever spent together. Maybe even more than we have in my life combined. I really got to know him and he really got to know me. We got in a lot of fights about everything, about philosophical stuff. I would ask and sometimes he had answers and other times he didn't. It was funny. I was the difficult child outside and I was still being difficult in prison.

Despite their disagreements on things like the format of the Friday *khutba* or the meanings of *hadith*, the time Mohamed spent with his father was the most precious. They spent a Ramadan together. They completed 16 recitations of the Qur'an and in the morning, his father would read from the Sahih Bukhari corpus. Together they would recite supplications:

To You, my Lord, I complain of my weakness, lack of support and the humiliation I am made to receive. Most Compassionate and

Merciful! You are the Lord of the weak, and You are my Lord. To whom do You leave me? To a distant person who receives me with hostility? Or to an enemy You have given power over me? As long as You are not displeased with me, I do not care what I face. I would, however, be much happier with Your mercy. I seek refuge in the light of Your face by which all darkness is dispelled and both this life and the life to come are put in their right course against incurring Your wrath or being the subject of Your anger. To You I submit, until I earn Your pleasure. Everything is powerless without Your support.

One night, during Ramadan, the officers came and carried Mohamed away. He had become weak and immobile from his prolonged hunger strike:

They came in and said yallah! I couldn't walk at the time. They grabbed me and put me on the wheelchair. They handcuffed me to the wheelchair and blindfolded me and started wheeling me away. And I lost it. I was finally looking forward to Ramadan, with baba who was always my spiritual safety net to carry me through it and hopefully find the strength to keep going with my stride. I screamed. It was a panic attack. I woke everybody up in prison.

The officers had instructions not to allow them to see one another. Mohamed's health was rapidly declining. One day in court, Mohamed finally saw his father:

I hadn't seen him in five or six months. I really missed him but he didn't recognise me. I had lost so much weight. He greeted me like he had greeted everybody else. I usually go kiss his hand but suddenly he moved his hand away because I was a stranger to him. As soon as he realised it was me, he gave me the biggest hug.

The prison authorities tried to instrumentalise their relationship and bond to break them – particularly at the height of Mohamed's hunger strike. Often, they would isolate them from each other and from the rest of the prison population.

As a prolific scholar and mentor, Mohamed's father wrote profusely on *tafsir* (exegesis of the Qur'an), *fiqh* and *hadith* in prison.
He would often hold study circles for young people on *tafsir* and
usul al-fiqh (the principles of Islamic jurisprudence). He also initiated a system of peer review for the books he wrote in prison.
On the way to the court sessions, he would wear two undershirts and a sweater. On one of the undershirts, he would write
a summary of his work. In court, he would take off that under-
shirt with the written material and give it to another inmate from
another prison ward who would advise him on the peer review
method. This was read by everyone in the other prisons and was
even leaked to scholars and intellectuals outside of prison. After he
received feedback from them, he would incorporate changes into
the main text.

The calibre and sophistication of intellectual life differs from
prison to prison. It relies heavily on the level of organisation in
these cells and the availability of scholarly voices. The most
common study circles include a study of *tajwid*. Prisoners with
*ijaza*s (authorisation to transmit knowledge) in the *qirat* (recitation) of the Qur'an would transmit this to other prisoners in study
circles. The person receiving the *ijaza* would sit and be examined
by the person transmitting the *ijaza* on their recitation and *tajwid*.
They would end the examination with supplications. Other prisoners would then hold parties celebrating the *ijaza*s.

Depending on the cell – and its theological homogeneity – *fiqh*
debates may or may not be amicable. Abbas recalls he was in a
cell that had both Muslim Brotherhood-affiliated prisoners and
Salafis. In this particular cell, debates were often heated but never
violent. In other instances where there were ISIS-affiliated prisoners or *takfiri*s, the debates often led to physical altercations. In
Abbas's case he describes the debates as more of a tit-for-tat:

> The biggest never-ending fight between the Ikhwan and Salafis
> was the permissibility of collective *dhikr*. Oh my days, we all just
> wanted them to shut up. The Ikhwan would do *dhikr* together
> and the Salafis would say that it is an innovation and ask for
> *dalil* (proof from the *Sunnah*). The Ikhwan would respond
> with that the Prophet encountered a people who sat together

in remembrance of Allah and did not stop them. That proves that it is not prohibited. The Salafis would respond with two things. First with a Hadith from Sahih Bukhari: 'O people! Don't exert yourselves, for you do not call a deaf or an absent one, but you call the All-Listener, the All-Seer.' And in *fiqh* of worship, you cannot worship God in a way that He did not prescribe for you to worship Him. The next issue would be the order of the *dhikr* then the content. There the Ikhwan would have a stronger argument because the *dhikr* is all based on *hadith*. Needless to say, this never got resolved.

Despite Abbas's characterisation of prison theological and *fiqh* debates as monotonous, out of boredom he too would raise debates. He chuckled as he recalled a debate he once raised that it was impermissible for a prisoner with a lisp to lead prayer. He explained, 'I told them that this guy would say *"Bism Allah a-wahman a-waheem"* because he could not pronounce the letter "r". I admit, I can be a bit of a bully. At the end they agreed with me and he didn't lead prayer again.'

Another debate that Abbas claimed irked him were those of the Azhari prisoners. The Azharis were predominantly *hanafi* then *maliki* and there was a small *shafi'i* minority. The Malikis and the *hanafis* would debate *sadl* (keeping the hands straight on the sides instead of folding them in prayer). They would also debate the time when *Du'a al-Qunut* (a special supplication done in prayer) is to be done. These debates were often tempered by *fiqh* books that were smuggled into the cell. Abbas recalls hiding a book called *Fiqh al-Sunnah* by al-Sayyid Sabbiq by hiding it in the cover of Abu al-Faraj al-Isfahani's *Book of Songs*.

The *takfiri* and ISIS-affiliated prisoners were the most difficult to deal with. For one, they often considered both inmates and officers to be outside the fold of Islam. That would facilitate their engagement with the authorities against the other inmates. On the outset, they would refuse to eat with other inmates, or accept food from their family in visitation based on the principle that one does not eat food prepared by the unbelievers. They would have a separate prayer congregation because they do not believe in the validity of other congregations.

The issue of prayer thus becomes very significant for the prison authorities to gauge the religious and political affiliations of inmates so as to better control them. This quickly became obvious to Hamza. The prison complex he found himself in was unique. There was a mosque on the premises – in which prisoners could pray, in theory. Sometimes, they would bring in an imam from the Endowment of Religious Affairs (*Awqaf*) to lead prisoners in prayer. In fact, one former detainee noted that the Egyptian president's adviser on religious affairs and renowned scholar Usama al-Sayyid Al-Azhari was involved in re-education programmes for detainees. In Hamza's case, the imam was not only an unknown scholar but also someone who was unable to recite the Qur'an properly:

So what happens is that usually, they bring these guys to gauge the affiliations of the prisoners. Based on whether or not you accept to pray behind him they can figure out to whom you belong. Whether you prayed in a congregation of your own or behind him, they would know how your mind works and what your affiliations were. And the more they knew, or thought they knew, the more they could hurt you. I liked to confuse them. One Friday, I would pray behind him. Another Friday, I would refuse. The next Friday, I would come to the mosque, but not pray at all. The officer would come and ask, 'Why are you not praying?' I'd just respond, 'I don't pray anymore; what has prayer ever gotten anyone?' He would be so confused: 'I thought you were Ikhwan!' I would respond, 'That's your fault for assuming.' The day I confused them all the most was one day I prayed a *raka'a* and just ended it there.

Hamza's attempts to disorient the prison authorities meant that he would repeat all the prayers in his cell. He knew exactly what was taking place, and wanted to subvert it as best he could – that the officers wanted to know whether or not he made *takfir* on the government-appointed Imam. For Hamza, however, it was a far simpler issue which made it easier for him to not pray behind the Imam: the conditions of the validity of the prayer were not fulfilled. The Imam did not recite the verses of the Qur'an correctly, so the core conditions for the prayer's fulfilment were not there. Hamza believed it was an act of religious humiliation at the behest of the prison authorities, whereby the prisoners were made to pray behind someone who could not even recite the short verses correctly.

Abdullah had the same observation about praying in the prison mosque. In congregation, each prisoner had two officers who stood by their side so they could listen in to their supplications when they prostrated (*sujud*):

> During prayer, the officer that had escorted me out of my cell stood praying next to me. Like every Muslim he began reciting *du'a* [supplication to Allah] for himself and his family. So I began to say '*Allahuma ikhreb bayto*' [O Allah, demolish his home]. We were both in prayer. He could hear my supplications and I could hear his. Every *du'a* he would make, I would make the opposite.

Many officers feared the supplications that the prisoners made against them. Former detainees mentioned that even while being tortured, officers become enraged if a prisoner supplicates against them. Abdullah added:

> When I was released, the head officer at my block came to take me. He held my hand. As we were walking to the gate, he said, 'Abdullah, please don't make *du'a* against me.' I smiled because that came out of nowhere. He said, 'Abdullah, please don't. I never wanted this for you.' Even the officers who would treat us badly have this lingering feeling that something is wrong.

While some officers insisted they were only following orders; others maintained their authority through domination. Mohamed would recite {Those who followed will say, 'If only we had another turn [at worldly life] so we could disassociate ourselves from them as they have disassociated themselves from us.' Thus will Allah show them their deeds as regrets upon them. And they are never to emerge from the Fire} (2:68).

During his hunger strike, the benevolence some officers showed was tempered by a sense of urgency by the prison authorities. A senior officer hauled Mohamed's wheelchair into his office:

> They started beating me so I would pass out ... Then he looked at me and said, 'You know, Mohamed, you and my wife are the same. This is a small piece of advice I want to give you. I tell my wife, 'Before I come home, clean the house, cook something nice, take a shower, fix your hair, put on a nice dress and some make-up; then wait for me to come home. If you're nice we will make love. But if I come home and the house is dirty and there is no food and you're in a bad mood and you haven't fixed yourself up, well, I will fuck you either way. I am telling you now, Mohamed, either way you will be fucked. Here, in this country, we are like God. We say Be! And it is [*kun fa yakun*]. Whatever we want we will get'. I never heard anything like that before. Someone comparing themselves to God. And using a prisoner. It literally reminded of the *surah* Ibrahim when the king said I give life and I take life.

The religious make-up of the officers differs and so are their religious justifications and understanding of their role as captors. In some instances, the officers are convinced they are waging a holy war against religious deviants. In interrogation, the officer recited to Mustafa the verses (5:130) {The punishment of those who wage war against Allah and His Messenger, and strive with might and main for mischief through the land is: execution, or crucifixion, or the cutting off of hands and feet from opposite sides, or exile from the land: that is their disgrace in this world, and a heavy punishment is theirs in the Hereafter}:

> This was the first thing he said to me in interrogation. When I laughed, he beat me harder. So I didn't respond. I would just say, okay! It was the strangest thing. He would torture me and when he heard the *adhan*, he would stop go pray and then come back and torture me again.

After Mustafa was sent to prison, he made friends with Khaled, a Palestinian inmate, who was detained under charges of espionage. After investigations cleared him of all charges, the officer in charge said to him, 'Khaled – there is no case against you and I believe that you're innocent but I found in your phone pictures of you with a lot of women and you're hanging out in bars and clubs. So I'm sending you to prison just so you can repent for your sins.' The Palestinian man spent five years in prison on the same espionage charges he was cleared of.

The month of Ramadan and Eid are bittersweet moments in prison. They are celebrated but some prisoners insist on not taking part in the celebrations. It is especially lonely for prisoners during Eid because it is a national holiday and so visitations are often not permitted. Mustafa recalled:

> The Ramadan vibes were intense in prison but to be honest, I was not happy. I usually spend Ramadan with my family so this was just very difficult. But people did celebrate it. Someone in the cell would always go to the window on the cell door and would recite Qur'an for those outside. The inmates would call on each other to congratulate each other. They would try and cook *iftar* and make Ramadan juices. Some people would even hang decorations in the cell, like paper lanterns and stuff. In visitations some families would bring in balloons. We would wake up, have *suhoor*, pray *fajr*, and then we'd sleep.

Mustafa had less fond memories of Eid:

> Some people would celebrate Eid but I was against it. Why would I be happy and celebrate while I was here in prison? I wouldn't pray with them even though I would be awake. People would call each other from different cells to congratulate each other for Eid. It would be two hours of happiness but then when reality kicks in, they are still in prison – they would feel intense depression right afterwards.

In Ramadan, prisoners typically pray *tarawih* prayers in the congregation, arrange for devotional circles of Qur'an and *dhikr* recitations. In Ola's cell, there was an inmate who had memorised the entire Qur'an. She would always lead the prayers. In *tarawih*, they completed the recitation of the whole Qur'an four times. Mona experienced high levels of spirituality in Ramadan but she also experienced another peculiar type of Ramadan: 'In the first Ramadan, our spirituality and worship were at all-time high. I prayed *qiyam* prayers, we studied Qur'an together. This was the first time I fasted the recommended fasts right after Ramadan.'

The following Ramadan, she was being punished. They moved her to a harsher cell with gang members. She was made to sleep on the floor under the fridge the prisoners used to store their food. This Ramadan also coincided with the release of a soap opera called *Sign al-Nisa* (women's prison): 'What was very strange was that the soap opera was filmed while I was in prison. This was very bad for us. They did not want the actors to see us. We weren't allowed to go out but sometimes we'd glimpse celebrities from the window; I guess that was nice.'

While some prisoners, like Mustafa and Layla were against Eid prayers being held, many others did pray. In the first Eid Layla spent in prison, she was not allowed to pray without permission. She would pray in her bed so as not to be detected. As she slept in bed, she heard the mosques that encircled the prison reciting *takbirs*. She could not join them because she was not free but she repeated 'Allahu Akbar, Allahu Akbar wa li Allah al-Hamd' along with the mosques in the outside. When she was moved to a better cell, in the following year, her fellow inmates tried to hold Eid prayers in the cell. Some *gina'i* prisoners tried to join them in the congregation. They were beaten as a result.

Munira had the fondest memories remembering Ramadan and Eid. She tried to explain:

In Eid, we would first wake up. An inmate would lead us in Eid prayers and then they would give *khutuba*. After prayer we would hand out sweets and chocolate to each other. I want you to imagine 30 crazy college girls in one room. They will find a way to party. Our parents brought us balloons and sweets. So we decided we are not going to be sad. We are going to sing and dance. Some of the *gina'i* inmates used to work in salons so we asked them to do our hair. We did henna. Another inmate was a belly dancer. She gave us dancing lessons.

Both male and female prison wards tried to maintain the practice of praying Eid in congregation; it seemed one of the few ways that they could find some semblance of joy within the community that they had experienced in freedom. This could take different forms, as the female-only congregations would not include the *khutba* – but what remained consistent, is the need to keep the rites of Islam flowing through the carceral veins of the Egyptian prison system, to always send the message that despite the best attempts of those in authority, they would continue to worship God fully.

4
Belief, Crisis and the Qur'an

THEODICY IN DETENTION

CIA Black Site – Jordan
Kandahar International Airport – Kandahar, Afghanistan
Bagram Airbase – Parvan, Afghanistan
JTF-GTMO – Guantánamo Bay, Cuba

In the darkness of his imprisonment, Sami Elhaj remembered the heroes of Islam's past as a way of infusing his 'spirit with tremendous energy'.[1] He cast his mind to the story of Bilal ibn Rabah, among the first converts to Islam, a slave in Mecca who hailed from Ethiopia – but more importantly, the companion of the Prophet Muhammad; Bilal's voice had been so melodious and strong, he was assigned the task of performing the first call to prayer. Sami knew well what Bilal had suffered, and recalled his cry of *Ahadan Ahad* – The One, The One – a cry that would become a banner call for the fledgling Muslim community of Mecca:

In those dark days, I called on the example set by the heroes of Islam. Bilal ibn Rabah who endured the boulder rolled onto his chest in the desert of Mecca. I could see him in my mind, lying under the boulder, defiantly repeating his faith in Allah: 'The One! The One!'

I saw Mus'ab ibn Umayr, holding the flag in his left hand after they cut off his right, then with his upper arm after they cut off his left hand. I recalled the heroism of Khalid ibn al-Walid whose body was so covered in cuts and wounds from swords and arrows that there wasn't an inch of clear skin. I saw them in my mind's eye, and I held on to them for strength.

... I remember the barbed wire, the clatter of weapons, dogs howling, the blood red of our clothes. Sounds of pain resonate in my ears, the pain of that place.

The place where my gaolers put me in solitary confinement, stripping me bare and throwing me into a cramped, freezing cell. I recall how, on that day when I was thrown into solitary, as I sat there shaking and trembling, I heard a voice from the cell on my right, entreating in a tone filled with endurance: 'The One! The One!'[2]

On his arrival at Bagram Airbase, Sami's welcome had been the insult of having a cross shaved into his head, part of the symbolism of a clash of civilisations that was evident in the actions of the US soldiers. He recalled the large wooden cross that had also been erected over the watchtowers of Kandahar – as if somehow these symbolic gestures would hurt the Muslim prisoners. Sami understood that this obsession was in some way to paint 'their "War on Terror" as some kind of extension of the Crusades'.[3] But it was never this symbolism that hurt him, it was much more the ritual humiliation that he and those detained with him were forced to endure at the hands of male and, crucially, female soldiers who would shout obscenities at them and make lewd remarks, particularly when the prisoners were forced to stand naked before them.[4]

Uncertain of their fate, many of the detainees believed that God had destined for them to die at the hands of the US military and the CIA. While detained at a black site in Jordan by the CIA, Mohamdeou Ould Slahi attempted to read his Qur'an to the best of his ability each day, but the extent of torture and anxiety he would feel meant that he could read up to 300 pages without understanding the words. His detention brought on a contemplation of death, and he realised that death was something that no one could predict, that even though he was 'at the hands of some of the most evil people in the world', his death would be something he could accept because he knew full well that they would be held accountable before God for what they had done to him in an afterlife.[5] This sentiment featured heavily in the thoughts of most of the prisoners who had been detained – they all believed that the torture and conditions of confinement would result in their deaths, but found ways of placing that within a larger metaphysics of their existence: 'I was sure that I was going to be slaughtered. Indeed, I was ready to submit to death, if Allah willed this for me. At least it would be an end to this unjust and savage cruelty that went against all human laws.'[6]

This is how Abdul Salam Zaeef felt about his time in Kandahar – that there would be an eternal recompense for what he was forced to endure. For him, though his treatment at the hands of the US was understandable, he had no expectation that they would treat him in ways that were humane. His thoughts instead turned to those *Muslims* involved in his abuse, whether in Pakistan, Afghanistan, or even within the US military, who had become his tormentors. Abdul Salam believed that what was happening to him was a microcosm of the condition of the Muslim *ummah*, 'I wondered about the disunity of Muslims, the alienation from Islam and the dependence and enslavement of Muslim leaders on the secularism of the West.'[7]

But while Abdul Salam's view of the *ummah* might have been somewhat bleak outside of a prison context, inside of prison there was a shared sense of struggle against an oppressive force, even if the detained men came from different backgrounds and traditions. Key among their joint belief was their stubborn refusal to cooperate with interrogators, even if it meant their own safety. From their time detained in Afghanistan through to Guantánamo Bay, the US military would consistently offer deals to the men, to give evidence against others, which most (though not all) would refuse – citing their belief in Islam as the reason for not acting in self-interested ways. Like Abdul Salam, Sami Elhaj was offered many deals to secure his own release:

'How would this work?' I asked him.

'That's easy,' he said. 'You'll get your job back at Al Jazeera when you leave here. Then when you're asked, for example, to interview Muammar Gaddafi, you'd describe to us the location, security precautions, his movements, expressions, and observations on what you see. If al-Qaeda contacts you to do an interview, look around where the interview is happening;

describe the room and manner of those you meet, their thoughts and behaviour.'

'We wouldn't need you to tell us your movements, we can plant devices in your body to follow you, and we can hear the conversation around you. We'd want reports from you on what the devices can't see. We'll train you to memorise numbers, to describe people and ways to win their trust. We'll organise a lot of training for you, and when you're back, there will be people in Qatar and in Al Jazeera to help you, you won't be alone. There are large financial incentives, and you'll be happy, you'll get what others haven't been able to after long years of hard work.'

'Fine,' I said. 'You want me to work against al-Qaeda and against those you mentioned.'

'Yes,' he said. 'But in a diplomatic way.'

'I fear Allah,' I said, 'and He is my witness: No Muslim is to cast their eye towards the sins of Muslims, and I am certain whoever does this work will quit the circle of Islam, lose his religion and his world.'

In Guantánamo, my interactions with Americans taught me to talk to people according to their mentality. Americans are materialistic, like their life. If I said: 'this isn't permitted in my religion,' they wouldn't care because they're distanced from religion, it means nothing to them. The same was true of most of the soldiers and interrogators we met. Materialistic people who spoke to the prisoners using their logic only.

I continued, 'I went to Afghanistan to cover the war. But what you're asking me to do is extremely dangerous. I would make money, but I would lose my soul, and I have one soul; if I lose it there's no point in money. I fear for my safety and my family's.'

'Don't be afraid,' he said. 'We here in America will protect you.'

'Excuse me,' I told him. 'If America was as great a nation as you say it is, why ask someone weak like me? How would you protect me, if you can't protect yourselves without me?'[8]

These offers would be made until the very day of their release, with prisoners being regularly asked to sign statements that confessed to their crimes. For most of the prisoners, signing such statements went contrary to their conception of their own lives and they would refuse to sign, preferring to remain detained than to sign a piece of paper that meant lying about who they once were. There were a few, like the Australian national David Hicks, who did cooperate with their interrogators, but this did little to speed up their release from Guantanamo. Cooperation was no guarantee of release.

Northern Correctional Institution Supermax – Connecticut, United States of America
Charleston Naval Brig – South Carolina, United States of America

The first night in prison is the hardest. Then the first day, the first week, the first month, then the first year. After a year, most people tend to accept it or they settle into a routine. When people go through calamities, there are three main things that they struggle with, especially if they have calamities that are an act of oppression by humans. People struggle to find meaning or purpose in their suffering, what they are going through. The second is that they feel this unfairness or frustration as to what has happened to them. That is the nature of oppression, that it is suffocating, that you have no recourse. The third one, is that they struggle to find how they are going to get through this. In my case, I realised that at some point, and this was through reading the Qur'an, that there was a great wisdom in what was happening to me.

Babar Ahmad knew that while you could fool people some of the time, you could not fool all people all of the time. He came to really understand what this meant when guards in the US would approach him after weeks of having observed his behaviour. They would never be able to help themselves with him. Why was he always smiling and in a good mood? Babar's response would always be to explain to them of God's wisdom, that he was only in prison by God's will, and that any of the injustice that he had suffered, would be taken care of on the Day of Judgment:

So the first thing that helped me to come to terms with it, was the understanding that Allah has a great wisdom behind what I am going through and I may not realise the wisdom behind it now, I may realise tomorrow, next week, next month, next year, maybe in ten years, or maybe even after I die, but I know that there is some wisdom. Just the fact that I don't know what that wisdom is, does not mean there is none. *Yaqeen*, certainty, and *tawwakkul*, reliance on Allah, comes into it.

The second thing that helped me to come to terms with things, was that whatever wrong had been done to me, that He would sort it out. I had two things that had been done to me, I had the injustice of my predicament, of my imprisonment, and then I had the injustice of the police assault case, of the officers getting off scot-free. I knew Allah would take care of it. It took me a few years to settle that in my heart because I believed it in theory, but for it to settle it took time, as in the beginning I went through the normal emotions of anger, bitterness, hatred, of wanting revenge, wanting all of these things. Eventually I settled with the belief that Allah would deal with it, and I just left it with Him to take care of. When I mention that to people, they always say it is good to forgive and forget, but I say no no no no, let's not get this wrong. I haven't forgiven anyone, and I'm certainly not going to forget; I'm just not tied to it, I'm not shackled to it. It's not like those officers, it's not like they came to me and they apologised and that I had the chance to forgive them, if it was genuine then I would forgive them. But for me to be expected to forgive people who did that to me, not only did they not apologise, but they covered up and they persisted in the wrong that they did. No, no way, there is nothing in our *din* [religion] that warrants that.

The third thing that helped me to get through it, again through the Qur'an, that whatever I'm going through, I'm not alone, and that there have been many many many people throughout history that have gone through something that I have gone through. The story of Yusuf AS is quite poignant because why does Allah mention a story in the Qur'an about a guy that was unjustly imprisoned, it's because Yusuf AS was not the first person to be wrongly imprisoned and he was not going to be the last. We talk about stigma, and that it's worse when you are accused of terrorism than other crimes, well no. There is one crime that is worse to be accused of, and that is rape, what Yusuf

AS was accused. By far, offences of a sexual nature are the worst viewed, because not only does society look down on you, but you are at risk from other prisoners who look at you in a weird way, but Allah mentioned that story in the Qur'an and it will be recited until the end of time, as there will be other people wrongly imprisoned who need to be given hope. When I would read the Qur'an or I would read the stories of other prisoners, that would give me a lot of comfort.

Despite Babar's hope and trust in God's plan, he was also realistic about his predicament. He knew full well that he found prison difficult at times, and that he needed others, and that there was little space for bravado in such a place. He strongly believed that anyone who said that they handled prison without feeling difficulty, was lying to themselves. He had seen the despair set in himself, as well as in fellow prisoners who would show their bravery publicly, and yet would be the ones who would break down during phone calls with their families and even start self-harming or taking drugs to cope with their pain. Babar's belief in God meant that he understood that feeling low, even in belief, did not mean that you had lost your faith, but rather it was part of the process of faith itself. In his own moments of difficulty, Babar made it a habit of knocking on the cells of others, asking for them to share some words that might uplift him, building a structure of care in his prison life that would help to inoculate him from the despondency of his surroundings.

Unlike Babar Ahmad, Ali al-Marri expressed much more optimism at his detention at the naval brig in South Carolina. Ali built routine, it was key to his own mental health, particularly after 13 years in solitary confinement. He would divide his days through physical exercise, cleaning his cell, reciting Qur'an and hadith, and studying Islamic books when he was finally permitted them after years of abuse. He did his best to be exhausted by the end of each day and while he missed his family, he had an intense conviction that it was God who was providing *sakinah* in his heart through the Qur'an and prayer – allowing him to pass this test. He felt that because he was only detained due to his practice of Islam, it somehow placed him in a different category than other prisoners who have been detained for criminal acts:

> I do believe that people have a problem in jail, I'm talking about Muslims and those who are in prison for their religion, not for other worldly crimes. I think the main problem is that if the man or woman has accepted Allah's judgement, and I mean accepted by his word, by his tongue, and by his heart, there is no internal fighting then. There are no ifs or buts inside. I accept total submission to Allah's judgement, and knowing, totally believing, that this is better for me, this is Allah's choice, this is Allah's judgement for me. This must be better than the alternative for that issue. If a man or woman has accepted the judgement, then it is like you are in a hotel, they will give you food, clean your clothing, no rent. *Wallahi*, you think sometimes people will think I am crazy in a way, by thinking that way, but that is how I felt, really.

Although he was fully aware of his own innocence, Ali never once opened the door to cooperate with his interrogators; he believed that his harsh treatment should never be rewarded with compliance, but rather that he was duty bound to seek justice for himself. In the end, Ali felt compelled to plead guilty to a small charge despite his years of refusal – he knew that in the US system, he could spend the remainder of his life outside of any conception of legal redress, and so he chose instead to enter into an agreement that would permit him to live a fuller life, one that was with his family.

For prisoners experiencing detention at the hands of the US, the legal limbo they were purposely kept in resulted in a range of struggles they had with their own mental and spiritual health. Ali al-Marri's positivity is perhaps very unique to his own circumstances, but most prisoners acknowledged the difficulties that came with being kept in lengthy periods of detention without charge or trial. Much like Babar, the ups and downs were seen as a normal part of the detention experience, rather than any kind of indication of a weakness in faith, and building a community proved to be central to holding on to that.

Rabaa al-Adawia Square – Cairo, Egypt

At first, I didn't ask the big question of 'Why are we here on earth?' or 'Why is there so much pain in the world?' After the massacre, I still didn't ask them. I was just angry. I was angry that the people died.

Layla was only 13 years old during the massacre at Rabaa. She had an intimate understanding of what happened because she was living with her family in the apartment blocks that directly overlooked the protest. It was there, from her bedroom window, that she witnessed the military raiding the sit-in, shooting and killing unarmed people – the utter carnage and devastation that was wrought on the peaceful protesters. She heard the screams and smelled the gas. In adjacent apartment blocks, her neighbours allowed soldiers and officers to use their houses to snipe at the protesters from above:

> Growing up, they would make us think that a martyr must be perfect. They must know the Qur'an very well. They must be great to their parents. Just because of that perception, I know it's weird, but I just never thought anything could happen to us, but then Hossam walked right passed me only a few minutes before he was shot. He was my friend at school. He was 13 as well. I remember looking at him and he was wearing sweatpants and singing this stupid song. I looked at him and thought: really are these the 'future generation' that's going to save us? And just like that, a few minutes later he was shot dead.

All the legends about martyrdom she was told as a child were happening right in front of her. The heroes were not the heroes of fairytales or books, they were her classmates and friends:

> I went to his house to give his mum my condolences and she had kept a handkerchief that had his blood on it. I smelt it and it smelt like musk. At the end for me, there was no defining moment for when the questions emerged but at some point I had to ask: what am I doing and why?

The stories of post-2013 detention cannot be told in isolation from the Rabaa massacre. The trauma of incarceration for most is a longer story of continued traumatisation. On 14 August 2013, around a thousand people perished in a single day. Thousands disappeared, and tens of thousands were detained. This was a defining point that transformed generations who witnessed and survived the massacre. Munira, an Azhari student, was detained when she was 20 years old. She recalled:

> After Rabaa and after Asmaa El Beltagy was killed, we were all broken. I felt like everything I had depended on was shaky. Nothing was stable any longer; not even our most essential beliefs. I didn't long for heaven. Something in my *aqida* [creedal beliefs] wasn't proper. Something was wrong. There was this lingering feeling that something was missing; we didn't know everything. There was a gap in our knowledge. I had faith but it wasn't the faith I wanted. I wanted a strong and conscious faith. I wanted to not be afraid of everything. I wanted so badly to have that serenity that there is wisdom in tribulation. The companions of the Prophet would get sad but they wouldn't be shaken to death with fear like we were.

Rabaa left the survivors like Munira scrambling for answers. Is divine justice or retribution real? Why has God not intervened to save the many innocent, faithful people who just died? If these were trials and tribulations, why did they have to be so violent and horrific? If it is up to free will and that God tests the pious and faithful, why then has God not given the faithful strength to fight back? How can human beings commit such horrific acts against each other?

Burj al-Arab Prison – Alexandria, Egypt
Enforced disappearance – Cairo, Egypt
Scorpion Prison – Cairo, Egypt
Tora Prison – Cairo, Egypt

When Ali was asked if his time in prison had changed his view of the nature of God's justice, he had more resolute albeit poignant responses:

We already knew we were fighting a losing battle. We saw the massacres in Rabaa. They had their guns and ammo and the most we had were a few rocks. Most of us knew we were fighting a losing battle. We knew what our end would be. We had to stand up because we knew this was unjust no matter the consequences. We always knew we were either going to die or end up imprisoned. At the end of the day, this was my decision to get involved. I knew there was justice and injustice ... you know the verse (3:140) {If a wound should touch you – there has already touched the [opposing] people a wound similar to it. And these days [of varying conditions] We alternate among the people so that Allah may make evident those who believe and [may] take to Himself from among you martyrs – and Allah does not like the wrongdoers}. Days rotate and there is a tax that has to be paid. Not everyone is obliged to pay the price but we made that choice.

The very nature of what it means to have volition and free will in prison becomes tenuous. Furthermore, the prison authorities act as supreme overseers of life, death, human becoming, and even the mundane, attempting to usurp God's power in ordaining human life. The prison environment elicited difficult questions, because the environment was so much worse than anything they could fathom – even worse than being killed. Mustafa had so many questions directed towards others, his captors, the prison itself and even God:

I don't know whether to categorise imprisonment as tribulation or just evil that generally just exists in the world. I used to think, if this was a form of tribulation then why is it so intense and so difficult? Why do I have to suffer this much? ... They say the Prophet was tried and suffered for years. Okay, but I am not a prophet or a messenger. I am a believer in God and He gives me strength but there were, at points, I would reach this place of extreme anger and resentment. I would be like why is He doing this to us? Why is He treating us this way? Like He does not need to show us, He exists. We worship Him already; what is He trying to prove? Why am I being put through this? Why are my family being put through this? He is punishing my whole family, not just me. Sometimes, I'd think maybe God has just lost His power. He is just not able to protect humankind. We grew up hearing [that] God will punish the oppressors but that doesn't make sense, human history is the history of human oppression.

In Bilal's five-year imprisonment, it was these very questions that haunted him. Like Mustafa, it took him a while to make sense of it all. The notion of free will seemed almost superfluous to even bring up in prison. All the while, he developed an internal dialogue with God. In the first two years of his imprisonment, he could not seem to escape the question of why this was happening to him. It was first: why, God? Then was when, God? He had been sentenced to 25 years in prison with no end in sight. Still, he found it difficult to share his questions and resentments with his fellow inmates:

My whole problem was *qada wa qadr* [fate and predestination] – whether we are predestined or if there was free will. Every time, I spoke with someone they would recite clichés or ask me if I believed in God. I am a believer but I had an issue – do we have free will or are we predestined to have things happen to us? If we are predestined, then God did not create me to be free; why would he choose something so horrible as prison for me? Is God not just? Well, if I actually do have free will, then how come I am in a place where I can't practice this free will? Why can't I just leave? If God is able – then why hasn't He used His power to free me? I started to think ... well maybe God can't. That took me down a whole rollercoaster. The one thing that enlightened my path was Surah Maryam. The verse said: {And, when the pains of childbirth drove her to [cling to] the trunk of a palm tree, she exclaimed, 'I wish I had been dead and forgotten long before all this!'} (19:23).
  This verse was about her giving birth to Jesus. She was scared they would call her a whore for giving birth out of wedlock. How did God respond to her? She said something (I wish I had been dead and forgotten long before all this) that if I had said in prison, people might say I lost faith in God but God responded to her: {And shake to you the trunk of the palm-tree [and] it will

let fall ripe dates down on you, readily reaped. So eat and drink and comfort your eye} (19:25–26).

It was like He was comforting her. It was like He was telling her, I know its tough but here just eat something, have a chocolate, have a date and try to forget. It was like God was telling her this had to happen. This is on me but I am sorry … It is tough but the young have to grow old, the egg has to become a chick and the chick has to become a chicken. There need to be a series of events that has to happen for something to occur and we don't know what that something is because we are limited as humans. How God comforted Maryam, just opened my eyes. Just as there is difficulty in childbirth, you have to go through a particular ordeal, but while you're in the ordeal, in the fire, you don't know, you can't know there is a more beautiful thing forming – gold is forming. Someone might come and change the course of history. I might get out at that time to meet this one person to have that one child so she can be my daughter.

For Bilal, the sequential realities that are revealed through calamities are an important indication of divine wisdom. However, the grander narratives of forbearance at the same time become unsettled. In a way, legendary tales of Prophetic forbearance, stories of the companions and the righteous become more mundane and more human thus giving the prisoners access to the very same pain. For Bilal, the very realisation that Maryam contemplated her death was very profound. Furthermore, pain and suffering are not evil in of themselves. They are subsumed in a larger story of becoming worshippers of God – ones that are able to locate difficult experiences within Divine Will.

Qanater El Khayereya Women's Prison – Qalyubiyya, Egypt
Leeman Prison – Minya, Egypt

Mona felt a sense of grand design as she put her head against the truck, taking her to court. The truck was torture in and of itself. In the summer, it was so hot that she would vomit and faint from suffocation and dehydration. This time, she was in a different vehicle. She could feel the soft breeze against the bruises on her face. Before her court session, Mona and her cellmates were being punished for reporting an officer:

> They called in the anti-riot squad to our cell. They encircled me and began to beat me. They stripped me of my clothes and hijab. They dragged me out by my hair. I was due at court that day. So they threw me a torn-up rag to wear and shoes that didn't fit. So I limped. You could see the bruises all over my face. I knew for sure that if I was in a different car, I would have died. It was by God's grace that they put me in a car with a large window. I felt the air hitting my face. It was at that point, I realised that every small detail – even a breeze – was to foretell something better that would happen later. I wouldn't have met my husband or became the person who I am today if it wasn't for what I have experienced. Without the sense of God, without the thought that there is something metaphysical, a purpose, maybe even punishment, without this idea that there is this God had an intention and a plan for me, I really wouldn't have survived. Without holding on to the comfort of *du'a* and prayer and without the knowledge that God brings ease, I would have killed myself.

Important to her, was her contemplation on a verse she had come across in the study circles with her cellmates (20:39) {And I endeared you with love from Me so that you would be brought up under My 'watchful' Eye}:

> We sat around in a circle and read the verse. We asked why is this happening? If we truly believed, then we must truly know that everyone from the officers to the guards to the judges that these people are not gods. So whenever an officer or judge would try to scare me, I'd think they don't actually carry my fate. They are there to fulfil what God has destined to happen to you. They are *asbab* [fulfilments of Allah's intent]. So in reality, all of this is happening to me so God can slowly bring me under His watchful eye. Slowly but surely and He brings you all these little tests and all these little helpings so He can perfect you under His watchful eye. This was so powerful to me.

The question that lingered for her – however – was not how God could let this happen but how human beings could be capable of such horrific acts. This struck her most, not when the officers tortured her but on a normal day when she was due for a court session. The officers transported her in an open truck, in order to parade her through the streets. Crowds gathered as soon as they discovered she was a political prisoner. They began throwing stones at the vehicle, aiming for her face and body. It was these acts, not by hardened soldiers, but by ordinary people that proved most shocking. She recalled the cruelty of the doctors at the prison ward, and especially of the inmate in the bed next to her who had breast cancer: 'I used to hear her cry when I was sent to the hospital. The prison doctor would take her painkillers away from her so he could sell it. She was in constant pain. She died soon after. The cancer killed her.'

The callousness of the prison authorities multiplied her alienation when they would show mercy in other contexts:

> It felt like, oh so you can be human? You just don't want to be a human to me. I felt like I had a weapon though, whenever they would beat me I would just say 'Sufficient for us is Allah, and [He is] the best Disposer of affairs.' And they would just lose it. They would say why are you making *du'a* against us? What have we ever done to you? The officer would just say, 'This [is] just my job. Do you think I have the power to get you out of here? I can't do anything.'

Like Mona, Mohamed Soltan's weakest moment squarely confronted him with the question of divine planning. Mohamed was months into his hunger strike. By then he was too weak to walk. The prison authorities wanted to punish him further, so they planned to isolate him from his father. They barged into their cell, and put him in his wheelchair, blindfolding him and handcuffing him to the chair. Mohamed began screaming. He was terrified:

> I couldn't tell where I was. I knew it was a cell because of the way the door closed. I was all alone. It was around *fajr* time and the first day of Ramadan; so I said to myself maybe I should

recite some Qur'an to calm myself down. So I began with *adhkar al-sabah* [morning litanies]. I have been reciting this my whole life, but now I couldn't understand it. The verse says, {God does not burden any soul with more than it can bear} (2:286) – but I am at my limit. I cannot bear anymore. This was the first time I started doubting God's justice. How can this be true? You [God] are saying it so confidently. You're stating it as a matter of fact with a language that is so unambiguous, that, you, God, are not going to burden me with more than I can handle. I told myself to continue reading – I was working myself up again and it was counterintuitive – to be handcuffed to a wheelchair and getting angry! Then I started reading the verse, {'Lord, do not burden us with more than we have strength to bear'}. I lost it! I was like, how can God claim in such confidence and such unambiguity that He is not going to burden you with more than you can handle? But then drive you to the point where you raise your hands and cry, 'God, please don't give me more than I can handle!' ... What have I been saying all these years? Eventually I checked myself a little bit and thought, let me just continue – and then, in the very next part of the verse, my faith that was being emptied was refilled again: {'Pardon us, forgive us, have mercy on us. You are our Protector'}. It was those three things. *Rahma, maghifra* and *afw* [mercy, forgiveness and pardoning (Qur'an 2:286)] – these words all come from the same family; they are different kinds of forgiveness. God knows our capacity more than we know ourselves; and why we don't have that knowledge is because our sins are weighing us down.

This sense of divine planning and human capacity stayed with Mohamed even after his time in prison. The conclusion he reached was that human notions of justice or even capacity lacked real knowledge – the knowledge of the unseen – the knowledge that God's plan is greater than any plan that a human can conceive. This thought left many of the prisoners with the sense that all they could do, was to act and behave dependant on the circumstances they were in, that the hardship itself was not the test; it was their own responses to the hardship that dictated everything.

THE QUR'AN

JTF-GTMO - Guantánamo Bay, Cuba

The Qur'an was the breath that Mansoor Adayfi breathed every single day throughout his incarceration, from the detention sites of Afghanistan to Guantánamo Bay. If he had one thing on his mind, it was his desperate need to hold the Qur'an and to read from it as a form of solace. He never once got bored of reading or reciting it. He knew that this was one of the miracles of the Qur'an itself, that every single reading leant itself to newer and deeper reflections, even if one read the same book for 15 years. There were so many stories in the Qur'an that spoke of the difficulties that previous nations of people had experienced. Mansoor could not help but feel humbled by their plight compared to his own; had he suffered the way they had, did he even have a right to complain?

The *sahaba* had come to the Prophet with their complaints about their treatment, and he told them the story of the people who would have their skin combed from their flesh and would have their heads sawed down the middle. Remembering this gave us all so much confidence in our own difficulties – because we knew we would be tested like people of the past. Surah Yusuf, for most of us became the most important Surah, and every time I recited it, I would cry. I remember being in solitary confinement, when no one could see me except for Allah, I would cry so much when I recited the verse of Yaqub: {*innama askhoo baththee wahuznee ila Allahi waaʿalamu mina Allahi ma la taʿalamoona* – I only complain of my grief and sorrow to Allah, and I know from Allah that which you know not}. When you are by yourself, all alone, this verse is such a strong reminder that Allah is always with you.

The treatment of the prisoners at the hands of US soldiers often felt like an attack on Islam itself; an attempt to abuse the religion through the way they abused the Qur'an and those they held captive. It was always reflected in the Qur'an that Mansoor would find his way to think through the immediate trauma he faced –

that if he withstood his torture with patience and gratitude, he would ultimately win. He would often reflect on the stories of Musa that were presented in the Qur'an – Musa, a prophet who was tasked with freeing an entire enslaved people – the Jews. For Mansoor, the story of Musa was one of relief from hardship (*faraj*), of comfort and relief that was sent by Allah at the moment that it was needed most:

> When I used to think of Musa, sometimes I would think that victory and relief are so close that they are in your hand, but it's just not the time for it until Allah determines that it is. When you look at Musa's story, look at him when he is holding the staff and Allah asks him what is in his hand? He said it is my cane. Allah then asks him to throw it and it turns into a snake. Musa was put through a very difficult test because (Pharaoh) and his crazy army had chased him all the way to the sea and trapped him and the Jews. Musa could never have known that his staff would open the sea before him and provide a pathway for their escape. He could have thought to himself that he was about to be captured, put into a black site, tortured, and I would say this to the other brothers all the time, but his victory was close to hand because it was always Allah that was assisting him – even at the moment of greatest peril. For us, what would one stroke of the sea with a stick do for us? Nothing most likely, but with Allah's help, it could change the world.

Mansoor was certain that the hubris of oppressors would come back to them, the certainty of this that was rooted in the Qur'an. He knew that Pharaoh stated that the Nile ran beneath him at his command at the height of his power, but he also knew that it was Allah who killed Pharoah through the very Nile he had claimed to control. The stories of the Qur'an became a matter of timing for Mansoor, that at the moment Allah wanted to change a situation, it would occur, and if He had to change the laws of physics to ensure that change, then nothing could stop His plan – that you could be thrown into a pit of fire, like the Prophet Abraham, and its heat would not touch you.

If there was one story that all the prisoners agreed on being significant for their imprisonment experience, it was that of the Prophet Yusuf. A story that has a complete chapter of its own and is described by Allah as *ahsan al-qassas* – the best of stories (Qur'an 12:3). This one chapter of the Qur'an was so compelling, that prisoners even began to refer to their own incarceration experience as *'Jamiat Yusuf'* – the University of Joseph. It was the first chapter of the Qur'an that Lakhdar Boumediene memorised while at Guantánamo Bay, specifically because it was about the unjust imprisonment of the Prophet Yusuf. Lakhdar was one of six Algerian men who had been unlawfully detained in Bosnia despite having no involvement with al-Qaeda or the Taliban. These men had settled lives in Bosnia, having married Bosniak women and even some having claimed citizenship after their participation in the conflict to defend Bosniak Muslims from the programme of ethnic cleansing by the Serbs.[9] Lakhdar's one solace of being separated from his family was the notion that he would one day be reunited with them – as the Prophet Yusuf had been reunited with his own after years of imprisonment: 'I would repeat to myself over and over lines from "Yusuf" about God's mercy and "His subtle ways," about Yusuf's dogged patience, his steadfast faith, his eventual victory over injustice, and his reunification with his family.'

The love that the Guantánamo Bay prisoners had for the Qur'an meant that at times they would have to separate themselves from the physical book in order to protect its defilement by the guards – they would rather not possess a copy than see it abused. They had protested, ripped their own clothes, fought with the guards, and gone on multiple hunger strikes, not primarily over their own unlawful treatment, but 90 per cent of the time over the desecration of the Qur'an by the US soldiers. The prisoners were forced to witness the Qur'an being rifled through, thrown on the floor, and the incident that sparked the first riot, the Qur'an being thrown in the toilet. After witnessing this regular treatment of the book, the prisoners chose instead to refuse copies of the Qur'an, returning it to the guards.[10] This was a profound act of sacrifice made by the prisoners, considering just how much they relied on the Qur'an for guidance, solace and hope. It was both an act of defence of the Qur'an – the literal word of Allah – and an act of defiance. And yet, it did not prevent them from learning or teaching the holy book. Those who'd memorised all or part of the book taught those who had not. In Islam, those who have memorised the Qur'an are known as *huffadh* – the protectors; their knowledge of the book meant that they were able to teach its words to those who had not memorised it fully. In this way, for a time, the Qur'an in Guantánamo was read and taught in the original way, in which revelation had first been transmitted by the Prophet Muhammad to his companions.

USS Bataan and USS Peleliu – Indian Ocean
MCC – New York City, United States of America
ADX Florence – Colorado, United States of America

Trapped for a whole week in the basement of the Qala-i-Jangi fortress located near Mazar-e-Sharif in Afghanistan, John (Yahia) Walker Lindh, had just managed to survive multiple attempts to kill him and those he was seeking sanctuary with. He had been among 400 soldiers that had been captured by the Northern Alliance warlord General Dostum, but following a revolt by a handful of prisoners, had managed to revolt and barricade themselves in the basement of the fort. A military operation led by US and British special forces supporting the Afghan Northern Alliance troops attempted to force the prisoners out, first by firing heavy artillery at the basement, and then by flooding the basement and electro-cuting the water. By the time Yahia emerged from the basement, again a prisoner of the allied forces, only 86 of the men he was with had survived the massacre.

Yahia had been paraded around the world and became the poster figure for everything that Americans feared: a white American man turned Muslim, even though he had no involvement in 9/11, and had entered Afghanistan before there was any notion of a conflict with the US. He had no idea of where he was being taken and at all times felt that he would be killed by his captors. From Qala-i-Jangi, he was transported to a hospital at Sheberghan, then to a makeshift special forces prison in an old Turkish schoolhouse, before finally being transported for imprisonment in two US warships located in the Indian Ocean. Beyond the jurisdiction of any laws, Yahia was being held incommunicado alongside seven other prisoners, and for the first few weeks, they had no access to any form of reading material. Eventually, after his persistence, he was granted an Arabic-English copy of the Qur'an. He would later find out that his great-uncle, who had been a chaplain for the US military during the Vietnam War, had intervened with the military to ensure that Yahia had a copy of the Qur'an during his detention.

On 11 January 2002, the other seven prisoners would be sent to Guantánamo Bay among the first group of prisoners to be held at the detention camp, leaving Yahia in solitary confinement. Free of any distractions, this period of detention opened the Qur'an to him in ways that he had not been able to predict:

> The period on the two ships, especially on the second ship when I was left alone with just the Qur'an, that I can remember, was when I really connected with Surah Yusuf – I can recall that very distinctly and recall being really moved by it in a way that I had never been before. Maybe because by that time I had been in my situation for long enough for it to really sink in, but also being alone helps – you are taken away from distractions and having nothing but the *mushaf* [physical copy of the Qur'an] with you. That is something that sticks very clearly in my mind. It was a type of encouragement, as I was thinking that they were in all likelihood going to execute me, or keep me in prison for life (which at the time I felt was the worse of the two scenarios). Reading Surah Yusuf was very reassuring on that level: it was soothing, like a peace of mind.

A year older than Yahia Lindh, Uzair Paracha's route to custody in the hands of the US would take a very different route. From a middle-class family in Karachi, Pakistan, Uzair had arrived in the US six weeks prior to his arrest in March 2003. Having finished his MBA in Pakistan, he wanted to dedicate himself to his working life, and while he was not religious, he found himself contemplating on his flight to New York that it was the right time for religious knowledge in his life. Uzair met his detention with disbelief: how could this happen to him, someone who did not even pray? He had only been in New York since February 2003, and so could not understand what he could have done to warrant arrest for terrorism. Uzair thought back to that time and to the words of the poet Robert Frost:

> Two roads diverged in a wood, and I—
> I took the one less traveled by,
> And that has made all the difference.

His first cellmate at the infamous New York Metropolitan Correctional Center had been a musician. A great lover of music, Uzair felt that he could use his time in detention to pick up a musical instrument, as he had always hoped to do. Yet, despite his most earnest wishes, he was soon separated from his musician bunkee, and instead placed in solitary confinement at the infamous 10 South section in an attempt to coerce him into a plea deal. All alone, he had requested reading material, but was denied any book except for the Qur'an, a book he had long neglected. Uzair only knew by heart three or four very short chapters, and only knew how to read the Arabic script in Urdu, which was close enough for him to follow. He smiled to himself, because he had been familiar with Surah al-Rahman – a relatively longer chapter – but only because his weekend morning cartoons in Karachi would be started by the first 15 verses of the chapter on the television. Ultimately though, he felt frustrated by his own lack of knowledge and how his pronunciation during his prayers was so difficult, this was particularly because he was far more familiar with the lyrics of Pearl Jam songs than he had been of anything related to his religion.

Uzair began a slow but meticulous process of memorising the Qur'an; it was the one thing that was keeping the madness of solitary confinement away. He found it ironic that he had to be arrested as a terrorist, a world very far from the one he occupied, in order to find his religion. Like Frost, he was now taking the road less travelled. Trying to memorise was giving him headaches though, so alien was this process that eventually he developed his own method of reading sections for two weeks consistently before even attempting to memorise them. The rules in New York were very strict, and so Uzair had to find ways of learning how to recite the Qur'an properly:

When I was in New York, I didn't know how to check if I was making mistakes, as I was only just learning again how to read the Qur'an. You need to be able to read it out [loud] to somebody who can check your mistakes, especially because I had never studied *tajwid* and so was using my Urdu instead. We were in isolation. There was a little room which was a recreation area and there was a brother whose cell was right next to the recreation area, so I would go there and take my *mushaf* and keep it on the side. We were not allowed to speak, but we were allowed to pray. Now we were not permitted to speak in Arabic, and because the guards knew I could not speak Arabic, when they saw me in this cell, they assumed that I was just praying when I was reciting. I would go there and melodiously say 'assalaamua-laykum yaa akhi, kayf-al-haal?' So that it sounded like I was praying to the guards. I would then sing Surah al-Ma'ida, etc., so that the brother knew where I was starting from. It would be comedic if it wasn't tragic. I would start reciting and he would correct me.

It took Uzair four years to memorise the complete Qur'an, but doing it by himself became increasingly difficult as he sought to retain the verses and chapters in his mind. He also required some form of checking to ensure that he wasn't making mistakes in his recitation, especially as he had learnt the science of *tajwid* from scratch – his Urdu had been more of a hindrance to his correct pronunciation than an advantage. When he was moved to the Supermax facility ADX Florence in Colorado to join Yahia Lindh and other Muslim political prisoners, he encountered new challenges due to the severe solitary confinement rules that were imposed on them. His cell was tightly constructed, but there were some small gaps he could take advantage of. Uzair at times would lie down on the floor and exploit a small gap in the corner to recite so that his voice would travel to one of the other inmates. At a key stage of his memorisation, he found another way of communicating that permitted him to allow his voice to travel:

One of the methods I would regularly use was through the drainage system. I would recite through the drainage system through the drain hole in my floor that was connected to the cells of other brothers who were close by – they would be able to correct my recitation through the same way. These were the ways we used to recite – imagine, I have recited the entire *mushaf* through the plumbing system to one brother.

There were other means too, but Uzair has come to understand that revealing all the secrets of prisoners is not in the interests of those who remain behind, so he holds on to those innovative methods of communication closely to ensure that the prison administration cannot further cut off contact in an already oppressive solitary environment.

Damanhour Prison – Buhayra, Egypt
Scorpion Prison – Cairo, Egypt

'Some prisoners said we are destined to be here to the end of days,' Abbas recalled as he explained the place of the Qur'an in Egyptian prisons. The prisoners were acutely aware that the very notions of prisons and incarceration appeared only twice in the Qur'an – in Surah Ash-shu'ara and Surah Yusuf. Both times were in Egypt and in both instances, a prophet of God faced an unjust ruler. As Musa relayed the message of God to Pharaoh – as in Surah Ash-shu'ara – Pharaoh responded {If you take a god other than me, I will surely place you among those imprisoned} (26:29). As waves of pessimism regarding their predicament prevailed, some prisoners declared that Egyptian prisons not only defy finitude but also that the oppressed in Egypt are destined to be imprisoned and humiliated to the end of times. Abbas and his friends would defy this interpretation. The chapters in the Qur'an do not foretell doom, but they indicate something more profound about the nature of injustice and tyranny – even as a tyrant attempts to usurp God's place in the universe – indicating something more reflective of the very nature of prisons.

For Omar, this was a reflection on the very nature of time. His devotional contemplation of the Qur'an transformed his understanding of temporality and finitude. At the outset, the prison authorities prevented the prisoners from receiving physical copies of the Qur'an. This was among the many ways the prison authorities attempted to exert control over the prisoners; in turn, this led prisoners to emphasise memorisation and orality. As Omar later explained, the prison authorities could not take away or control what the prisoners knew in their hearts. With the absence of physical clocks or watches, prisoners would often arrange time through prison rituals – from amongst them was having a *wird* of the Qur'an. Omar noted:

> Another thing that became more clear is how erroneous and fickle the idea of *zaman* [time] is. As humans, we pray to God and expect an answer quickly: {Man is made of haste. I shall show you My signs, so do not seek haste from Me} (21:36). But this very idea of *zaman* is meaningless; to Allah, time is infinite. I understand this through the hadith: Whoever passes away, indeed his *Qiyaamah* has commenced. See, Allah responded to Yunus as he was in the stomach of the whale and Ayyub after many years, but in the Qur'an, there is an impression of haste. Time is therefore not true in of itself. This world [*dunya*] and the afterlife [*akhira*] are a part of the same continuum. They are not temporal ruptures. Even if the oppressor is not punished in the *dunya*, they will get their due in the Hereafter; that is because time is infinite.

Despite the illusory nature of time, divine consolation through the Qur'anic narratives is ever-present through the prisoners' devotional contemplation. For Mohamed Soltan, this occurred in his lowest moment at prison, when his father was sentenced to death. Mohamed was once again isolated from his father. He went back to his solitary cell. There was a single blanket on the floor. Usually, he would go back to his routine. He would make ablution, pray, read the Qur'an and then sleep. This time he could not. He was alone and his father was sentenced to death. He began to think of everything he had been through:

> I was like if there was any sort of justice in the world, half of this shit wouldn't ever happen. I had been through so much up to this point: an impromptu surgery without anaesthesia or sterili-

sation by a fellow inmate doctor. I've been beaten, tortured; I had cigarettes put out on my back, I have seen people die. I've experienced all of this just in prison; I hadn't even begun to process the horror and death in Rabaa. I thought for a second, if there is a God then He has either forgotten about me or forgotten about us. None of our prayers counted. I think the highs and lows of religiosity and closeness to God are a function of prison life. The lows are very low and the highs are very high. It fluctuates until you reach your end. I had this sudoku word search thing that had names of cities and bible verses. I had finished 168 pages of it and I so badly needed a distraction. Then I opened it where I had stopped. It was a word search of a Qur'anic verse. I was like no way, get the fuck out of here. I remember thinking this is insane. I think this was the first time I read Surah al-Duha in an English translation. It was like {By the morning brightness, and by the night when it grows still, your Lord has not forsaken you [Prophet], nor does He hate you} (93:1–3). I immediately got up, made *wudu*, and prayed. I have seen too many clear signs in the Qur'an; somebody saying something at the very moment you need to hear it. Even a puzzle book that has a verse. It goes to show our awareness is so limited: {We created man – We know what his soul whispers to him: We are closer to him than his jugular vein} (50:16).

Enforced disappearance – Cairo, Egypt
Burj al-Arab Prison – Alexandria, Egypt
Scorpion Prison – Cairo, Egypt
Tora Prison – Cairo, Egypt
Qanater El Khayereya Women's Prison – Qalyubiyya, Egypt

The Qur'anic narrative persists and animates the lives of all prisoners in Egyptian prisons through Surah Yusuf. This is not just true for political prisoners but also *gina'i* prisoners too. In more than one account – in both female and male prisons – *gina'i* prisoners would recite Surah Yusuf among themselves and would often ask political prisoners to relate the story of the Prophet to them. Both Ali and Khadija recalled discussing the Surah with them. Khadija recalled:

I would read Surah Yusuf often. One time, an older *gina'i* auntie sat next to me and asked, 'Can you please tell me the story of Prophet Yusuf?' I told her the story, even though she knew it already it made her very happy and it made me happy to tell it to her.

I asked Ali what the significance of Surah Yusuf was for the *gina'i* inmates he shared a cell with. Ali laughed a little and said: 'There were two main things they liked. First, that he went to prison but actually got out. Then they also liked that all the women wanted him.'

The meanings prisoners derive from the story vary. However, principally the very fact that a Prophet too found himself in an Egyptian prison was the source of comfort and consolation to all prisoners – regardless of background or status. Mona said:

> Keep in mind we were really just kids at the time. We neither had the knowledge nor experience to sit around and think analytically. But there were things that spoke directly to our condition – especially Surah Yusuf. The very fact that he was here like us in a prison in Egypt. That meant a lot. Each time we would sit and try to gauge simple lessons from it.

Surah Yusuf, for Omar, perfectly encapsulates the temporal discrepancies – between God's promises and human expectations. The internal symmetry in the Surah indicates a divine promise that is eventually fulfilled. It begins with Yusuf's vision {As Yusuf said to his father, 'O my father, surely I saw [i.e., in a dream] eleven planets and the sun and the moon; I saw them prostrating to me'} (12:4), and ends with the fulfilment of vision: {and took them up to [his] throne. They all bowed down before him and he said, 'Father, this is the fulfilment of that dream I had long ago. My Lord has made it come true and has been gracious to me – He released me from prison and He brought you here from the desert – after Satan sowed discord between me and my brothers. My Lord is most subtle in achieving what He will; He is the All Knowing, the Truly Wise'} (12:100). Despite this fulfilment of divine promises, the issue of temporality persists as central to this narrative. Omar noted:

> I see that there are two stations in the Surah that reflect the reality of prison life. The first station is {Mention me in the presence of your lord} (12:42), and the second station is {Return to your lord and so ask him} (12:50). The first station indicates the pressures and the difficulty of prison life that makes it unbearable and the second station shows certitude in divine retribution. In time, you can train yourself to move from one station to the other – where there is certainty in God and serenity in Hs decree. Meaning the first station is one where you are in a hurry to leave prison and the other is acting through conviction and trust in God. For that reason we used to recite a *du'a*: Allah release us as you have released Yusuf.

Like Omar, the ambiguity of temporality in the Surah struck Bilal:

> Consider the verses {As Yusuf said to his father, 'O my father, surely I saw [i.e., in a dream] eleven planets and the sun and the moon; I saw them prostrating to me', and he replied, 'My son, tell your brothers nothing of this dream, or they may plot to harm you – Satan is man's sworn enemy} (12:4–5). At the beginning, Allah tells two Prophets their fate. Put yourself in Prophet Yaqub's position. He knows the end but he does not know the middle. His older children take his son, lose him, and tell him that his son is dead. He says,'I know you're lying because one day you will kneel before him. He knew they were lying for forty years still he was blinded by grief. Does this mean that God was not merciful to him? Does his sadness mean that he did not have faith? This is the *sunnah* of the world. His son needed to be kidnapped and displaced, to endure prison just so he would end up in a place where he would rule Egypt. In your immediate situation, you could be tired, you may get sad but that does not mean that God has taken you out of His mercy. If you read through the Surah, there is a lot of pain but God shows His mercy.

Bilal reached a resolute conclusion about the nature of tribulation in his encounters with the Qur'an: forbearance and struggle are not absolute. God shows His benevolence in the midst of struggle:

Another beautiful story that became closer to my heart is the story of Musa: {We inspired Moses' mother, saying, 'Suckle him, and then, when you fear for his safety, put him in the river: do not be afraid, and do not grieve, for We shall return him to you and make him a messenger'} (28:7). God inspired her and foretold that he will be safe but still he recognises: {The next day, Moses' mother felt a void in her heart – if We had not strengthened it to make her one of those who believe, she would have revealed everything about him} (28:10). It was the *lutf* [benevolence] of Allah that made her bear it. Despite that, her heart was broken and even though He had foretold everything, He did not abandon her: {So We turned him back to his mother so that she might comfort her eye and not grieve, and that she might know that the promise of Allah is true} (28:13). The whole narrative feels like He is consoling her. He didn't doubt her faith. The whole Qur'anic narrative is ripe with God consoling; saying 'I'll be there, try to forget for now. It will all be okay.'

For Asmaa, the significance of Surah Yusuf was less a question of finality and more the truths that were revealed to the Prophet throughout his incarceration. When I asked Asmaa what was the greatest truth that struck her most of Surah Yusuf, she raised her eyebrows a little and tried to hide a cheeky smile: 'Siblings are snakes! Look at Prophet Yusuf's siblings: their dad was a Prophet and their brother was a Prophet, yet still, they were snakes! It's okay that people betray you.'

Asmaa got more serious and added:

Some people were inspired by the fact that he left prison to hold the highest position in the land. I never really saw it this way. He was human and wanted to leave prison; he was weak but at the same time he had *sabr* [forbearance]. These two things don't negate each other. I felt like I could relate to the Prophet, I felt this incredible sense of contentment in God's plan but I still wanted to get out.

The second Qur'anic narrative that persisted with the prisoners is the story of Yunus. Khadija and Mustafa both recalled the *du'a* that had an enduring presence when they were first incarcerated: {There is no God except You. All Extolment be to You! Surely, I have been of the unjust} (21:87):

> I felt like it was going to be my salvation and truly, it made it easier. This was the *du'a* that delivered Yunus from the belly of the whale. I thought, this is what will save me. I remembered that this is what my mum always used to tell me. At the very least, it just means that God will not leave me. I had this resolute belief that God will only test me in a way I can handle, not more. So that is the *du'a* that stayed with me.

Marwa would experience moments of weakness and fear. In her first visitation, after being forcibly disappeared, her older sister came to visit:

> My sister said maybe you should just take off the hijab and start smoking or something, so they won't think you're Ikhwan. I was already questioning the hijab and had taken it off before for a while but then I wore it again. When my sister suggested that I started considering it again, I thought about it, as I was so terrified in prison. I thought, maybe if I took it off they would release me. My mum said, 'I don't think this is a good idea but no one is going to judge you either way.' After the visitation was over, I went to read my *wird*. It was Surah al-Ahzab:. {you were afraid of people, but it is more fitting that you fear God} (33:37).

Marwa teared up as she recalled, 'I felt so ashamed of myself. I wore the hijab because I knew it was an obligation. I can't just take it off because I was scared of prison.'

5
Ethereal Beliefs

DREAMS

Birmingham, United Kingdom
JTF-GTMO – Guantánamo Bay, Cuba

In Birmingham, in 1995, Moazzam Begg was awakened from his sleep sobbing. The visions that had been sent to him in his dreams were truly horrifying. His wife gently spoke to him, telling him not to worry, soothing him back to sleep. It was the image of the concertina wire that would remain most deeply ingrained in his mind, a wire that would come to dominate the images that would emerge from Guantánamo Bay. His dream had the quality of a premonition – a minor form of prophecy sent by God as a reassurance and form of guidance to believers. The details of Moazzam's dream would come to pass, but seven years after his sleep had been broken by them:

The concertina wire is ingrained deepest in my memory. As we strolled meaninglessly around the enclosure, cameras surmounted with machine guns, and guards in military uniform followed our every move. The situation was hopeless – without a foreseeable end. The dismal monotony of daily existence was becoming unbearable. The uncertainty of the future compounded the atmosphere of apprehension and fear.

I whispered to a fellow detainee, 'How much more of this can we take? It's becoming impossible. If we don't make a stand now, we'll lose our self-respect, in addition to our freedom.' My companion sedately replied, 'Patience, my brother, we must have patience.'

And then it began. The firing was indiscriminate; rounds whistled overhead, the bodies fell around me. Turning back towards my confidant, I began to spurt out muffled words about running, but he was already on the ground like the others, dead. Everyone was getting shot – except me. I felt unable to do a thing, but then I did. I called the *adhan* as loud as possible, for the world to hear. It did hear – eventually.

I had known all along that my wife was expecting a baby, and I still had some hope of being present for its birth. But when I heard someone yell across the wire that the child was about to enter this world – with its father captive amongst coils of razor wire – I knew that even if I survived this massacre, it would be a long while before I was reunited with my family. At this thought, I was oblivious of the surrounding carnage. I raised my hands, in the traditional Muslim way, towards the sky, and began to weep. Voices in my head whispered to me to seek help from Allah and beseech His mercy. My hands rose, and continued to do so, passing the clouds. And still I wept.[1]

For Moazzam, there were so many elements to this one dream that would come true, he would never be able to shake the shadow of it in his memory. From the concertina wire and military detention in the compound to having witnessed the murder of the taxi driver Dilawar, the experience of imprisonment ran true. The timing of the dream was unclear though – his wife had been expecting a child in 1995, but it was her pregnancy with their youngest in 2002 that would herald the fulfilment of the premonition.

Belief in the significance of dreams became an integral part of the way that Muslims detained at Guantánamo Bay came to take meaning and succour from their detention experience. In the Qur'an, there are a number of stories that indicate the importance of dreams in predicting future events, not just for believers. Warnings and visions of future events are sent, most significantly to the Prophet Yusuf who only sees the fulfilment of his dream after experiencing years of difficulties, including imprisonment. The prisoners understood from the traditions of the Prophet Muhammad that truthful visions were a small part of prophethood, but that especially for those in the future, 'Prophethood and its effects will be so far away in time, so the believers will be given some compensation in the form of dreams which will bring them some good news or will help them to be patient and steadfast in their faith.'²

As in Moazzam's dream, the idea of *sabr* (patience) and *thabaat* (steadfastness) being central to the purpose of premonitions became part of the vocabulary of prisoners, that their dreams carried significance they were not able to understand at the time they received their visions. Sometimes these visions would be described as having an immediate manifestation in the real world, and at other times, as with Moazzam, they would manifest years later. There was at times a sense, however, that some of the men took their obsession with the dreams too far. Moazzam himself became critical of the extent to which his fellow prisoners would speak of their dreams, feeling that such emphasis almost became debilitating to their everyday survival and mental health:

Another of Uthman's abilities was the interpretation of dreams. He was chief dream interpreter in the whole area. Daily, even nightly, someone would ask him to explain some obscure-sounding dream. At first it was a little intriguing, but I soon lost interest and got really sick of it. Feroz did too. He used to say to me, 'Some of the Arab brothers are always dreaming.' I had had two dreams in my entire life that were worth recalling, and I have mentioned them in my story. But there were some people who were always having amazing dreams. I could see that Uthman tried to be very careful about the interpretations. Some people would make important judgements and decisions about others, based on a dream. People would decide that somebody was an agent of the Americans, or some such thing, based on a dream. I heard Uthman tell people that they had got to put a stop to this, that it was all nonsense. Other dreams he would just interpret as a good omen, or as a bad omen. But one day, when all this was irritating me, I said, 'Uthman, you know what the problem is?'
'What?'
'You know why people dream so much?'
'Why?'
'Because they sleep too bloody much.'

He replied, in all seriousness, 'No, no, no, it's not that, it's because of the situation and people want to see things, and thoughts come into their subconscious.'

The significance of dreams for the men detained at Guantánamo Bay became not only a coping mechanism for the everyday difficulties they faced, but further, tied them to Divine reassurance that provided meaning to their suffering. Through images of the plan that God intended for them, they could find ways to seek hope in the mundane monotony of prison life.

Female Unit, Hillsborough County Jail – Florida, United States of America

Palestinian (US-resident) academic, Sami al-Arian, was under pressure to enter some kind of deal from his lawyers during the period of trial on terrorism charges by the US. He had been accused of being involved in materially supporting the killing of civilians in occupied Palestine and had been intimately involved in his own defence. However, by 2005, he had come into conflict with his lawyers over defence strategy. Sami, confident of his own innocence, refused to concede any ground to the US government, and that in part placed him in conflict with his lawyers, who were keen on finding him justice in what they knew to be a discriminatory judicial system. He felt under further pressure, largely because he was being housed at a female detention unit in complete solitary confinement. All the wings of the unit were empty except for his, and all his guards were women. There was no option of privacy for attending to his personal hygiene, and so Sami felt the humiliation of being under the constant gaze of female guards whenever he had to use to the toilet or take a shower. These conditions were specifically designed to break his will.

In February 2005, at the height of the conflict with his lawyers, Sami had one of the most vivid dreams of his detention experience. He was accustomed to be woken every day at 3 a.m. by the medical cart in order to ensure he received medication for his diabetes. On the occasion of this dream, he awoke to the cell door opening to a man with a rock, coming to crush his head:

Of course you think this is reality and you are about to die. So you have one of two reactions that came to my mind, either I try and stand up and try and wrestle with that person and defend myself, or just accept my fate and pray and then whatever happens, happens.

It was only three steps between me and that person. And during these times I remembered a very long *du'a* actually, but I don't have time to say it, so I take a very small part it and I say 'God is Great, God is Great, God is Great. I seek refuge from bad things to happen.' So this person is coming now and I see the footsteps and I feel the fear and I hear the breathing, and they are right there on top of my head about to crush my head with that rock and I continue my prayer when suddenly the breathing stops and suddenly I open my eyes and see the door is open and the lights are out.

This is when I wake up and see exactly the same thing, but this time with the door shut. So I tried to make sense of what that meant, and I was guided to the fact that the message I was getting was 'do not fight, just pray.' From that moment on, I decided not to fight my lawyers; let them defend the case the way they see it, just pray. So I concentrated on just praying. Really, every day, and my wife, God bless her, she gave me a book of prayers that was very helpful, as it has all kinds of prayers even if you are in prison.

For Sami, this dream did not serve the role of being a premonition, as much as it took on the feeling of guidance that he was in need of during that period. It permitted him to surrender the oppositional position he had taken to the expertise of his lawyers, allowing them to dictate how it might be best to proceed. Significant dreams served different purposes for Sami at different stages of his detention. On 11 November 2005, two days prior to the jury's verdict in his joint case with two other defendants, Sami again received a dream:

I saw myself in a courtroom, but without clothes, just underwear and underpants, covering myself with a prayer rug. And then the judge is reading the verdicts – not guilty, not guilty, not guilty, but too much for my co-defendants – not for me. So I'm asking my lawyer, 'Why is he not saying anything about me?'

Sami was convinced that this was a positive sign for his co-defendants at least, and with two days to go without seeking his permission, his lawyers attempted to file for a mistrial, unsure about how to read the jury's reactions to the evidence that had already been seen during the trial. Ultimately, the judge refused the mistrial and the jury was still in deliberations. What Sami did not know at the time, was that the deliberations were in their favour, and the judge sought a partial verdict in order to ensure the government's case did not collapse completely. By this stage, Sami was fully aware of what was going on, and so congratulated his two co-defendants, informing them that Allah had sent him a dream that they would both be acquitted, as they were. This was among a number of premonitions that Sami would have during his detention, all providing him with a degree of succour that he would be vindicated by the end of his ordeal; his visions led him to write a book of poetry entitled *Conspiracy against Joseph* – referencing the Prophet's Yusuf's dreams and ultimate vindication.

Tora Prison – Cairo, Egypt
Qanater El Khayereya Women's Prison – Qalyubiyya, Egypt
Burj al-Arab Prison – Alexandria, Egypt

Years after his release, Mohamed Soltan would recall the enduring power of dreams in the bleakest moments of his confinement. Prisoners would reflect on the story of Yusuf as they too recounted their visions and premonitions to one another. They would seek the pious and knowledgeable from among them to act as deciphers and interpreters of their visions and dreams. Any prison ward that would have access to books – either by the consent of the authorities or smuggled – would have a copy of the treatise on dream interpretation attributed to Ibn Sirin, who lived in the eighth century CE.[3] Muhammad Ibn Sirin, a scholar and contemporary of Hasan al-Basri, is widely held as the foremost Islamic authority on dream interpretation. Ibn Sirin, son of a captive freed by Anas ibn Malik, would later too become a prisoner and languish in the prisons of Basra.

For Mohamed, dreaming in prison encapsulated blessings, even if it would not foretell release:

> Dreams are a divine function of prison; they allow you to escape. By God's mercy, they take you to an alternate reality – one where you are free. You're out and about with your family; you are with your loved ones; you're meeting people that you have not seen or met in forever. You are remembering people that you have forgotten ... When you start waking up, you're halfway between your reality and your alternate reality. It is the worst moment in prison; it was like a curse every day. It is a daily renewal of your detention, because you realise, damn, I am actually in this place. You try to force yourself back asleep, but then reality harshly pulls you into itself.

Mohamed found himself oscillating between attempting to find solace in dreams and escaping the harsh reality of waking up to a prison cell and bars. Like Mohamed, Abdullah also felt that dreams were a divine blessing to the prisoners in the midst of the solitude and desperation of confinement:

> Besides supplications and the Qur'an, prisoners saw dreams as one of the ways they communicated with God and God communicated with them. And what can they do? People cling to any speck of hope. Dreams are narrated across prisons. It is all a part of a spiritual act that people cling to, because what else can they do? They look for rays of hope, but there is power in that. If they are helpless because human power does not exist, then even the authority of your captors does not really exist either. It is a dual thing.

Abdullah, like many prisoners – including some who are sceptical about the proliferation of dreams and dream interpretation – saw a vision he believed would foretell his release. He was in solitary confinement and in the depths of his hunger strike. He saw himself going up a mountain in three circles until he came across a man selling a notebook. He asked the man how much the notebook would cost. The man responded that it would be 45 pounds. In the dream, Abdullah tried to haggle, but the man refused and said the price was fixed. Suddenly, the man gives Abdullah the notebook along with a horse which he rides to the top of the mountain. Three days after seeing this dream, a fellow inmate knocks on the window on Abdullah's cell door and asks if he needs anything:

> I said 'Actually yes, do you know someone who can interpret dreams?' He said, 'Yes there is someone who is good at dream interpretation here.' I asked him to get me a pen. Because this is a maximum-security prison, there are no pens and no paper, but he gets me a pen and a tissue. I write down my dream and he takes it to the dream interpreter. He comes back a while later and says, 'This will be the last place you will be held before you are released.' This will be your last 45 days in prison. The notebook signifies a decision or court ruling and the horse means freedom.

Abdullah would only be in prison for another 45-days before being released.

Prisoners oftentimes seek dream interpreters to decipher their visions. These are typically pious, well-respected, older inmates. In the prison ward where Munira was held, the dream interpreter was an older inmate called Auntie Iman. Munira had no hope of ever being released. During Ramadan, she was reminded of the supplication Yunus made in the belly of the whale: 'There is no deity except You; exalted are You. Indeed, I have been of the wrongdoers':

> I felt so stupid. Why did I never make this *du'a* before. It was God who saved Yunus from the belly of the whale. That can't be more difficult from what I am experiencing right now! I felt like it was a sign. I said it over and over. I really felt it and I really believed it with all my heart. Allah brought me to this *du'a* so I can be released. I had no questions, only *yaqeen* [certainty].

That night, Munira went to sleep. In her sleep, she saw herself holding a plate of dessert as the sun was rising. Munira went to

Auntie Iman and told her the dream. Auntie Iman had Ibn Sirin's book with her:

> She said, 'Well, why don't we open the book and see what it says about your dream.' She opened the book and said, 'This is a good omen! You're getting out.' In prison, there was a *Hudhud* [Hoopoe bird] that would appear whenever someone was about to get released. That morning, I saw the *Hudhud*. My detention was already being renewed for another 45 days, but that day they called my name. They called my name and I was so scared and told everyone to pray for me.

For the very first time since her arrest, Munira had some hope. For the first time, she was not alone in the transport vehicle. There were other inmates there beside her, which brought her immense solace. That day, she did not see her dad in court like she had expected. She did not get out. She went back to her cell and felt an overwhelming sense of sadness and hopelessness. That night, she had the same dream. She woke up confused but continued to pray. It was only until later that day, she was sent to another court and found out that she was being released.

Asmaa experienced dreams and visions in prison very much like Munira. In the ward where she was held, there too was an older auntie who would interpret their dreams:

> I dreamt I was wearing white and I was dancing in front of a crowd of people. When I left, I found myself in a very narrow corridor. I felt very scared and alone. At the end of the long narrow corridor, I saw myself on a stage and there were microphones and cameras. By her right was an Egyptian actor and by her left was an American.

Asmaa went and consulted the auntie who interprets dreams. The dream interpreter explained that when a prisoner dances or when someone wears white, that indicates glad tidings. The narrow corridor foretells a personal crisis that Asmaa will have to overcome. The stage, camera and microphones indicate that she will experience recognition for the struggles she has endured:

It all happened. I left prison three weeks later but I was put under house arrest for a year and three months after I got out. These were some of the most difficult times in my life. After house arrest, I left Egypt, and the actors I saw in my dreams held a conference in support of human rights and I was given an award.

Visions, inside and outside of prison, do not always foretell glad tidings. For some, they would foretell tragedy or even their own incarceration. Hamza would recall that he never used to dream prior to his imprisonment, but in prison he had many dreams: 'I see dreams in general as something from God to give *sabr* [forbearance] to the prisoners. I see it as provision and sustenance from God. There are some people who go too deep and take it too far to the point that they lose their minds a little.'

The first vision Hamza saw was one week before his arrest. He saw Saad El-Katatni – the former Speaker of the People's Assembly after the revolution – open the door of a prison cell and invite him inside. One week later, Hamza was detained and the first person he saw by the cell door was El-Katatni. Hamza was shocked and told El-Katatni that he saw him in a dream doing what he was doing at the time. El-Katatni stood in utter confusion. In the cell with them was an older shaykh – Shaykh Ra'fat who had seniority in prison. He was in his late seventies and was first imprisoned by Hosni Mubarak. He had been in prison for over 25 years. Shaykh Ra'fat was skilled in dream interpretation and would decipher the visions of the prisoners in the prison ward.

One night, Hamza had a dream that disturbed him. He dreamt he was in Mit Ghamr station at Ain Shams. He went out onto the bridge and saw one of his good friends standing there beside him. Under the bridge, he saw the Prophet Muhammad carrying a casket and behind him were thousands of people walking in the funeral. He left the bridge and went into the metro. There he found the girl he was in love with and wanted to marry and the train left. Hamza asked Shaykh Ra'fat what the dream meant. Shaykh Ra'fat listened to the details of the dream, and then explained. First, his friend whom he saw on the bridge would be arrested and would only get out of prison at the same time Hamza would:

He then said 'One of your friends will be martyred. The Prophet and the angels will walk in his funeral.' I asked him, 'What about the girl?' He only said 'Have *sabr* and God will show you the way.' I asked him, 'What does that mean? Does that mean we will end up together?' He said, 'I didn't say that. I said have *sabr*.' My friends laughed at me so much for taking the dream so seriously. Next week when we were all in court, journalists told me that my friend died. He was shot by security forces in Ain Shams University and that before he died, he told them to say hello to me. I was taken aback. I then asked, 'So who was taken?' They were so surprised. They asked me how I knew. My friend would become a prisoner with me and he would later be released with me.

Hamza and the girl he loved never married in the end. But for Hamza, visions are a way God gives prisoners forbearance and strength. He noted, however, that people do often go overboard. Ali too explained that the proliferation of dream narratives in prisons would often have adverse effects on people's sanity. Prisoners would desperately look to interpret signs that may or may not be there, hoping that somehow this would indicate their release:

If we went by these guys' dreams, the Aqsa would be liberated three times over! There was this one guy, he was always dreaming these big dreams. I just went up to him one day and said, 'For the love of God just please stop dreaming.' He got upset and called me a materialist!

Ali was laughing hard at this point, as he was recalling this story. Once, he dreamt of the number three. He went to a prisoner who interprets dreams, who said, 'You will be free in three weeks!': 'I went to court and was sentenced to three years! I was so confident as well. I told everyone I was leaving; the brother assured me. But I got three years!'

For other prisoners, like Mustafa and Mona, dreams were not a form of release. They had no escape in their sleep. They only had nightmares. For that reason amongst others, they could not relate to the culture of dreams and dream interpretation. Like Ali, they felt that there was a more sinister side to an over-emphasis on dreams and signs for many prisoners clinging on to any semblance of hope. Mona explained:

> Mind you, some people follow signs to the point of halluci-nation. One girl was convinced that God was communicating directly with her. For example, if a breeze moves a branch and she sees its shadow, she thinks it's a message. The problem with following signs and engaging [with] their supposed meanings is that when it doesn't work out in the way you want it to, you can fall into really deep depression and even become resentful.

This was a realisation Marwa came to after prison. In prison, she was convinced that a vision she saw was a message from God fore-telling that she was destined to be with the man she loved. When their marriage did not work, she was less certain. She felt that perhaps she was manifesting signs rather than simply deciphering them: 'I was a big believer that one connection a person in prison has with the outside world is through dreams. It is like the story of Prophet Yusuf. I still believe it is, but sometimes we read signs not because they are there but because we want them to be there.'

JINN AND BLACK MAGIC

JTF-GTMO – Guantánamo Bay, Cuba

For the 14 years that the Kuwaiti national Fayiz al-Kandari was detained at Guantánamo Bay, he was considered a scholar among the inmates who were detained alongside him. Part of his routine was to provide spiritual advice, Islamic legal opinions, and even help whenever some disputation arose between the prisoners. Regularly, he performed *ruqya* (spiritual healing) to help those who were exhibiting ailments, especially if their ailments seemed as if they were caused by *jinn* possession* or through *sihr* (black magic). During his time in detention, interrogators attempted to

---

* A *jinn* is an ethereal being made of smokeless fire imperceptible to the sight of humans.

disturb and disrupt him by focusing on hurting him through his own system of belief.

Fayiz and other prisoners would be taken to darkened interrogation rooms with very low lighting, and on the middle of the floor would be a hexagram or pentagram within which a number of prisoners would be placed. On the walls of the room, the interrogators would place sexually explicit pictures, as well as images of dismembered children. Fayiz would describe the music played as devil-worshipping and the smoky atmosphere created by the burning of incense alongside the placement of amulets around the floor. Fayiz could never be sure if these were actually rituals of black magic, but he understood that at the very least, they had been placed in order to give such an impression. Fayiz, himself, was largely unfazed by these tactics. He had heeded the advice of the Prophet Muhammad to perform his *adkhar* (remembrances of Allah) and to recite the chapter of the Qur'an, Surah al-Baqarah, as a way of warding off evil.

There were, however, instances of *jinn* disturbing the prisoners, with Fayiz witnessing the way that one sleeping tier had been affected on a single night:

Once, I was awake sitting in the middle of the night and the young men were sleeping in front of me on the first tier which had cells open to one another. So I heard a scream from there, and everyone was covered with their blankets. It was in the middle of the night and it was all calm. I turned and saw that a brother had woken up. Then a second brother shouted and woke up, and another shouted and woke up, then another. I question what's happening, when one shouts 'Ah, my leg!', until it spread across the blocks and I am amazed at the spectacle. One of them claims that someone kicked, and then others claim that someone kicked them on the leg, the third and the others too. All of them are experiencing the same thing and I am laughing and saying to them that a *jinn* is kicking you all from the first one to the last one.

The *jinn* were there initially, but they eventually left, as nearly 24 hours a day the Qur'an was being recited at Guantánamo Bay – the brothers were buzzing like bees with their recitation. One of the brothers saw a dream where the *jinn* were all leaving the island in a convoy, one who had his eye popped out, and another whose hand was broken, another with a torn face. While they are departing, they are turning back and looking at the brothers, depressed at being forced to leave the island due to the war bringing all the brothers there.[4]

The tactics used by interrogators against the prisoners at Guantánamo varied greatly, but sometimes the information they were given by their own cultural advisers simply did not correlate to anything the Muslim men understood about their beliefs. It was clear to Ahmed Errachidi from the very beginning that they would make every effort to exploit his faith, particularly during interrogations:

At this point a different officer, one I'd not previously met, came in and ordered that two seats – one made from iron and one from leather – be brought in. He told the soldiers to give me the comfortable leather seat while he took the iron one. He had two cigarettes, one of which he lit and the other of which he put on the ground. Then he did the oddest thing. While facing me, he spread one of his hands across his face until he was looking at me through his fingers. He moved this hand to left and right while saying: 'I can't see any *jinns* or angels with you.' I didn't know what he was talking about but he didn't care. 'You're on your own,' he said as he continued to jiggle the hand. 'You're weak. Other people have *jinns* and angels to protect them, but I can see you're alone.' It was the most ridiculous spectacle I'd ever witnessed. He was acting as if he believed in black magic, and as if I did as well. I couldn't quite credit it that a grown man should choose to make such a fool of himself. I told him I didn't need spirits or angels. This made him furious. He ordered the guard to swap our chairs, so that he now had the leather one while I was on the iron one. 'I deserve this more than you,' he told me as he sat down again.[5]

The farcical displays of the guards in relation to the beliefs that the Muslim prisoners held did not stop the guards from having their own beliefs in the spiritual world, which were observed by the detainees. An amusing incident took place where a newly arrived female guard was watching a prisoner with very long hair and a long beard rocking back and forth while reciting over a bottle of water – performing prayers for the purpose of healing. It was a moment of pathetic fallacy as a storm raged outside and thunder and lightning provided the atmosphere. A prisoner called the guard over and offered to explain what was taking place, that the prisoner was a sorcerer and he was summoning a thunder and lightning *jinni*, and as the thunder clapped outside, the prisoners could see the blood drain from the guard's face and she jumped out of fear.[6]

Metropolitan Correctional Center (MCC) – New York City, United States of America
ADX Florence – Colorado, United States of America

Uzair Paracha's hands were involuntarily clawed tight as he sat in the early days of his detention at the New York MCC. He did not understand what was happening to his hands until he thought back to his life in Karachi, when a relative was in touch with a spiritual man who claimed he could provide healing for a range of issues – as far as Uzair knew, the spiritual was a euphemism for a *sahir*, a practitioner of black magic. This was not uncommon in Pakistan; although strictly forbidden in Islam, people would often turn to sorcerers to heal ailments or to cause harm to others:

There was a relative of mine who claimed to have been in touch with someone in Karachi who was said to have been some kind of spiritual figure. Apparently, this spiritual man had helped someone else with an issue they were having, but he seemed to be someone who was into black magic. That relative of mine, his demeanour had changed after this interaction. He would have tics, would sit in certain ways and would have clawed fingers that were tight, his physical appearance had changed. After I got arrested, I am aware that I am doing those exact same things in the first few months of my arrest, and I don't know why and I can't stop doing them. I started reading the Qur'an a lot, and eventually came out of it; in fact, that Qur'an helped me to change my whole demeanour and gave me a lot of strength to stand up for myself. I became bold and confident, even mentally healthier. I think that this is the many benefits of reading the Qur'an. I spoke to my mother many years later, and she mentioned a relative who got in touch with the same spiritual man (who I believe was a *sahir*) and they approached him about my incarceration, and so they did things in my name, and I displayed similar symptoms. I can only think now that this was some kind of manifestation of *sihr* – I found out about this ten years after the fact.

By the time Uzair had come close to the end of his detention experience in the US, he had accumulated a great deal of knowledge by learning from the more scholarly men he had been detained with, but also by reading almost every single Islamic book he could get his hands on in the prison library. He was very familiar with the contents of the library, and so when a new Muslim prisoner arrived in his unit for a drug-related case, he was able to diagnose that there was a potential *jinn* issue at play. The prisoner's bunkee had been complaining that the new prisoner had not been sleeping at all, and so there was clearly a problem. New prisoners sometimes complained of problems, in order to be moved into the hospital wing, as a form of reprieve from the difficulties of their new prison environment. Uzair explained that it was impossible to fake four days of complete sleeplessness, and so there might be something else at play. He remembered there was a book on black magic that one of the other prisoners had, and so he borrowed it to help heal the new prisoner. The removal of black magic or *jinn* can be a violent process on the body of the one afflicted, so Uzair took two very large Muslim prisoners with him to hold the man down while he performed the exorcism:

I borrowed the book and took two very large brothers with me to hold down this man who was suffering while I read the Qur'an over him. He started beating himself up when I put my hand on his forehead and tried to read the things in the book. I did that for a week or two weeks, and eventually he started sleeping. This was not a direct encounter with *sihr*, but it may well have been a *jinn* issue. I wasn't trained to help, but we had a book so we tried our best to help.

Scorpion Prison – Cairo, Egypt
Mansoura Prison - El Mansoura, Dakahlia, Egypt
Qanater El Khayereya Women's Prison – Qalyubiyya, Egypt

'It was rumoured,' Khaled explained, 'that Scorpion Prison was built on top of a burial site.' Stories of *jinn* inhabiting the prisons and possessing prisoners were ripe in many prisons and, in particular, Scorpion Prison. Mustafa was bemused as he recalled the stories of *jinn* inhabiting the prison cells. He recounted what an older inmate had told him: 'These prison sites were their [*jinn*] home long ago. We are the ones who have intruded on their homes. They don't understand that we [prisoners] are here against our will. They try to force us out of their homes but we can't leave.'

Mustafa never saw a *jinni* himself but stories of *jinn* proliferate in prisons to a large scale. He explained that within that space, it is very easy to slip into alternative realities, or even hallucinate. Some prisoners who claim to witness supernatural phenomena – like a broom levitating, or a shadow of a person that is not really there – could be making credible claims. The very trauma of prison life, however, can lead people to see things that may or may not be there.

In the first few days of his incarceration in Mansoura Prison, Amin felt like he was losing his mind. There were faint, shrill screams escaping through the walls. He felt like his brain was playing tricks on him. However, each night the screams grew louder and louder. He could make out the words. These were satanic rituals. The ceiling began to slowly drip a red liquid resembling blood. The slow blood that dripped from the ceiling was now flooding their cell. They were on the top floor of the prison complex (or so they were made to believe). The inmates spent each night in complete terror at the sound of the screams, possession, and the blood that flooded their cell. Even the most sceptical among them was frozen with fear: 'We later found out we weren't the top floor at all. There was a room directly above our cell that the guards used. They were simulating *jinn* possessions to terrify us. Then through the pipes they would spill faux blood which would flood our cell.'

The Qanater Prison complex too was filled with stories of possessions and black magic. Layla explained that the execution ward – the ward where those sentenced to death spend a lot of their sentence – was known for being a place ripe with the presence of *jinn*. She added that it was well-known in prison that whoever saw the execution ward *jinn* would be killed that very same week. There was the story of another *jinn* who would only appear to political prisoners:

> They would only see her [the *jinn*] in *fajr*. She did nothing. She would only pass by. This one girl, who was really annoying, went to the toilet and heard the *jinn* scratching at the door. Everyone freaked out. I just laughed. I said, 'God bless that *jinn*, because really that girl was so annoying.' I was not as scared of *jinn* as some other prisoners were. I believe they are beings who exist in a different realm and that's okay.

In her cell, she encountered convoluted myths involving the occult – the most convoluted of which involved a woman nicknamed 'murderer of the cemeteries' from Upper Egypt. This woman was part of a gang that illegally traded ancient Egyptian artefacts. A myth had developed after the British colonial archaeologists' campaigns, where they opened ancient tombs and plundered their remains, and these archaeologists mysteriously died not long after. This myth arose in peripheral occultist circles that human sacrifice must be made before attempting to open the tomb. Layla explained:

> The female officer nicknamed this woman 'murderer of the cemeteries'. According to other prisoners, she was a part of the artefact mafia, and to open up these tombs you have to engage the occult. Sometimes murder is involved. So police officers often wait for the mafia to open up the tombs because they are too scared to and once they do they arrest everyone. The female officer said that the *jinn*, who the 'murderer of the cemeteries' was in communication with, asked her to sacrifice a child to open the grave, and so she killed a street child. I have no idea if

any of this is true. I just know that that woman was really weird. Everyone just stayed away from her.

Layla was irked by the power those who claimed to possess supernatural powers yielded on even educated and pious prisoners. One prisoner, who was imprisoned on sex crime charges, preached a gospel of crystals and energy. Many prisoners gravitated towards this, which Layla felt was irksome but not necessarily dangerous. However, none of the occultists would bother her more than Lamis, a Syrian woman. Lamis was a Sunni woman who fell in love (and/or) seduced a Druze man. She subsequently conspired with her brother – who may or may not be her lover – to kill her husband and her sister-in-law. That is how she ended up in prison. Lamis would recite the Qur'an daily but would never pray. When Layla asked her why she would not pray, Lamis would respond that she was exempt from prayer:

> She used to correspond with *jinn* and had bizarre control over prisoners. Rich prisoners would pay all of her expenses in prison and because she made friends with all of the officers so she was protected. She came to me one day and said, 'I can talk to him and ask him when you're getting out?' She was gesturing to *jinn*. I said, 'No thanks; I'm good.' If she was so amazing and so connected, she would have helped herself.

Lamis befriended a political prisoner – who was a member of the Egyptian *Tablighi Jamaat* (known as *Jama'at al-Tabligh w-al Da'wa*). Layla became dismayed that an educated and pious woman was ensnared in Lamis's occult practices:

> [Lamis] told the *Tablighi* woman that she saw her grandfather in a dream. The grandfather said that if she read Surah Maryam until verse 34 {That is Isa son of Maryam, in word of truth, concerning which they are wrangling}, for forty days straight she will be released. I really did not think she would do it, but she did. After forty days nothing happened. [Lamis] then came and said he came to me in my dreams again and said it would be another five days. She did it and yes she was released afterwards.

The history of Egyptian prisons – past and present – is replete with stories like Layla's. In 1981, the renowned, charismatic, blind Islamic preacher and orator – Shaykh Abd al-Hamid Kishk – was imprisoned among many after Anwar El Sadat ratified the Camp David Accords with Israel. The prisoners he shared a cell with conducted a plan to mess with the guards. Before the guards locked the door each night, they would obstruct it in a way that was not obvious. Every night, the guard would lock up only to come back in the morning to Shaykh Kishk sitting meditatively outside the cell while all other prisoners would stay in the cell. The officer would go back the following night and make sure that the doors were locked, only again to find Shaykh Kishk sitting outside the cell the following morning. The prisoners whispered to the guards that Shaykh Kishk was a blessed man who possessed supernatural powers that enabled him to move across locked bars and so it was not right to bother him. The guards became terrified of his powers. They became convinced that Shaykh Kishk was a saint and that he was manifesting saintly miracles (*karamat*) by teleporting across. No officer bothered him after that.

Mohamed Soltan recalls a similar story with his father – Salah Soltan. An officer grabbed the copy of the Qur'an Salah was carrying, tearing out a page:

> Baba shouted: the guards are tearing up the Quran [*mushaf*]! He made a very direct prayer [*du'a*] against him: he said, 'May God paralyse the hand that tore the Qur'an.' Two months later the guy got in an accident and he couldn't use it anymore. Then he quit and told everyone that this was because of the prayer of Salah Soltan. It then became a legend in prison. No one upset Salah Soltan after that.

Cairo International Airport Deportation Cell – Cairo, Egypt

One approach to spiritual healing and blessing that prisoners shared with one another was *ruqya*. The practice of *ruqya* is the practice of reciting Qur'anic verses on a person afflicted by evil eye (*hassad/nazar*), black magic, or even physical ailments.

On her way out of Egypt, Khadija was detained. She was forcibly disappeared in a deportation chamber at the airport. The chamber had migrants and refugees from all over the world. There were whole families sleeping on the floor:

There was a Palestinian woman being deported. She looked so very much like my aunt. I was crying hysterically and banging on the locked door. I was crying, 'Let me out! Let me out! I don't want to be here.' She came over to me, hugged me as I fell on the floor crying. I put my head on her lap and she started comforting me. I was crying and crying. She started to recite Qur'an over me and then started doing *ruqya*. I began to yawn. She told me I was experiencing *hassad* (evil eye) and that I will be okay. I started to feel better.

In the worst moments of his time in prison, Bilal had a similar experience. Three years into his imprisonment, Bilal's appeal was accepted. What on the surface seemed to be a good thing pushed him towards cycles of renewed incarceration. Bilal was on the Presidential pardon list; the appeal nullified the pardon. This meant that he would be in prison for at least another two years. Bilal's anger exploded when his parents went to visit him that day:

This was the lowest point for me. Three years of pent-up anger exploded. My mom said, 'I made you the food you like.' I told her I didn't want anything from them. They must be happy that I was there. That they didn't care. Imagine a mum and dad, helpless, going to visit their son in prison and all they get was this ill treatment. I remember my dad began to cry and I couldn't look him in the face. I couldn't continue. I was so ashamed of myself. I asked to be taken to my cell.

Bilal entered his cell looking like a ghost, to the point that his cellmates asked if someone had died:

You know the sobbing that comes right from the gut. That was me. This was the worst moment in prison. I hid under my blanket to escape my shame and cry. Somehow, I don't know how, God inspired me to say the *du'a* Prophet Ayyub in the *ayah* (38:41) {And remember Our servant, Ayyub – when he called his Lord saying, 'The Satan has inflicted weariness and pain upon me'}. I kept on saying it over and over. That day, I fell asleep and it was as though angels descended upon me and they told my cellmate to perform *ruqya* on me. I tried to say, 'I seek refuge in Allah from the cursed Satan.' But my tongue was twisted. I woke up and I felt like I was no longer in prison. The next day, I saw a dream in which the judge – Nagy Shehata – who sentenced me to 25 years, was humiliated and working a menial dirty job. He was begging me for my forgiveness. I asked him why he did this to me? He just kept on repeating, '*Wallahi*, I am sorry.' It was as if I was now the judge and he was the prisoner. I woke up, and somehow after that I felt free.

6
Torture

CULTURAL HUMILIATION

Kandahar International Airport - Kandahar, Afghanistan
Bagram Airbase - Parvan, Afghanistan
JTF-GTMO - Guantánamo Bay, Cuba

On arrival at Kandahar, one of the first forms of ritual humiliation that the Muslim men detained were subjected to was forced nudity and forced shaving – both of which caused deep distress to all the men who had been careful throughout their lives of their own modesty and self-grooming. Murat Kurnaz used to visit the *hamam* (Turkish bath) during his years in Bremen, but due to his consciousness of his duties in Islam, he would protect his modesty by covering himself from his navel to his knees, choosing to shower with shorts so that no others would be able to view his private area.[1] In those initial moments, he was held naked along with sixty other men in a pen, with many crying over the shame they felt, in many ways worse than the fact of being detained. This would only be a precursor to their torture, as Murat would come to repeat the litany *'hasbe Allahu wa ni'mal wakeel'* – reminding himself that God is the ultimate protector of his life. It was these words that would come to his mind in Kandahar, between each dunking of his head beneath water, as his American interrogators mock-executed him by simulating drowning between their questions. 'Where is Osama?' Dunk. 'Who are you?' Dunk. With each emergence from his near drowning, his mind reiterated *'hasbe Allahu wa ni'mal wakeel'*.

The experience of those who were taken to Bagram was no different; almost immediately forced shaving and forced nudity became the norm for newly arrived prisoners. Moazzam Begg understood what was happening, and the way the Americans were completely aware of the effect of their forceful abuse of the men:

> I was then moved under a wooden shelter, and sat down so they could take portrait pictures for their detainee album: one with all my hair, and one after it was shaved off. The barber sadistically enjoyed his job, and as he shaved off my beard with a machine, he commented, 'This is the part I like best.' I wondered why he would say such a thing, but realised that he knew the beard was an important symbol of Muslim identity, particularly in this region. He'd obviously seen plenty of distressed reactions from others. As he pushed my head around to shave it, I tried to adjust my feet, so that I wouldn't slide off the stool. A guard shoved my feet further away from the stool and stamped his boots on them, really hard. 'Who gave you permission to move, mother-fucker?' The most humiliating thing was witnessing the abuse of others, and knowing how utterly dishonoured they felt. These were men who would never have appeared naked in front of anyone, except their wives; who had never removed their facial hair, except to clip their moustache or beard; who never used vulgarity, nor were likely to have had it used against them. I felt that everything I held sacred was being violated, and they must have felt the same.[2]

This abuse of the prisoners would continue at Guantánamo Bay, where forced shaving and nudity would become routine practices. The men understood this had nothing to do with hygiene in the prison, but was directly related to efforts to humiliate them. Lakhdar Boumediene spoke of this humiliation as the guards would often shave their heads and beards, but leave large patches, 'Hitler moustaches', or even a patch in the shape of a Christian cross.[3] Writing of his experiences alongside Lakhdar, Mustafa Ait Idir described how he had his own red line that he established before challenging their treatment at Guantánamo Bay:

> All detainees in Romeo were required to go barefoot. I did not protest; I handed my flip-flops over without complaint. The others did not seem to mind either.

The soldiers' next demand, however, was unacceptable. They told us to remove our slacks and hand them over. We were unwilling to do that. Men are supposed to cover their *awrah*, the area from the navel to the knees, during prayers. If the soldiers took our slacks and did not return them, we would not be able to pray as our religion instructs us to.

'I am not going to give you my slacks,' I told the soldier standing outside my cell. 'It is impossible. It is not going to happen. How do you expect me to perform my prayers without my slacks?'

'These are the regulations,' he insisted. He told me that his authority came directly from the men in charge of Guantánamo.

'I don't care if President Bush himself said to come take my slacks,' I said. 'There is no way that it's going to happen.'

The soldier I was speaking with left and returned with a higher-ranking officer.

'Are you going to give me the slacks or not?' the officer asked. 'I am not going to give you anything,' I vowed. 'Then we're going to take them by force.' 'Go ahead,' I told him. 'If you want to take them by force, go ahead and do it. But I am not going to give them to you.' 'Fine,' the officer shrugged. He and the first soldier walked away. Minutes later, a mass of soldiers swarmed Romeo Block. They had sent in the IRF [Initial Reaction Force] teams. A group of soldiers went to each prisoner and demanded his slacks. One man complied; he was sickly and knew that his body could not endure whatever punishment the rest of us were about to suffer. The rest of us refused.

The IRF soldiers started going into one cell after another, beating detainees and forcefully removing their pants. The sounds of violence grew louder as they worked their way across the block, growing closer and closer. When they reached my cell, one of the soldiers demanded my slacks. I knew it would earn me a beating, but I simply could not bring myself to hand them over. Some things are just too much.

'If you don't hand them over,' the soldier threatened, 'we're going to come in and take them.'

'Go ahead,' I replied.

'We have six guys here, and we're all coming in.'

'I hope you'll be first,' I said, anger coursing through me. I am not a violent man. For me, karate has always been about competition and physical fitness, not blood-sport. But every man has his limit.

I stood there in my cell, barefoot, listening to the screams and cries of my fellow detainees being savaged, disrobed and humiliated, I had reached mine. I wanted to hit this man. I wanted to hurt him. I was ready for a fight. I took off my slacks and ripped them into pieces. I would rather destroy them than let these bullies seize them from me. I threw the shreds into the corner of my cell, behind me. To get what was left of the slacks, they would have to come through me. I stood on the tiny bed in my cell and waited, in my boxers, silently challenging these six armed, armoured soldiers.

The soldier again demanded that I hand over the shreds. I again told him that I would not.

'Why?' he asked. Obviously, they were of no use to me now.

'Because I want you to come in and get them.'

An order was given, and the soldiers started piling through the narrow door to my cell, trying to rush me. When the first soldier came within range, I struck him. Hard. He tumbled backward into the rest of his team before most of them had even cleared the door, and they all scrambled back out. I suppose they had not been expecting a barefoot prisoner in his underwear to put up quite so much of a fight. A short while later, another IRF team arrived outside my cell. I could tell from the emblems on one man's uniform that he was a high-ranking officer. 'Are you gonna give us your slacks?' he asked.

'There is no way I will give them to you myself,' I told him. 'If you want them, come in and get them.' The officer started talking to the other soldiers. They spent a long time in conversation, trying to figure out what to do. Eventually they settled on a tactic. First, they hit me with pepper spray, or something like it. I tried to turn my head, to shield my eyes, but it was no use. Soon I could hardly see, and there was a terrible stinging pain in my eyes.

Four of them rushed me. That was when my training took over.[4]

Mustafa's martial arts training would eventually not be enough to ward off the attacks, although he would give the soldiers something to think about in the future. His actions did signal to the authorities that there were lines (mostly related to religious practice, but also of his basic humanity) that, if crossed, would result in forceful responses from the prisoners – ones that might lead to their own harm.

ADX Florence – Colorado, United States of America
Terra Haute CMU – Indiana, United States of America

They never explicitly admit that their abuse of our faith is systematic, but they all but admit through their actions – that their hate is directed towards Islam. If they could crush out every last trace, they would do so, but they don't because it's not practical, so that's why they create these notions of radicals and extremists and create separation between Muslims, giving the visage of honouring certain aspects of Islam while denying others. If they had their way, they would not let anyone utter the name of Allah or express the slightest aspect of Islam in any circumstances.

Yahia Lindh experienced restrictions on his faith in manifold ways. A key restriction was the complete ban on him speaking a word of Arabic to anyone inside or outside of prison – it touched every part of his life. Any breach of this rule resulted in his punishment, even going as far as extending his detention by a few weeks as he was found to have contravened the rule close to the time of his release. This was not a rule against significant amounts of Arabic being spoken, the simple words of '*Assalaamualaykum*' or even the requirement of Muslims to respond with '*wa alaykumasalaam*' resulted in punishment.

At the Communications Management Unit (CMU) at Terra Haute, Indiana – often referred by the prisoners as Guantánamo North – Yahia spent close to twelve years of his detention. During his time, he was denied praying *salat-ul-jama'ah* (congregational prayer) with the other Muslim prisoners – being punished if they were ever caught doing so:

It was considered to be a dastardly deed, to be praying in *jamaʿah*. Even after we won the lawsuit to permit the prayer, their hatred towards Islam did not diminish, it was expressed in a variety of ways. Even after we won, the prison refused to implement the court order. It got to the point where we had to go back to the judge and hold the warden in contempt. Initially, when they allowed us to finally pray, they set it up in such a way that it would be as inconvenient and humiliating as possible. They permitted us to pray in one specific place, which was a cage, and there would be a guard sitting in front of us. We couldn't pray without the guard sitting directly in front of us. From our perspective, we had a *sutra** and so felt that it was ok, but from their perspective, you could tell they believed that they had positioned themselves in a way to make it look like we were making *rukuʿ* and *sujud* to them. That's how it seemed. At the very least, it was a type of humiliation that they wouldn't let us practice without supervising in every moment. This was in addition to the cameras and microphones being everywhere.

Many of the rules that Muslim prisoners were subjected to impacted on them in particular because of Islam's specific ritual requirements, and so it was easy for the prison administration to enforce rules specially designed to this effect. A specific policy was implemented that permitted all non-Muslims to behave in one way, but explicitly restricted Muslims from also doing the same. As Muslims, many believed that the rule of *isbaal* meant that they were not permitted to wear their trousers below their ankles due to a narration of the Prophet Muhammad, that the clothing worn below the ankles would result in hellfire. In 2004, a policy initiated by the Federal Bureau of Prisons on Religious Beliefs and Practices stated explicitly: 'Islamic inmates may not hem or wear their pants above their ankles.'[5]

The rule was finally changed in 2015, after a legal challenge brought by Yahia was successful, leading to a formal change in the policy documentation. Little so explicitly gave an insight into the way that Islamic beliefs and culture were weaponised against

---

* A *sutra* is a barrier for the imam, designating the physical prayer space.

Muslim prisoners as the direct wording in the rule against hemming their trousers. This was particularly stark, as non-Muslims were permitted to do so without issue – reinforcing the institutional Islamophobia that permeated the US prison system.

SEXUAL HUMILIATION

Bagram Airbase – Parvan, Afghanistan
JTF-GTMO – Guantánamo Bay, Cuba

The cavity search was a humiliation that was too much to bear for Muslim prisoners. During processing at Bagram, Mohamedou Ould Slahi was forced into a position and raped by his guards and interrogators – compounded by the sounds of their laughter and comments as the prisoners were subjected to this torture one by one. He hated that this was how he began to learn the language, through the lewd and abusive language that his captors were using against him. Mohamedou didn't feel ashamed of himself despite the humiliation of the moment. He knew that those who should be ashamed were the ones who were carrying out the torture. It was more difficult for other prisoners, who had been so traumatised by the experience, to move past the pain and shame. Many could not even speak about what had happened to them.[6]

Sexual humiliation at the detention camps in Afghanistan became a routine part of prisoner life, with threats of sodomy, rape and rape of others being deployed regularly. Moazzam Begg described how he was led by his US interrogators to believe that his wife was being raped in the interrogation room next to his own. By the time the men arrived at Guantánamo Bay, US interrogators had learnt much of what might impact on the psychology of Muslim prisoners – often relying on Raphael Patai's deeply racist and Islamophobic book *The Arab Mind* as a way of learning and dominating the culture of the prisoners. Mustafa Ait Idir, the Algerian kidnapped from Bosnia, was routinely sexually harassed by a female interrogator. Shackled to the floor, this woman would sit silently a few feet away, unbuttoning her shirt and exposing her chest – this happened on a number of occasions. Mustafa understood what was taking place, they wanted the men to 'feel like sinners, to make us feel humiliated and guilty, frustrated, weak and broken.'[7] Mustafa's belief did not permit him to lewdly ogle at the woman, but he had also lived in Europe, and so had already been subject to the images of hyper-sexualised societies.

Within his first year at Guantánamo Bay, Mohamedou Ould Slahi became familiar with Sergeant First Class (SFC) Shally and her superior Staff-Sergeant (SSG) Mary, interrogators sent to use their sexuality against him. SSG Mary would press herself against Mohamedou, giving him warning that she would rape him if he refused to talk. Attempting to seduce him by speaking seductively in his ear, SSG Mary offered herself fully to Mohamedou, saying that having sex could not be considered torture, only to have her efforts rebuffed.[8] True to her words to escalate her harassment if he did not cooperate, SFC Shally and SSG Mary attempted to break down Mohamedou together:

'Then today, we're gonna teach you about great American sex. Get up!' said SSG Mary. I stood up in the same painful position as I had every day for about seventy days. I would rather follow the orders and reduce the pain that would be caused when the guards come to play; the guards used every contact opportunity to beat the hell out of the detainee. 'Detainee tried to resist' was the 'Gospel truth' they came up with, and guess who was going to be believed? 'You're very smart, because if you don't stand up it's gonna be ugly,' SSG Mary said.

As soon as I stood up, the two women took off their blouses, and started to talk all kind of dirty stuff you can imagine, which I minded less. What hurt me most was them forcing me to take part in a sexual threesome in the most degrading manner. What many women don't realise is that men get hurt the same as women if they're forced to have sex, maybe more due to the traditional position of the man. Both women stuck on me, literally one on the front and the other older woman stuck on my back rubbing her whole body on mine. At the same time they were talking dirty to me, and playing with my sexual parts. I am saving you here from quoting the disgusting and degrading talk I had to listen to from noon or before until 10 p.m. when they turned me over to Mr X, the new character you'll soon meet.

To be fair and honest, the two women didn't deprive me of my clothes at any time; everything happened with my uniform on. The senior interrogator SFC Shally was watching everything through the one-way mirror from the next room. I kept praying all the time.

'Stop the fuck praying! You're having sex with American whores and you're praying? What a hypocrite you are!' said SFC Shally angrily, entering the room. I refused to stop speaking my prayers, and after that, I was forbidden to perform my ritual prayers for about one year to come. I also was forbidden to fast during the sacred month of Ramadan [in] October 2003, and fed by force. During this session I also refused to eat or to drink, although they offered me water every once in a while: 'We must give you food and water; if you don't eat it's fine.' They also offered me the nastiest MRE [meal ready to eat] they had in the camp. We detainees knew that JTF interrogators gathered Intels about what food a detainee likes or dislikes, when he prays, and many other things that are just ridiculous.[9]

In the same year, the former army sergeant Erik R. Saar exposed some of the tactics that were implemented by Major General Geoffrey Miller during his tenure as the commander of the detention camps. Saar described how he witnessed a female interrogator attempt to break a Saudi prisoner by exposing him to a tight-fitting t-shirt and rubbing his back with her breasts, eventually humiliating him by commenting on the prisoner's eventual erection. The prisoner spat in her face, and the interrogator left the room very angry. Saar witnessed her approaching a translator to find out how she could break the man, and the linguist advised that she pretend to smear menstrual blood on him, and then to shut off water in his cell so that he could not wash himself – leaving him ritually unclean and thus unable to pray.[10] The interrogators saw the prisoner's ability to pray as the salve that fortified them against tactics to harm them. Ultimately, they were largely unsuccessful because the prisoners had a narrative of relying on the mercy of God when they were subjected to treatment that left them in situations outside of their own control.

MCC – New York City, United States of America
CMU Terra Haute – Indiana, United States of America
ADX Florence – Colorado, United States of America

Strip searches became a routine part of Uzair Paracha's detention experience, from his time at the New York MCC through to ADX Florence. There was no modesty permitted for them as prison policies were constructed to always have complete sight of the imprisoned men. Strip searches would humiliate them, but there were also the cameras directly above their toilets and in their showers. Uzair would wear his bedsheet as a reverse superman cape as a method of attempting to provide some degree of cover for himself as he would use the toilet. Even then, he would hear the laughs of guards – particularly female guards – as he would wash himself with water while using the toilet, or have comments made about his body. Uzair's need to cover his cell with a sheet while showering was heightened after he heard a guard commenting on a non-Muslim prisoner masturbating during a shower in his own cell, confirming how little the guards cared about the prisoners' personal privacy:

There was a book I read in prison by Sylviane Diouf called *Servants of Allah* about the experience of black Muslims in the transatlantic slave trade. I used to tell brothers that I've read so many books on Islamic history from the time of the Prophet through to the time of Salahuddin Ayyubi and many others, but I could not relate to anyone as much as the brothers and sisters who were sold into the slave trade. I am not saying that I went through what they went through. They were maimed, beaten and raped; they went through so many hardships, but at the same time there were so many things like the issue of no respect for their clothing, their need to cover themselves. There were so many things that I could really relate to. Ayuba Suleiman Diallo was in Maryland, and I knew brothers who were being held in Maryland, you feel that they were on the land we are on. They obviously went through something much worse than us, and I'm not trying to make the claim that we are on the same level, but I feel that I could relate to that.

Yahia Lindh thought of the Standard Operating Procedures that had been instituted by Geoffrey Miller in Guantánamo as he considered the purpose of strip searching at the Supermax facilities he had been detained in. He had come to understand strip searching as an exercise of power, of their omnipotence – language that Miller had laid out in stark terms: 'Stripping consists of the forceful removal of detainees' clothing. In addition to degradation of the detainee, stripping can be used to demonstrate the omnipotence of the captor or to debilitate the detainee.'[11]

Omnipotence – it was a word that summarised well the behaviour of the prison administration towards Muslim prisoners. Yahia only learnt many years later, that some of those working in the federal prison system had once been part of the administration of Guantánamo Bay, reinforcing the travel of policies between prisons:

> That's the thing, it's not like Guantánamo was another planet with a different species of Americans operating it – these were the same people. Initially the strip searches were not the case, but they introduced it after a few years of operation. They started to use this as a weapon, and again it was not used against everyone; it was predominantly used against Muslims and in a way that was entirely irrational. We had visits that were behind glass, and with almost no ability to come into contact with your visitors, yet they would conduct a full strip search on the prisoner before and after the visit. It was not everybody, it was specifically Muslims, and even among the Muslims, it was certain Muslims. This is part of their playbook, and I would say it is an important part. Specifically, this is about hurting Muslims in their belief. They know how sensitive this issue is with us; they have psychologists and experts who study these things and they know where to hit a person where it hurts. This is why the use these specific lines of attack.

It would take legal challenges to provide partial relief from the treatment the men faced. In 2016, Yahia won a partial victory after judgment in the case of *Yahya (John) Lindh v Warden, Federal Correctional Institution, Terra Haute, Indiana*. By that stage, however, he had already been subjected to 14 years of humiliation by the federal prison system.

Miscellaneous Locations – Egypt[12]

On 20 February 2019, the guards woke Mahmoud Al-Ahmady at dawn. Born in 1994, Mahmoud was 25 years old. However, these were to be the last moments of his young life. He was not alone. There were eight others beside him, all being marched to their death. The courts had made their judgment and the Grand Mufti of Egypt – Shawki Allam – had ratified it. These young men were to be executed. One by one, they were marched to the execution ward, and there, one by one, they were hanged. We do not know what Mahmoud's last thoughts were, nor do we know his last words. We do know, however, that two years earlier the presiding judge – Hassan Farid – in rudimentary Arabic recited verses of the Qur'an before he handed them a death sentence: {And he who kills a believer premeditatedly, then his recompense is Hell, eternally [abiding] therein, and Allah will be angry with him, and will curse him, and has prepared for him a tremendous torment} (4:93).

These young men were *Kharijites*, the proponents of chaos, Farid exclaimed – stating that it was the court's responsibility to prevent the proliferation of extremist ideas that the men purportedly represented. Still, these young men seemed unfazed. In the court, they screamed '*Allahu Akbar*' – Allah is greater. For journalists and observers, the trial was unsettling. This was not merely due to the fact that these young men were wholesale handed to the execution ward, but that a few months prior when a slight opportunity presented itself, they were able to tell their stories of torture and sexual assault. One of those later executed told his lawyer:

They beat me with an electric rod. They beat me with their hands and with their feet. They stripped me naked and began to electrocute me all over my body. They kept on electrocuting my penis and inner thighs. They humiliated me so badly. They beat me with slippers on my face. I was stripped completely naked and they tied each arm and each leg to a chair and put me on the ground. They electrocuted me but just kept on focusing on my groin and thighs. They wouldn't stop for two full hours. They said, 'Are you going to talk or will we have to get someone to fuck you?' They sent me to the doctor afterwards. I couldn't go to the toilet for four days afterwards because my testicles were swollen.

In Mahmoud's statement, he detailed abuse consistent with the accounts of the prisoners placed in the same case. He, too was electrocuted all over his body but especially on his genitals and thighs. Another prisoner on death row detailed his torture:

They electrocuted me for two days straight. They threatened to hurt my family. They said they could kill me and throw my body in[to] the desert. They electrocuted my genitals, thighs and knees. They bound my hands behind my back and suspended my body from the ceiling. They then raped me. They put something in me from behind.

For the presiding judge – Hassan Farid – and for the Grand Mufti, these accounts were not credible, nor did they matter. After all, they had confessed to a serious crime. They conspired and killed the former Prosecutor General of Egypt – Hisham Barakat. Farid went on to add that prison and government hospitals investigated these men's seditious allegations of torture and coercion. They were categorically unsubstantiated.[13] Farid was seemingly unfazed by the monumental significance of this sentence, but the tension around him was palpable. Mahmoud Al-Ahmady – who was now being informed of his impending death – stood before Hassan Farid, detailing his torture: 'I will stand as your adversary on the day of Judgment before God. You know very well that I – and everyone else on trial here – are innocent.'

Judge Farid retorted, 'Mahmoud, but you confessed.'

'Give me an electric rod in front of all of these people, I can get anyone to confess that they killed Sadat. We have been electrocuted with enough electricity to power Egypt for the next twenty years.'[14]

It is hard to untangle – in the case of Egypt – physical torture from sexual abuse and humiliation. Primarily, torture takes on a sexual nature. This is true for men, women and children. It starts from the very first encounter with the police and continues through the life cycle of detention. It encompasses not just those targeted, but their families as well.

The police marched into the home where Maryam was staying. She was pregnant with her second child at the time and was concerned for the well-being of her unborn child as officers demanded Maryam disclose where her father was. She didn't know. Her worst nightmare materialised as the supervising officer looked at her and ordered the low-ranking officers to tear off her clothes. They wanted to break her completely, so they used her child as a weapon against her. They brought her little daughter into the room so she could witness her mother's assault. Maryam cried, as she felt their hands grab her breasts and genitals, and her cries for her unborn child's safety went unheeded; more than her own humiliation, she was desperate to protect the life growing within her. She finally fell to the floor after they pushed her defiled body, hearing the screams of their profanities – calling her a whore. Maryam thought it might be over, but then came their final salvo, they began to target her stomach and beat her with a stick, punishing the unborn baby for daring to grow inside her, for being a threat to their futures.

There is more to torture and sexual abuse than attempts at eliciting information from a prisoner or even their family. The very threat of impending assault is one of the most significant modes of domination. The security apparatus of the state fashions rituals of humiliation for political opponents of the state – both real and perceived – as well as their families.[15] This allows for complete control of the wider population, since the boundaries between prison and everyday life is porous. The state and security apparatus can exercise these rituals of domination and humiliation on anyone; in the same way it can render someone non-existent – through enforced disappearance.

Abdullah Boumadian was twelve years old when he was forcibly disappeared. He was sleeping at home when military officers raided his home and took him from his bed, seeking his older brother. Abdullah was disappeared for over six months and his mother looked all over Egypt for him. During his time in disappearance, he was moved between different detention and military centres, always being kept away from any prospect of the rule of law. Abdullah was subjected to severe torture – even by Egyptian standards. He was brutally beaten by the officers who even before asking any questions, would begin by using an electric rod to electrocute him, especially his genitals. His body became an ashtray for the officers, as they proceeded to put out their cigarettes all over his body. Abdullah was strung up, like a piece of meat in a freezer, handcuffed and suspended from his right arm – which had a disability. The officers then filled the torture chamber with water and threw in exposed wires over the water and forced him to lie in it. The officers also tied him to a metal bedframe which they set on fire. Abdullah was exposed to starvation tactics – a tool the prison authorities would sometime use against the prison population. He would be fed once every three days, only enough to keep him alive. Abdullah told his lawyers later that he also saw his father – who was also forcibly disappeared – early on in his detention. He watched his father being stripped and tortured. After Abdullah was transferred to a police station in Cairo, he was placed in solitary confinement for a hundred days. His body developed boils as he was prevented from showering or gaining access to medical attention.[16]

While some female prisoners are also exposed to electrocution and suspension by the arms and feet, as in the case of Layla mentioned in Chapter 1, this practice is almost systematic for male detainees when they are first detained. These rituals of degradation are a form of initiation into prison life. Yahya recalled the first 14 days of detention in the National Security Agency (NSA) headquarters:

I was tortured really badly there. They electrocuted me all over my body and especially my private area. They stripped me naked. They insulted my mother and said very bad words about her. She is a really kind old lady; who is 80 years old and completes the Qur'an every three days. When they would electrocute me, they would make me take off all of my clothes and they would put a chair in between my legs. They would handcuff my hands from behind and proceed to torture me badly; all the while they would be listening to music on their phones. They would call my wife horrible names. They would also suspend

me from the ceiling for two days straight. They would say, 'We
are the National Security Agency, we can kill you right now and
wrap you in a blanket. We can throw your body in the sewage
and no one would know.' I was so scared. They would say this all
the while I was blindfolded. In other days, they would keep me
naked in the middle of the office while they would take turns
beating and punching me.

In other instances, the officers would photograph prisoners after
they stripped them naked or while they were sexually assaulting
them. In fact, this has been a long-standing tactic that was used
during the Mubarak era. In 2007, police officers arrested minibus
driver Emad El-Kebir. They tortured him, sexually assaulted and
sodomised him. They recorded the abuse on camera on their phone
to blackmail him. The video of his assault was leaked. Contrary to
what the officers anticipated, Emad El-Kebir was not ostracised or
humiliated by the public. Instead, there was an upsurge of anger
towards the authorities for the crimes they had conducted against
him.[17] The practice of recording sexual abuse still seems to be, by
and large, used to blackmail prisoners – especially in NSA detention centres. This happened to Ashraf when he was first detained:

When I was first arrested, I was hauled into the transport truck,
and there was a barrage of insults. They tore off all of my clothes
and began to hit me really badly. The officer threatened to rape
me and electrocute my penis. I was so scared, I told them that
I would say whatever they wanted me to say. They took me to
an office and made me lie down on the ground; then they all
began to beat me. They would kick me with their feet. I begged
them to stop and said I would tell them everything. The officer
took photos of me naked and said if you give us any trouble, I'll
upload these pictures to the internet and he got his rifle and put
it to my head and said they could kill me any second. I don't
know why they had to take off my clothes if they wanted to beat
me. They did not need to take off my clothes.

Although NSA detention centres and headquarters are sites of
the most horrific accounts of torture and abuse, torture is rife

throughout the lifecycle of detention. During visitation, Abdurrahman's mother sensed that her son was not okay.[18] He looked sickly and shaken. He slipped her a letter detailing what happened to him. He apologized profusely for telling his mother what he was about to say. Abdurrahman Al Shuwaikh had befriended some of the *gina'i* inmates and was dedicated to helping them learn the basics of religion. He devised a way to teach them and somehow be less lonely in prison. Every day, he would teach the prisoners in the adjacent cell a *hadith* narration. But one prisoner was tasked with being an informant, who reported Abdurrahman. With great reticence, he wrote to his mother of the consequence of the quisling's betrayal:

Mama, I was very hesitant to write these words to you because it was the worst thing that could have happened to me on 06/04/2021. This wasn't just torture; it was sexual assault which made me unable to withstand myself. I will leave my affairs to Allah. Please mama, this might be the last time you will see me because I will go on hunger strike and I will stop drinking water. Do what you can, mama.

Abdurrahman told his mother that the informant was upset that he was teaching other prisoners *hadith* narrations. They got into a fight and Abdurrahman was first sent to a disciplining cell. After being released from the cell, Abdurrahman found out that the informant was stealing money that his parents had sent him and began to argue with the informant:

He said, 'I will teach you to raise your voice.' He got the guards and officers and they bound me, blindfolded me, they tore my clothes. I was exposed. I screamed and begged them, please for the sake of Allah cover me up. But they didn't; they assaulted my honour. They forced my eyes open so they could humiliate me. They forced me to prostrate before the informant. I was forced and bound ... I told them God will judge them for what they are doing to me on the Day of Resurrection. This made them angrier so they assaulted my honour by force; they grabbed my head and put under his feet while he was sitting down on a chair.

Praise be to Allah. Allah suffices me, for He is the best disposer of affairs. Allah is greater and He is the most knowledgeable. Please forgive me, mama for telling you this.

Abdurrahman's mother, frantic, posted her son's letter on the internet, hoping that someone would advocate on his behalf. It had the names of the officers and informants that tortured and raped her son. Soon after, she too was arrested.

In prison, women face a myriad of abuses and like men, these abuses are often sexual in nature. After Samia was detained, she was taken to the NSA headquarters where officers began to interrogate her, wanting her to confess to crimes of their imagining. It would be later that Samia would tell her brother that in the NSA headquarters, she was beaten, stripped naked and blindfolded. Painfully, she described to her brother how the officers electrocuted her in her genitals so that she would confess.[19] The most common and egregious forms of abuse occurred with female inmates during cavity searches. These cavity searches would often be conducted by female officers under the watchful supervision of male officers. In other times, the prison authorities would outsource the torture to other prisoners acting as informants. The informants would conduct cavity searches and hymen checks sometimes to the point where they may break the inmate's hymen. They would use an unclean object – like a plastic bag – to do the cavity checks. The same plastic bag would then be used on all the prisoners, exposing them to infections and diseases. Talia, a young female detainee recalled these cavity checks:

As soon as we arrived at prison, they took all of our belongings, and we were stripped of all of our clothes. The presiding correctional officer grabbed a plastic bag from the floor and proceeded to check my vagina in a very demeaning way. I started screaming, 'What are you doing, I am still a virgin and haven't been married yet!' and continued to yell at her until she left me alone.

Lara, like Talia, experienced the sexual humiliation that occurred during the cavity searches. These – as she described them – were akin to rape. The female officer had decided at one point to search all the inmates in the cell:

She held me by the stairs and told me to take off my clothes. I told her, 'I can't. There are male officers standing right there.' She said, 'Either you undress or I will tear your clothes off.' I burst out crying. She was so terrifying. She tore my clothes off and she grabbed my breasts and said, 'And they call you a virgin? No honey, these are the breasts of a whore not a virgin.' She grabbed me and she stuck her fingernails in me like she wanted to tear the skin from inside. She then insisted, I urinate in front of her. I was unable to talk for four days after that ... This same woman would get a plastic bag and she would use it to check all of the prisoners. She would put it inside them and they would get infected with viruses. She did not insert one finger; she would insert two or three. And she didn't do it slowly – she would thrust it in them until they bled. One girl with us kept on bleeding for one week straight. We did not know how or when the bleeding would stop.

Lara's trauma had only just begun. She found herself in the police station, alone with a detective who locked her in his office and began to grope her body. She couldn't resist as he forced himself on her and tried to kiss her neck. She screamed. He then tried to pass it off as a joke. The next day, the same detective called her in. He said he wanted to take a picture with her. She tried to keep a distance, afraid that he would attack her again. He then proceeded to grab her breasts and laugh. This particular officer held back with Lara because she was a political prisoner. He did not want to get in trouble for doing something unauthorised. Lara recalled, however, the horror that other inmates detained on criminal charges had to endure. She heard the screams from his office as he raped them.

The restraint is contextual. Meaning, that being a political prisoner does not entail protection. Rather the officers may need – in certain situations – to be given permission before they can abuse prisoners. That is because these abuses are often calculated modes of domination. This is what happened with Sumar, who was 15 years old when she was arrested. In the NSA detention centre, she confessed to crimes she did not commit. Later she wrote: 'I would not have liked to write this. I am still scared of the repercussions. I still do not know whether it is right that what I know should be known by others. Leaving aside the lame introductions. That day was the worst day of my life … .'

The officer proceeded to interrogate her about things and people she did not know. Then he brought up the name of someone she did know, but decided to pretend that she didn't:

> The officer then began to take off my hijab. He whispered in my ear, 'You are such a big girl Sumar.' I was only 15 and he began to say things to me he wouldn't to a prostitute. I began to scream. Then I found that he had put a strange thing [his penis] in my mouth! At that point I had no clue what was happening! I just wanted to kill him and kill myself afterwards. I was on my period that day. He pushed me to the floor, tied my hands behind my back and then stomped on me. I began to bleed all over the floor. There was blood all over the place. He threw soap on me and told me to go clean myself. I pretended not to hear him; I was crying so hard. He picked me up and sprayed his perfume on me. He told me that was an honour to be sprayed with his perfume. I told them everything afterward. I couldn't go through this again. This is why I confessed.

At times, torture and abuse are kept at the discretion of the officers. In other cases, like with Yusra, the torture is based on top-down orders to purposefully break a prisoner. Yusra was detained because her father was a well-known figure and the authorities wanted to hurt her – not to extract information or even elicit a confession – but purely for the exercise of control and humiliation. Yusra had been stripped naked by the officers and then they proceeded to electrocute her all over her body. She was detained with two other women, Alaa and Rawan. The female officer conducted a cavity search so intrusive that Rawan began to scream, 'I am not married yet; you're going to ruin me.' The officer did not care. The practice of enforced nudity and cavity searches means that most female inmates have experienced some form of sexual harassment or assault. Suzanne – a young housewife – was pregnant when she was first detained. The officers kept her naked for two full months in her cell. They would grope her breasts and genitals. The officers would beat her repeatedly in her stomach. After she had her baby, the authorities put the child in an orphanage and to this day, no one knows the whereabouts of the child.

Dahab also was eight months pregnant when she was arrested. She was on her way to the doctor when she found herself stranded at a protest. As the police began shooting at the protesters, she hid in the lobby of a building. The tenants reported her to the police for hiding out and she was caught and sent to the police station. Dahab pleaded with the officer that she was not part of the protests. He said, 'You will give birth here. Just so you know.'[20] Soon after, handcuffed to a bed, Dahab gave birth to a baby girl she called Houria – freedom.

Everything about prison life – beginning from the metal container trucks to interrogation, and then the unsanitary living conditions and lack of medical access – is part of the process of coercion and control. The transportation truck particularly is used to torture prisoners. In the summer, especially if it is packed, it cooks prisoners inside. In the winter, it is so cold that the inmates freeze. Mona recalls that she would often faint inside and that they would have to revive her. One day, they moved her in an open-topped vehicle. She had been branded by the officers as a political prisoner, and a mob of people gathered around the car and began to throw stones at her, aiming for her face. She could not understand why ordinary people – who were not officers – would hold such intense feelings of anger:

That feeling of injustice never left me. I was beaten so badly in prison. Even after I left prison, my dad was so harsh with me. I started to feel, why is all of this violence directed at me? Why do they think they can all hurt me? Is it because I am a girl? I almost lost my hearing in prison from the beatings. We were just kids. I was only 20 years old. You can imagine; our bodies were changing. They stripped me completely naked and every time they did a cavity search, they would put their fingers deeper and deeper in me while the male officers were watching. They wanted to break me.

Maryam was visited by a delegation from the National Council for Women after human rights organisations reported on the conditions of female prisoners. Mervat Tallawy, the president of the Council at the time, berated her. Mona recalled: 'She was so aggressive and said you must have done something to deserve it.'

The Council concluded that there were no female political prisoners in Egypt – aside from one leftist activist – the rest were either criminals or terrorists. Later, renowned feminist scholar Nawal El Saadawi presented the Council's findings at a conference in Madrid, where she affirmed that indeed Egypt did not imprison women for their political views.

7
Faith and Resistance

RESISTANCE STRATEGIES

Bagram Airbase – Parvan, Afghanistan
JTF-GTMO – Guantánamo Bay, Cuba

From the very beginning of his detention experience at Bagram, Abdul Basit was intent on resisting his unlawful imprisonment. He had a strong sense of his own righteous indignation, and felt it was important that he express his position to his captors. The majority of the time Abdul Basit chose to show the guards he was enjoying life, that he had taken optional leave from life and that he was on holiday. He became famous among the prisoner population and guard force for clicking his fingers at the guards and ordering them to bring him things, as if the entire prison complex had been constructed for his own particular pleasure. In reality, he knew that he had no power, but he wanted his interrogators and guards to believe that they held no power over him and the other men, that they could reframe their abuse in any manner of their choosing.

Abdul Basit would go on to join hunger strikes to assist those who felt it was an important method of striking, but generally took the position that such a method was counterproductive. He could not understand why his fellow prisoners would want to make themselves weak, when instead they could express strength in the face of their captors. His weapon of choice was his body, but not in the way those on hunger strike would use it; he preferred to use his own faeces:

> If you want to strike, then strike the soldiers in a physical way, make their lives difficult and not your own. In all my five years, I had the label of instigator because I would always pick on the

guards. To be honest, I preferred it when we would use our faeces in order to carry out strikes on them – I am saying this proudly that I was one of the experts at such operations. This was a big humiliation for the soldiers, and so I always felt that these strikes were the best way of getting our rights. If you throw shit on them, it is the best way to harm them. This is a much bigger punishment in my eyes than using the hunger strike. I was able to throw it very accurately. We didn't really worry about whether or not it was correct Islamically to do this, because we were trying to gain our rights and to defend ourselves and our brothers – the person who was able to do this was very much respected. If you will allow me to say, but I was very accurate in my throws and hitting the guards – I must have done it over one hundred times! I was *kaamyaab* [skilled] at these attacks. In particular, I was able to target their mouth, and they had no real way of protecting themselves.

As Muslims, we are very clean and we don't like to do something that will make us feel ashamed. But we were in a circumstance that was already shameful, and so I always wanted the guards to know that they were not safe to do whatever they liked to us. It was our belief that with every strike we carried out, that Allah would give us multiple reward[s] for doing so. We used to talk about how our own Muslim countries are so scared of America and these American soldiers, but as soon as you throw shit on their faces, you really show them to be nothing.

We even had a person who we called 'factory'. He was an expert in mixing the faeces by making it thinner. There was a person who we called 'hunter', he was our expert in accurately throwing the faeces, so it would hit the guard between the eyes, ears, or mouth. We would challenge one another as to where we could hit the guards.

One day we had a meeting with the colonel in charge. He was a very arrogant person by the name of John. He came to those of us who were cell representatives, and began to tell us all about how the US nation was the best nation on Earth. I agreed with him, and said you should ask me how, which he did. I told him that it was the one nation that was consistently eating the shit of

Afghans, in the entire world. We defended our rights with this, it was the only way we could exercise our own *quwwa* [power].

Although not used as regularly at Guantánamo Bay, faeces splashing was used as a technique of resistance to express anger at the prison administration, but only against guards and interrogators who were acting in abusive ways, or those responsible for the running of the detention camps. Murat Kurnaz recalled General Geoffrey Miller coming to inspect Oscar Block, flanked by several high-ranking officers and other officials. As they reached the centre of a corridor, one prisoner used their bean-hole to fling a mixture of water and faeces that they had collected for precisely this moment. Miller attempted to turn away from the cell, only to be splashed by a prisoner on the opposite side of the corridor.[1] As the officials made their retreat through the corridor, they were treated to a series of splashes being hurled at them. As a tactic of resistance, it was generally considered distasteful to use such a method for their own personal hygiene reasons, but in the circumstance they found themselves, the prisoners felt they had little option.

During his time at Guantánamo Bay, Ahmed Errachidi was given the *nom de guerre* 'The General' by the prison administration for his ability to organise the other prisoners in collective action through building solidarity with one another. In the early years of their detention, the guards began to remove the clothes of prisoners for 24-hour periods in order to humiliate them. Ahmed encouraged the prisoners to make life as difficult as possible for the guards, so that it would take them a long time to process the removal – meaning only a few prisoners could be impacted each day:

On another occasion when I was in yet another punishment block and we were involved in a protest, they set about removing our clothes. We fought back and so they only managed to strip four or five of us a day, returning the next day to do another batch. Because new prisoners kept joining the block and then, seeing what was happening, also joining in our protest, it took over seven days to remove all our trousers and many prisoners sustained injuries in the process. It was so exhausting; after seven days we no longer had the energy to resist, with the result that newcomers started voluntarily giving up their clothes. Even so, we prisoners found ways round this imposed nakedness. At times of prayer, we'd take off our shirts and wear them round our legs while others would pray in their shorts. But there was nothing we could do about the toilet: prisoners on punishment would have to use it naked and without a veil while soldiers, including women soldiers, stared and jeered.[2]

On refusal, the guards would send in the Extreme Reaction Force (ERF), who would go through the process of pepper-spraying the prisoner as they entered his cell, cutting his clothes off his body while five guards would hold him down. Ahmed had been left completely naked on a number of different occasions due to his insistence that he would not comply with the order to pass his clothes on, often being beaten and beating back the guards to the extent he was able.[3] Ahmed's ability to organise the prisoners meant that he would never give up thinking of innovative ways to gain rights for all those who were being abused. He would consider their situation and the weaknesses of the prison administration very carefully before mooting collective action the prisoners might take:

I'd already been working on an idea for a few weeks – pacing my cell, three steps one way, three steps the other, figuring out my reasoning – so I was prepared. I proposed that we rip up our orange shirts.

Since the main thrust of our protest was to put an end to the punishment of having our clothes forcibly removed, this must have sounded like a peculiar idea. But I laid out my arguments in a methodical manner, I told my fellows that one of the reasons we were prohibited from removing our clothes was because they were visible and helped the soldiers to identify us. If, I argued, we managed to get the bulk of the prison population to join in the removal and destruction of up to five hundred shirts, this would not only confuse them but also send a strong signal about our refusal to put up with punishments, and it would undermine the camp authorities who'd given us the orange kit. Since, I continued, it was compulsory for them to clothe us (I told my fellow prisoners that this was written into the Geneva Convention – I didn't know if it was but thought it might be), a prisoner being escorted to interrogation or clinic without a shirt would be an embarrassment to the army. Although we never met them, we knew journalists and their like paid frequent visits to the prison and if they were to see us dressed only in our trousers this would make a huge impression. The orange clothes were also a visible sign that we were their prisoners: by removing our shirts we would be sending the administration a message that we were no longer prepared to be their captives. And finally, I argued that if every one of us tore up our shirts at the same time, and if we then tore up any new shirts issued to us, they'd have a serious problem, not least because the Pentagon would start asking why they were spending so much money on shirts.[4]

As with the faeces splashing, optionally removing their own clothes was counter-intuitive to the cultural and religious practices of the detained Muslim men, however, their desire to gain justice for themselves meant that they were forced to take actions in ways that privileged gaining justice over performing rituals in the perfect way possible.

ADX Florence, Colorado, United States of America

Yahia Lindh was aware of the debates that had been staged within the US prison system, especially among prisoners who were not being held for political reasons – that obedience to the governmental authorities was a religious obligation – irrespective of the status of the government in question. This was a view that was heavily promoted by the Muslim chaplains who would come to visit the prisons where the men were detained – and even a small number of political prisoners were eventually influenced by this way of thinking. Their argument rested on various verses of the Qur'an and traditions of the Prophet such as {O you who believe, obey God and the Messenger and those in authority} (4:59) but they conveniently neglect to mention the subsequent words: {among you}.

Yahia realised that the Qur'an was being misinterpreted in order to build a compliant and subservient prisoner that would not complain of being abused of their rights. In his own understanding of Islam, resistance was a necessary part of the prisoner experience, not just as a matter of gaining rights, but also to fully be able to worship God:

> Resistance is a constant. In prison, you are in a situation where most of the power is with your enemies, and so you have to calculate very carefully whether something you do is going to lead to greater harm or if there is a potential for some good coming out of it. You have to take every situation and you have to analyse it very carefully before you take any action. But, resistance is a constant, but what changes is what tactics to use, what situations, what moments in any given situation. To hold on to your *din* [faith] in that situation, is resistance. To be a Muslim is a type of resistance. They don't explicitly try to make you renounce Islam (although sometimes they do) but essentially that is what it all boils down to, so to continue to practice your *din* becomes resistance in itself.

There were key differences, however, from the experience of those held at Guantánamo Bay. As the prisoners in US custody had largely been found guilty of crimes (often in politically constructed cases or through FBI entrapment), they were subject to the rules of the prison system, not regarded as prisoners of war. Resistance that involved some form of abuse or harm of the prison administration carried the very real risk of having their sentences increased by many years if it was proved they had committed an assault. Thus, although faeces splashing was used by those facing life imprisonment in the non-political prisoner population, it was a tactic that the political prisoners did not use.

Building solidarity in the federal prison system required a different approach, where a general strike had to be coordinated between different groups – not explicitly Muslim-only, as they were never the majority population within the prison system. A general strike would mean that the prisoners would refuse to go to work, which would mean the prison would shut down, because the operation largely runs off the labour of prisoners themselves. The day-to-day operation, the work, is done by the prisoners. Refusing to work was often a successful attempt at shutting down the institution. This became a way of Muslim prisoners trying to gain their rights without having their sentences increased for criminal behaviour – a constant risk that they might become subject to. Building solidarity with other prisoners in order to gain their rights became the mechanism by which they could support others who were being oppressed, but also improve some of the conditions of confinement.

Tora Prison – Cairo, Egypt
Burj al-Arab – Alexandria, Egypt

Each day, in the Tora Prison complex, each prisoner was given a small piece of soft cheese and a piece of bread for breakfast. The living conditions had become increasingly difficult. One officer – Sami – was particularly cruel. He not only subjected prisoners to ritual humiliation, but also began to harass their families during visitation. He would sexually harass the women visiting their relatives in prison. When they brought food, he would stick his fingers inside the food to contaminate it. At first, the prisoners tried to level with him, but he did not care. Day after day, they saved their cheese from breakfast. While Officer Sami was doing the nightly checks, a few of the prisoners grabbed him from the metal bars and smashed all the cheese they had hoarded on his face and hair. Officer Sami stood bewildered; he could not compute that there was cheese on his face!

The very notion of prison resistance is tenuous. Particularly for one to merely survive an institution built to break them is resistance. Abdelrahman ElGendy was 17 years old when he was first detained. He recalled the day of his detention:

Guards poured into the cell, screaming and kicking us out, then left us with one guard holding a digital camera. It was file-photos update time. Standing in a long line in the hallway, one by one, we held the black sign with our inmate numbers on it in white chalk … I decided to do something meaningless, a tiny act of resistance. When I held my sign, I stared at the camera and smiled as wide as I could. The sight was infuriating for the menacing guard. He yelled at me to shut my mouth. I did not. He shoved me in the chest and threatened to throw me in solitary confinement. He went back and pointed the camera, and I again smiled, as wide as I could. My braces gave my smile a childish look that further provoked him. It was reckless and risky, but I had acted without thinking, so I decided to follow through. Suddenly, there were snickers in the hallway, and my fellow inmates started laughing. I could instantly see the guard unsettled. The guard who controlled our fates and could do anything to us, was suddenly not in control. I could sense the shift in the power dynamics in the place. It was subtle; nothing has changed, but we were somehow more enabled.[5]

Like ElGendy, prisoners often express their everyday acts of resistance in a manner that breaks the seeming hold and monopoly of power and surveillance of the prison authorities. In Hamza's case, for example, he would praise the senior prison officer's acumen and intellect in private, but would refuse to do so in front of the junior officers. This would often provoke the senior officer, who was hoping for an ego boost from a college graduate in front of the junior officers. In a more extreme case, prisoners tried to take a more drastic step in their resistance to the officers. The officers had been mistreating the inmates' families during visitation and the situation was becoming increasingly dire. A few prisoners began to document personal information about the officers in charge. They wrote their names, addresses and details about their families on paper. They then sent the paper to a senior officer – to show them that they too know everything about them. The prison went into complete lockdown as a result.

Much of the motivating factors behind prison resistance is to defy rituals of humiliation that other prisoners or family members during visitation have to endure. Ali recounts that Burj al-Arab Prison was brutal by the end of 2014. The prison population consisted mainly of older inmates who were subjected to immense abuse and constant humiliation. In 2015, there was an influx of prisoners from the student movement at universities:

We didn't wait for things to get better. We said, no we deserve better living conditions. You can't just humiliate people. We will respond. We would protest, go on strike, bang on the doors, anything really. We began to get some gains. We decided that if any of our families got humiliated we would respond.

At the time, because of the student movement, the prison was becoming highly organised into sophisticated networks of resistance. To quash the resistance, the authorities decided to force 400–450 prisoners into *taghriba* – a form of punishment where prisoners are relocated to far away and remote prisons – so they can longer communicate:

They brought in the anti-riot squad from Tora Prison. These guys were huge. It looked like they were preparing for war. I was shocked. They had no idea we would fight back and resist. They were armoured, trained to break bones and had dogs with them. We made a plan to resist. We used everything to defend ourselves, even the light bulbs.

The anti-riot squad began to throw CS gas canisters into the cell:

I began to suffocate. My whole body was on fire. What came after was a massacre. They were beating us as if we weren't people. The funny thing, the cell next door was watching. They really wanted to help. So they began throwing soap, water and washing liquid into our cell. As if that would somehow trip the officers. Problem is, I was the one that tripped over the soap. And once I was on the floor, it was like the whole of Egypt was gathering around to beat me.

Munira faced a very similar situation in prison which culminated with her hunger strike. Conditions had deteriorated dramatically in women's prisons after Sisi was elected as president. The oversight or even potential refrain that the officers may have shown initially in some cases ceased. For some of the officers, this meant exercising their power and even vengeance:

After Sisi won the elections, the female guards began to pick fights with us. They beat us and the *gina'i* inmates. So we fought back. The next day, the anti-riot police came in. They forced us out of our cells. They beat us badly, stripped off our hijabs. One of the older aunties with us was stripped and beaten really badly. This made me stop eating. I didn't even think of it as a hunger strike at first. I just felt like we are not cows that they would treat us this way. We were violated and we couldn't defend ourselves. I felt humiliated. They knew we wore hijab, but they made the decision to move us without our hijab.

As she was being stripped and beaten, the officers were yelling at her: *Khawarij, Khawarij*. She felt like that they were trying to strip her very claim to her faith by stripping off her hijab. That is why she decided to go on a hunger strike.

HUNGER STRIKES

JTF-GTMO – Guantánamo Bay, Cuba

… someone unexpected visited us in our cages while we slept. The hunger *jinn* whispered into our ears, Hunger strike. I'd never heard of Mr. Hunger Strike before, but other brothers had.[6]

Mansoor Adayfi had never heard of a hunger strike before. He heard in whispers around him how some believed that it was a sin to harm your own body on purpose. Others close to him began to debate the issue from different perspectives, whether they be military, political, or religious. It was the young boy in the cage next to Mansoor – so young he wasn't able to grow a full beard or moustache – who refused the first meal one morning. Mansoor looked at the example of his neighbour and decided that he too must take action. Despite receiving criticism from their elders, soon others would join them, even though they themselves were unsure of what they were really doing:

Every day the number of brothers refusing meals increased and so did the number taken to the medical tent. Mr. Hunger Strike walked the blocks happy with what he had started.

The Muslim chaplain brought us a *fatwa* he printed in Arabic saying that it was against the teachings of Islam to harm ourselves with hunger. Then he recited a verse from the Qur'an: O you who have believed, do not consume one another's wealth unjustly but only in business by mutual consent. And do not kill yourselves. Indeed, Allah is to you ever Merciful.

This was the Pakistani chaplain who watched us get stripped naked and beaten, who watched us get punished for practicing our faith, and as far as we knew had never said a word in protest.

'As you know, it is our religion to pray together,' we said. 'Why do you sit by and watch them beat us for practicing our faith?'

He had no answer for this. So none of us listened to him.

Ten days passed, and we knew the hunger strike was serious when the marine general Lehnert walked the blocks with an interpreter talking to prisoners. When he came to our block, he knelt down in front of our cages and talked to us through the interpreter. He had the squarest jaw I had ever seen, and sharp eyes, but when we talked, he nodded his head and listened.

It surprised me that he would kneel down and talk to so many of us. Our demands were simple. We wanted to be able to practice our religion praying together.[7]

Years later, Mansoor's guards would question how it was possible for the prisoners to go on strike for months at a time, how they managed to cope with the loneliness and hunger of solitary confinement as they were punished for striking? His answer to them was always simple, *Allah*. The prisoners would see the camp administration change, rotation of guards, but always, the one constant for them was the mercy of God, He was the one nourishing force that reinforced their bodies and their hearts.[8]

The hunger strikes across the different prisoner blocks at Guantánamo Bay differed for the reasons they were initiated and the length of time they were carried out. As the blocks started to become increasingly organised, they would appoint an *amir* (leader) for each block who would decide the point at which a hunger strike would be initiated.[9] While the hunger strikes were often organised as collective actions, there were also those who were detained in solitary confinement who chose to carry out their own individual strikes in order to complain of their conditions and abuse of their religion. The Al Jazeera journalist, Sami Elhaj, very much saw the hunger strike as his own way of exercising autonomy over his own body and life. His hunger strike gained international attention as he chose to strike for long over a year, as he 'brandished the hunger strike in the face of our executioners'.[10] In his own mind, it was the one weapon that his captors could not take from him, the one that he could deploy at his own choosing to hold them to account:

> I decided to begin a hunger strike at roughly the same time as the opening of Guantánamo's Camp 6, around the first week of January 2007. It is crucial for me to remember those days and dates inside the cells. So I made an effort, to the extent that I could, to commit everything to memory. It was extremely difficult during the days of solitary confinement, spent almost continuously in the dark.
>
> I prepared for my strike by reducing the amount of food I ate, then the number of meals, refusing some. I was slowly going down to eating nothing, determined to reach my goal of being on full hunger strike, in spite of the fact that I was severely constipated by the lack of food and that aggravated my haemorrhoids.
>
> After I was refusing all meals, they cleared the cells to my right and left to make sure that nobody was passing me food in secret. An officer and doctor came to see me and explain that they would be testing my blood pressure every day, sometimes three times a day.
>
> On January 6, 2007, one day before starting the hunger strike, I sent my five demands to the General: first, respect for Islam; second, our right to the rights in the Geneva Convention on the treatment of prisoners of war; third, the right to advocate for ourselves in front of a civil court; fourth, to return the brothers who had been isolated in Camp Echo; and fifth, an investigation into the deaths of the three prisoners who died mysteriously on

June 10, 2006. I raised these demands and stopped eating as the sun rose on January 7, 2007.

That first month, I was exposed to the administration's preliminary tactic, neglecting the hunger striker completely to make him despair and abandon his demands, pressured by hunger and thirst. At the end of the month, they began to try to tempt me, telling me that I would leave soon. They tried to reason with me: 'You're a young man with your life ahead of you. Don't kill yourself. Isn't suicide haram in your religion? Your family is waiting for you.'

They were disappointed; I bore all their ploys with the support of Allah and resisted their temptation. I ended the month with unswerving determination, and they realised that I would continue my strike into the second month, especially when they saw my weight had dropped from 90 to 56 kg. So they moved me to hospital.

In the hospital, in contrast to the deliberate neglect of the days before, they began a programme of care, and force-feedings. First, they were doing it intravenously, sticking me with needles several times a day. Soon, they decided to change to using a feeding tube, as my health condition had deteriorated to a point where it was necessary.

They would threaten me during the sessions: 'Those you hold dear will die, you will die as a result of your refusal to eat.'

The hunger burrowed into me, from my flesh to my bones. But I was armed with faith in Allah and remained calm while they went about their business nervously. It was time for my first force-feeding.

That was a sombre, bizarre day. The doctors and hospital staff gathered around me and held me down on a horrible seat that resembled an execution chair, restraining my four limbs so that I couldn't move. Then, in what felt like an enormous violation, they painfully inserted the feeding tube down my nose. The feeling is indescribable, horrible suffocation as the metal-tipped plastic tube was forced down my nose, seemingly cutting off my oxygen till I felt faint. Then it passed the back of my mouth and started to go down my throat, inflaming it and irritating my oesophagus.

I, to this day, cannot say if what they did was intentional or a mistake, but there were several occasions when the tube ended up in my lungs instead of my stomach, and a few drops of feeding liquid would be forced into them. Even when the tube when to the right place, the intense burning pressure caused by the feeding liquid being emptied into my stomach was almost as suffocating and brutal.

To be extra cruel, an attendant would deliberately mix three or four times the required amount of water with the feeding liquid base, sending four times as much liquid as recommended rushing into my stomach, now minuscule after over a month of not eating. I would feel I had entered a state of death, life and colour receding from my face, from my body, my breath ebbing, sweat pouring out of me, then paroxysms of vomiting would begin.

They would persist in the feeding until they were satisfied, needing to follow their procedure so they could fill out their forms. My intense intestinal pain did not seem to deter them; their faces remained grim, coated in cruelty. That first day, and in spite of the pain I was in, I asked them to remove the restraints so I could pray. They refused, citing security, claiming I would behave violently if they removed the restraints. All I could do was cry out: 'What can a man in my situation do? Don't talk to me about security!'

They retorted: 'We don't want to let you pray.'

There was a moment of complete silence. I called on God in my heart, thanking him for all my trials and for showing me the truth of their hearts.[11]

Female Unit, Hillsborough County Jail – Florida, United States of America
Pamunkey Regional Jail – Virginia, United States of America

From the moment of his arrest in 2003, Sami al-Arian thought that he may need to go on hunger strike. He had heard about the tactic previously in other political contexts, but it was not a tactic he had studied in any great depth. He understood that he was now facing a political case, one that would have resonance across the world. From the very beginning he decided that he should start a hunger strike, in order to make it clear that he was determined to defend his rights at all costs. The prison administration immediately deployed their doctors and imams in order to convince him not to pursue this action. Sami negotiated his first hunger strike down to one where he would take the protein drink Ensure, rather than a full hunger strike that would be reduced to water. Due to the complexity of the initial period of legal challenges, Sami felt that he needed to break his strike in order to give his full attention to his case.

It wasn't until his second case in 2007, having beaten the first, that Sami felt the need to go on another hunger strike. By this stage, it was clear that the Bush administration was eager to pursue every angle they could to persecute and prosecute him. By Ramadan that year, he had been transferred to a jail in Virginia where they were attempting to coerce him to appear before a grand jury – which he was refusing to participate in. At the time his family were promoting the film *USA v Arian* – a documentary about his case and their struggles in supporting him. Sami felt that the promotion of the film would be the best time to stage such a strike, highlighting the political nature of his plight further:

Once they decided to initiate a grand jury and bring me in, I decided to go on hunger strike. I refused to testify the second time. I said, I'm not going to go like this. They wouldn't monitor me and so after 22 days, I was just on water. One day I was making *wudu* for *fajr*. And then I passed out. So my head even hit the seat and I didn't even wake up until maybe seven or eight o'clock in the morning when I awoke in the prison infirmary.

They began to bring me food three times a day to entice me, then they come and check your vitals twice or three times a day and all that. But you're sitting in solitary. That's when bringing me an imam to convince me every day, this is *haram*. He was African-American, educated in Saudi Arabia, *Wahabbi*, they'll have set up a really nice person. And he was leading the prayer in prison.

I had the doctor coming in each day, threatening me that they're going to put [a] tube through the nose and it would be very painful. They told me they would put it through my nose, I said do what you have to do, I'll do what I have to do. They wanted to bring me to testify, but it's no condition to testify, so they kept postponing it. And that's the point I was trying to make. In addition to the publicity we're generating, I knew all along that at one point I'm going to break, but yeah, I'm trying to prolong this to make the point, otherwise no one cares.

Sami's hunger strike had the effect of prolonging the process of the grand jury, as his captors were keen to ensure that he was not presented to the world in such a weakened state. They attempted to send an imam again to him to convince him away from the path he was on. The imam claimed that the verse *wa la tulqu bi aydeekom illa al tahlukka* (of not *ruining* oneself) did not permit him to take this path, but Sami explained that he had no intention to kill himself. Sami had read of the hunger strikes taking place at Guantánamo Bay and knew that the prison administration would intervene to force feed if they had to, in order to ensure that he did not die. Despite his weakness, to the extent that he would experience blackouts and severe immobility, Sami thought of this period as one of the peaks of his spiritual experience, particularly in relation to his reflections on the Qur'an – he knew that he must struggle in any way he can – and his body became the final site of contestation with his captors.

A year and a half after ending his second hunger strike, Sami al-Arian went on his final strike, except this time he took the extreme step of going on a hunger and thirst strike. He went for 18 days without food or water, resulting in a severe deterioration of his body. The attempt to coerce him before the grand jury again forced him to take this step, but he was still taken, entirely disorientated – not able to answer their questions due to his physical condition. This tactic was generally looked down on by other domestic prisoners due to the severity of impact on the body, but Sami decided that the political situation surrounding his case required such a response.

Scorpion Prison – Cairo, Egypt
Burj al-Arab – Alexandria, Egypt
Qanater El Khayereya Women's Prison – Qalyubiyya, Egypt
Leeman Prison – Minya, Egypt
Tora Prison – Cairo, Egypt

During February 2016, 57 inmates in the infamous Scorpion Prison (*aqrab*) announced an open-ended hunger strike. In the previous year, at least six people died due to medical neglect and the situation was becoming increasingly dire. The prison authorities began implementing systematic enforced starvation tactics and banning prisoners from access to medicine. They had no blankets, and the material of the prison clothes was so light that they effectively froze. Those who were healthy survived but fell sick, and many others who were already weak could not survive.[12] When they died, the prisoners gathered around to pray funeral prayers for them. Omar recalls before he made the decision to join the hunger strike:

I was isolated for a few months prior. The circumstances were very difficult. Food was very limited. There were days we didn't have any food at all. We were hungry and in these days, it used to be especially cold. We wore very thin material and weren't allowed any underwear. We didn't have blankets and they kept the windows always open.

Omar – who was in his fifties at the time – decided to join the collective hunger strike. There was a myriad of reasons that led up to this decision – which was not taken lightly by anyone – that culminated in the death of the inmates: the prison authorities' enforced starvation tactics, brutal torture, medical neglect and the banning of visitation rights:

Being engaged in some form of resistance automatically gave me a sense of contentment. As long as I was resisting in situations of injustice, I felt I was okay. Yes, of course, general health is also important – especially for someone like me – who is a bit older – and the older you are, the harder the hunger strike will impact you but I couldn't shake this *ayah* from my mind: {Fight them!

191

Allah will torment them at your hands and disgrace them and grant you victory over them and cure the breasts of a people [who are] believers} (9:14). This is my personal conviction; it is not necessarily the case for everyone else.

For Omar, there was a distinct difference between two modes of hunger strikes – collective action or individual hunger strike. Collective hunger strikes are geared toward collective demands on the living conditions within the prison, while individual hunger strikes are geared toward individual demands. This means that collective hunger strikes could potentially yield more permanent and structural changes in prison; or, in turn could open prisoners to collective punishment. Both were true in Scorpion Prison. At times, the prison authorities would be open to negotiating and responding to the demands of the hunger strikers. At other points they would use brute force. On 2 May 2017 at 7 a.m., the prison authorities stormed the prison cells along with an anti-riot squad. They were armed with live bullets, electric rods, teargas and police dogs. They let the police dogs loose on the prisoners and they began to charge and tear into them, biting them. The officers demanded the prisoners sign a paper stating that they forgo their demands. When the prisoners refused, they were sprayed with a chemical and they began to suffocate.

Like Omar, Ali found himself a part of a collective and highly organised effort inside prison. Although they were more successful than those in Scorpion in their struggle against the prison authorities, they employed similar methods:

There are two types of hunger strikes in prison – one is like Soltan and El Shamy's hunger strikes. That is, striking for freedom and release. The second type of hunger strike was one I was involved in – that is, demands for reform inside the prison. We founded a committee that included 60–70 young people; subcommittees were formed within these committees. We communicated in code. We had two major red lines: our families won't get harassed in visitations and no prisoner – especially older prisoners – will be humiliated.

These were mainly student activists – who had been very organised and sophisticated outside prison and continued to be so inside. They had a long-standing rivalry with the police and so the feud ran deeper than prison. The committee decided that if the officers did anything to provoke them that they would fight back:

One Friday, we knew something was going to happen. We were ready. And before they could call for backup, each of us began beating whichever officers came at them. Four minutes later, their backup came. In the middle of the fight. a big guy stood up and began screaming on the top of his lungs, so all of the other cells would know what was going on. They began to beat us badly. The other cells started chanting and beating at the doors. Next day, we announced a hunger strike. At different times, each person would announce they were on hunger strike. It began to disorient the authorities.

Ali began his hunger strike on the second day. It was not designed to be a long-term battle; rather, to cause enough havoc to force the prison authorities to negotiate. The cells erupted in protests and chants. Not everyone was on hunger strike, but in each cell, there would be at least five or six people who were:

We knew this wouldn't last and that they would crumble. The prison authorities did not have the resources to deal with such a large-scale hunger strike in a huge prison like that. Either they will escalate or crumble. And sure enough, after eight days, the negotiations began and they gave in to some of our demands.

The dynamics shift dramatically when the prisoner makes the decision to go on hunger strike on their own and not as a part of coordinated collective hunger strike, as in the cases of Mohamed Soltan, Abdullah El Shamy and Ola al-Qaradawi. These range from highly organised strikes such as that of Mohamed to more organic and less organised – like Ola's.

Ola was in her early fifties when she was first detained. She was in a state of shock. She could not comprehend what was happening to her. In those early days, she tried to recount supplications or verses to soothe herself, but her mind was completely blocked. She tried to get the female guard to give her a Qur'an, but she refused. It was a difficult reality to grasp. Her time in solitary changed her. Her hunger strike occurred slowly:

> Look, as soon as I was arrested, I was put in solitary confinement. I did not see anyone and I did not know what was happening in the world. I was in a room that was 1.5 x 1.7 metres. It was completely silent. There was a steel door and bars on the ceiling. I did not have a toilet; there was a small bucket in my cell. The cell opens at 8 a.m. for ten minutes so I can use the toilet. I just stopped eating and drinking completely. I just couldn't imagine myself ever using that bucket. I just couldn't reach that stage. At first, it wasn't so much a strike; I couldn't comprehend what was happening. I couldn't believe it, so I didn't eat.

When Ola first decided that this was going to be a hunger strike, she was alone and afraid. She didn't tell anyone:

> I would just go on hunger strike and sit alone, silently. I was done with the world. I didn't want to continue like this. I didn't want to be alone. On the fourth or fifth day, I went to the prosecutor's office and I just collapsed. I had to tell my lawyer. He told me not to continue my strike but I decided to anyway. When the prison authorities found out, they were terrified. That's when things started to get better.

The officers would try to bring her lunch and eat with her. She began to understand that they were trying to get her to end her strike:

> They tried to convince me that hunger strikes don't get people released but it does! I just had to persevere. I heard about Mohamed Soltan and Abdullah El Shamy; they went on hunger strike and got out. I told myself that if I resisted long enough, I could also get out.

Mohamed Soltan and Abdullah El Shamy were the longest and most successful cases of hunger strikes in Egypt. Mohamed's hunger strike lasted for 489 days and Abdullah's hunger strike lasted for 130 days. They coincided in prison. Mohamed smuggled a letter to Abdullah. He began:

In the Name of Allah, the Most Beneficent, the Most Merciful.

{And [He will give you] another thing, which you love: Help from Allah, and victory, near at hand} (61:13). My brother Abdullah, I call on you for the sake of Allah – He in whose hand is dominion and goodness – do not be attached to worldly consequence. Attach yourself only to Allah. For He has the real power. Be free of all consequences and humanly paths. Do not preoccupy yourself with them too much. By Allah, the moment of victory will not be deferred or hastened for a single second: {Then they will shake their heads at you and say, 'When will that be?' Say, 'It may well be very soon'} (17:50).

My brother Abdullah, make your *khalwa* [spiritual solitude] a form of *i'tikaf* [devotional seclusion] to draw nearer to your Lord. And to besiege Him to free us and the whole community of Muslims and to accept us in peace – if not above this earth, then close to the Lord of the Heavens.

For both Mohamed and Abdullah, hunger strikes were a tactical mode of resistance that invariably raised the question of their mortality. In the outset, as the prison routine began to set in, they had to come to terms with a new reality. They were now prisoners. Abdullah's detention was in the process of being renewed and there seemed no end: 'I wanted to leave prison and I thought to myself even if I were to leave prison – because of the hunger strike as a dead person, then fine. I have achieved my goal. I've achieved freedom.'

The question of death loomed – although this was neither their intent nor desire. Like many other prisoners, they faced their mortality many times – whether during the Rabaa massacre or throughout the lifecycle of detention. This war of attrition was different. Either the prison authorities lose and they are free, or they lose and potentially die. Mohamed recalled:

A part of getting ready for a hunger strike is to be ready to see it to its end. Its end means my end. This meant I was not going to go to God in a terrible spiritual shape. I had to be on top of my prayers. I had to genuinely be close to Allah because he is the only one that is going to be the true judge of that. It had to be a real, solid connection.

He began to see a snapshot of his life and experiences. This was not going to be the end: withering away in prison, alone and immobile. He was very close to dying many times. In his weakest and most vulnerable moments, the officers would slip razor blades under his door. They would shout and scream: 'Kill yourself, end it.' Somehow, despite the vulnerability of the space, this only strengthened his resolve. Before taking this step, Mohamed got in touch with former Irish and Palestinian hunger strikers through his family. They gave him advice on how to properly conduct a long-term hunger strike and manage the manoeuvres of the authorities:

I read up on Irish and Palestinian hunger strikers before starting. I had my family reach out to their family members to see what they did. The single most important advice they gave me was: salt water! Don't jump into it; wean yourself off food gradually. So the calculus was made; I didn't need to invent anything. I was very clear-headed about the decision, so even if I were to go, I wouldn't go in vain. A lot of work on the outside went into it, a whole campaign – videos and content. I would document and write everything that was happening to me, so if I died it wouldn't be in vain. Now, I had a timeline I could prepare my physical body but also spiritually. So if I lost, I can go to God at least having tried my best to salvage my relationship with Him. *Subhan Allah*, I didn't think it was going to work. I fell into a hypoglycaemic coma a dozen times or more. I had a pulmonary embolism but the authorities would use medical interventions to inflict as much pain as possible. They were so detail-oriented with the torture.

The prison authorities too employed everything in their arsenal, from forced medicalisation procedures to media and disinformation campaigns, to mobilising religious discourses. Months into his hunger strike, the official state media released photos of Abdullah El Shamy eating on the floor. Later, he discovered that he had been drugged and moved by the prison authorities during their medical intervention. They staged pictures of him eating to discredit his hunger strike.

Omar scoffed when I asked him whether or not prisoners debated the religious permissibility of undergoing a hunger strike:

> There were only the *ijtihadat* [making legal decisions by independent interpretation of the scriptural sources] of the prison authorities. No one was asking whether this was *halal* or *haram*. I didn't encounter this question between the prisoners. However, the prison authorities would bring this up a lot. They would say this is a form of *tahluka* [self-destruction] which was *haram*. They would often attempt to use the mechanisms of *fiqh* as a form of pressure. Prisoners just debated whether it was effective, not if it was *halal* or *haram*.

The prison authorities would constantly raise the question of permissibility – either via a prison chaplain or imam, other prisoners, or through appeals of paternalistic figureheads – in every hunger strike case. When Ola al-Qaradawi first announced to the prison authorities her intent to continue her hunger strike, the authorities, trying to persuade her to end her strike, told her it was impermissible and akin to suicide – 'Even ask your father!':

> I asked baba once. From what I understood is that yes hunger strikes are permitted, but you should avoid self-harm as much as possible. I thought, okay my goal is not self-harm. My goal is to apply enough pressure to get them to do what I need them to do. They care that I stay alive. If something happens to me, it's a bigger problem for them. I just need to reach a point where I can threaten them with this.

As with Ola, the prison authorities employed a paternalistic religious tone with Abdullah to dissuade him from hunger strike.

The minister of interior's assistant came to visit me in prison, and he tried to act fatherly. He was like 'Abdullah, hunger strikes are not for Muslims. We are Muslims. This is *haram*. You are a young man, and I'm speaking to you like you're my son.' You know the rhetoric officials use to try and lower you into confidence as another way of violence. He continued, 'Now tell me an example of someone who went on hunger strike and actually was released?' I said, 'I think the Irish people did it.' He said, 'Irish are not Muslim.' And then I said, 'Palestinians do it as well.' He said, 'No, but Palestine is a different story.' This all happened just four days before they then took me to solitary confinement.

The verse that the prison authorities cite as scriptural evidence to the impermissibility of hunger strikes is {And spend in the way of Allah and do not throw [yourselves] with your [own] hands into destruction. And do good; indeed, Allah loves the doers of good} (2:195). The debate centred around the meaning of 'destruction'. Mohamed recalled, 'They got these shaykhs from Al Azhar; you know the ones that lead prayer. They said, "Do not throw [yourselves] with your [own] hands into destruction." I didn't take them seriously. So is what I am going through now *halal*?'

Both Mohamed and Omar noted that 'destruction' did not mean suicide, as they intended to indicate it was. Instead, abstaining from *jihad* was the destruction that the verse meant. This is based on a narration on the life of the companion Abu Ayyub al-Ansari:

> When a man from amongst the Muslim army in the first expedition of Constantinople charged into the first line of Roman [Byzantine] armies, Muslims screamed, '*Subhan Allah*, he has thrown himself into the destruction, and giving an interpretation to the verse {Do not throw yourselves into destruction} (2:195).' Abu Ayyub al-Ansari replied 'Destruction is leaving *jihad* and refraining from supporting Allah and His Messenger.'

Mohamed went on to add that when the advice of the prison chaplain did not work, they called in prisoners affiliated with ISIS to dissuade him:

When they figured out this *halal-haram* stuff did not work with me. They started bringing in the ISIS guys. They would bring those guys because they were aligned with the authorities. They would say only resistance is resistance. Everything else was futile; these people only respect the gun and power. The state of weakness you're in right now they have no respect for. You must have strength to resist. It makes perfect sense because if the prison authorities can't convince you it is *haram*. If you decided to go the violent route, it plays into their narrative.

Conclusion

Religion and the Deification of the National Security State

For a moment, I started thinking. Why is everyone just watching us? Is that it? A few hours ago, almost one thousand people were just killed – just like that. People are just going about their life like nothing happened ... And then the moment you leave the square, people are fine. Cafes are open. You would think as someone who has just witnessed what you've witnessed that people might be angry that people are being killed just a few kilometres away but that just didn't happen.

Abdullah El Shamy in the aftermath of
the Rabaa massacre, 2013

This was not a case of art imitating life imitating art – there was something more of a prescient quality to *The Queue*, written by the Egyptian psychiatrist Basma Abdel Aziz. Written in 2012, a year prior to the military coup instigated by General Abdel Fattah el-Sisi, and the massacres he would order at Rabaa in Cairo. The novel could have been mistaken for a contemporary dystopian version of the events – rather than what it turned out to be – a premonition. Written by Abdel Aziz as a warning, and as a concern that the former Mubarak era had not fully ended, she could foresee that all it would take for the resumption of the Egyptian security state was one act that could be relabelled a national security emergency – Morsi's short term as president and the subsequent protests proved to be that very excuse.

Conclusions to books often attempt to summarise the key findings of the main body of the work, to extract some key ideas, themes and ways forward for readers to take away. What we want to do is to reflect a little on Basma Abdel Aziz's novel in relation to the instrumentalisation of national security and religion as an operating form of control and violence over the lives of prisoners. This book has very much sought to bring to light the everyday experiences of prisoners in practising their faith – but the book has been in a constant duality, one where the national security state is equally engaging with religion – but purely as a means of exercising violence.

Abdel Aziz's novel itself is set in a nondescript Middle Eastern country, and so in some ways could be transplanted to the current political situation in countries such as Tunisia and Syria, and even further afield, Pakistan. The security state operates as a malignant virus that has spread through the body; highlighting the harm that it causes in one area does little to expose how utterly corrupted the body as a whole has become. Abdel Aziz's novel understands that central fact completely.

The Queue sets the scene of an invisible despotic regime that controls society through 'The Gate', a municipal structure that deals with all the daily bureaucracies of citizens' lives – all laws, regulations, permissions, citizenship approval, hospital care, etc. It is akin to every *baladiyya* [municipal council] in the Arab world, structures that are as important to daily life as they are infuriating. A long queue stretching for miles forms outside The Gate after the 'Disgraceful Event' – an event in the recent past that is only given a brief description, except that we can glean that it is related to the brutal crackdown on protesters who were shot and killed – very much prescient of the future events at Rabaa in 2013:

The Events had begun when a small group of people held a protest on a street leading to the square. There weren't many of them, but they boldly condemned the Gate's injustice and tyranny ... They chanted with passion, their numbers grew, and the protest started to move, but they were quickly confronted by the Gate's newly formed security units. These accused the protesters of overstepping their bounds, and said they wouldn't tolerate such insulting behavior. Then the forces attacked, to 'return people to their senses', beating them brutally. When the injured protesters scattered in retreat and ran into the side streets, they were accused of 'spreading chaos', and attempting to undermine the blessed security that had finally—thankfully—returned under the Gate's rule.[1]

As a form of punishment, The Gate effectively closes, shutting down civil administration and forming its own form of social control, as citizens and non-citizens wait in a long queue for their lives to be able to function; but they are left waiting for the Gate to open for months on end. Wanting to get on with their lives, a micro-existence emerges in the queue, that magnifies the logic of the national security state as those in the queue attempt to form solidarity with one another, while simultaneously being under the constant fear of one another and the security forces of the state.

The national security state centralises all aspects of public goodness to itself, so the actions, behaviours and beliefs of citizens are always tied inextricably to the perpetuation of the status quo – particularly in the case of religion. National security states monopolise religion for the purpose of maintaining their hegemony, even where those states are ostensibly secular. The divide between the secular and the religious is arbitrary, as the state, not scripture, is always the final determinant of the limits of religiosity and its own accompanying goodness. The narrative of the ethical boundaries of the state are determined through the language of religion and piety, thus those who kill, murder, detain and torture on behalf of the state are pious by virtue of their carrying-out orders.

This comes into sharpest focus as the agents of state personify omnipotence in their dealings with captives – even with some Egyptian interrogators quoting the language of God in the Qur'an by claiming divinity – akin to the Qur'an's presentation of Pharaoh proclaiming {I am your Lord most high} (79:24). The Egyptian prisoner Mohamed is wheeled into the office of a senior interrogator, who shocked him by claiming divinity for the national security state, 'Here, in this country, we are like God. We say Be! And it is {kun fa yakun}', explicitly referencing God's language in the Qur'an that He is the One who creates all. The prisoners saw their guards as mimicking the despots presented in the Qur'an, such as Nimrod, who would portray themselves as having total omnipotence, of their prisoners' very lives and deaths.

In a more secular setting under the custody of the US, the camp commander at Guantánamo Bay explicitly sought to deify his officers to the prisoners by establishing a relationship of omnipotence over them in the standard operating procedures he established at the camp, 'degradation of the detainee, stripping can be used to demonstrate the omnipotence of the captor or to debilitate the detainee.'[2] In the same way, on the US mainland, Ali al-Marri was systematically abused in order to establish this god-like power dynamic between him and his need to access basic amenities.

Abdel Aziz understands the connection between the state and its instrumentalisation of religion – for her, a soldier who dies in the process of carrying out a massacre of protesters, is the only one the state will recognise as a martyr; if the state is deified, then dying for it becomes the ultimate form of *shahadah*:*

If he'd been in Mahfouz's shoes, he would've done what Mahfouz had done and more, and if Ines had been defending the nation in his place, she'd know how to obey orders. She would've learned that when you're given an order there's no discussion, no question, and barely enough time to carry it out – and even if there were time, the Commander wouldn't let you waste it with stupid questions. If he'd ever heard the things she said from one of his men, he would teach him a thing or two and then lock him up. If this woman had any honor, she would know that to obey your Commander was to obey God, and that insubordination was a sin greater than any mortal could bear and would lead to her own demise. But she was probably corrupt, morally and otherwise – no scruples, no religion, not even wearing a respectable headscarf; he could see a strand of hair hanging down beneath that pitiful scrap of fabric on her head. Yes, she was definitely one of the people the Commander had warned him about, just talking to her was dangerous, she might mess with his mind, try to brainwash him. If she wasn't one of them, why was she defending them and insulting his cousin, why was she happy

---

* *Shahadah* – witnessing, in the context of witnessing and ultimately a declaration of faith in one God (Allah) and His messenger, including martyrdom.

that he was dead? She wouldn't agree that Mahfouz was a martyr, didn't think his family deserved to be compensated or that he was worth anything at all. It was possible that she had participated in the Disgraceful Events, too; he'd heard rumors that there were women saboteurs.[3]

The daily inconveniences created by the national security state create a whole class of obsequious citizens who prefer to privilege their own daily convenience and existence over the need for building a society with more just and equitable systems of governance. The national security state, in fact, requires it. *The Queue* depicts a population that is tired of The Gate, but is also scared to do anything to confront it, and scared to be placed in a position where others who confront its abusive system of bureaucracy, might result in a delay to their own needs.[4] This fear brings about the form of politics of obedience that Étienne de La Boétie wrote of in the sixteenth century, a form of mindless acceptance of the status quo, but more than that, a daily complicity.

Egyptians have been forced to endure this daily complicity since the coup in 2013. Asmaa's sexual assault on the streets of Cairo by a police officer, and the reaction from bystanders that she should simply remain quiet about the assault is indicative of the fear that populations live in, but also their simultaneous propping up of that very system – it is a dialectic that self-perpetuates the power of the state. Mona recalls ordinary citizens chasing her as she was transported in the open-top truck; people throwing rocks at her and aiming for her face because they were told she was a political prisoner.

The complicity took place at a number of different levels of Egyptian society. Within the prisons, other prisoners, such as the more institutionalised *gina'i* would be forced by officers to take part in the ritual humiliation of female political prisoners by conducting cavity searches – an act they would regret. The complicity of the *gina'i* takes place in an environment where they have very little agency of their own. However, there are other complicities to be found in the upper echelons of society, such as that of Mervat Tallawy, the president of the National Council for Women who would deny the experience of torture. These 'liberal' Egyptian women actively chose to deny the experience of female political prisoners by providing cover to the national security state.

Ali al-Marri intrinsically understood the way that complicity of the everyday person operates after he was visited by the FBI after 9/11. For him, there was something obvious about his fellow passengers reporting a Middle Eastern man after seeing him at the airport with a large trunk – not that he thought this was acceptable. Across the Western world, hundreds of thousands of phone calls began to be made to security agencies, whether to the CIA, FBI, police, etc., reporting anyone who was considered to be mildly suspicious by virtue of their faith or ethnicity. The reality of the War on Terror is that the national security state was built directly on top of a pre-existing oppressive structure – the carceral state. The prison industrial complex in the US has seen the over-criminalisation of hundreds of thousands of people of colour – particularly since the Reagan administration in the 1980s. The US is now the primary carceral state in the world, and after 9/11 has expanded the geographies of its carceral reach – an archipelago of detention. Thus, we found Guantánamo Bay, Baghdad, Bagram becoming centres for thousands of direct detentions, while countries such as Morocco, Egypt and Syria became partners to the US for the export of torture and detention – effectively becoming proxies for the US carceral state by expanding its reach.

Adjacent to the deified national security state that Basma Abdel Aziz writes of, sits a mechanism by which The Gate is able to centralise moral authority to itself – religion. *The Queue* presents the most overt use of religion as a means of control through two means, the first are the *fatawa* that are issued directly by The Gate, but this is accompanied by the office of the High Sheikh – whose signature ratifies the religiosity of any of the rules pushed by The Gate. Sitting alongside the idea of the deified national security state, Abdel Aziz presents it as a paternalistic entity – one that knows best for its children – and so the notion of trust in the state operates at multiple levels, the level of theology in it having moral force, but also in the sense of family – it is the caregiver who knows best and from whom nothing should be hidden.[5]

Religious justifications for the actions of the state have been a consistent feature of the global War on Terror. It could even be said that the entirety of a state-centric narrative on its relationship with its Muslim communities has been an attempt to 'own' the space of Islam, and thus what is and is not considered to be righteous – out of a sense of doing what is best or right for Muslims, and on behalf of Muslims. Thus, in France we currently see the Imams' Charter as a way of curtailing religious freedom by centralising the Muslim identity to notions of French *laicité* and allegiance to the state. This type of ethico-religious narrative can be found in many permutations of the War on Terror – for example, with the US claiming that they were following Islamic law by dumping the body of Osama bin Laden into the sea, instead of permitting him to be buried in a regular grave. The announcement required a certain degree of justification from within the laws of Islam to be presented – usually in the form of a *fatwa* – stating that they had consulted and that in order for his grave to not become a shrine, he should be buried in the sea. As the late Saba Mahmood explained, the state operates as a 'de-facto theologian authorizing practices and doctrine as legitimate', only when they are able to control the boundaries of what that doctrine means.[6]

The *fatwa* itself thus becomes a site of control, one where the national security state is able to dictate how the Muslim citizen can respond to egregious forms of violence – by attempting to limit the scope of what they can do. *The Queue* captures this perfectly through the role that is played by the High Sheikh in issuing *fatawa* through the Fatwa and Rationalizations Committee:

> The High Sheikh invoked a few passages from the Greater Book, explaining that if a believer were to be struck by a bullet (despite his prayers and supplication), his faith would guide him to the understanding that it was God himself who'd struck him down. A wounded believer should not despair or oppose God's will. Nor should he question the unquestionable – such an act could lead him down a perilous path toward doubt. Instead, the believer must accept the will of God. He must acknowledge how lucky he was to be struck by a bullet, and exalted to a place in heaven ordinarily reserved only for the most dutiful.[7]

Fatawa played an important role in Guantanamo – they were the means by which interrogators would attempt to curtail the resistance of the Muslim men detained there. The interrogators found that the torture, raids and isolation could only work so far, and instead they would have to use a form of soft power to enforce compliance. Somewhat akin to the role of the High Sheikh in Abdel Aziz's novel, Guantánamo had its own Muslim chaplains who were stationed there in order to help the regime manage the men – their presence was primarily to support the detention and interrogation teams. Once the hunger strikes started at Guantánamo, the Muslim chaplain at the time was immediately deployed in order to convince the prisoners that going on hunger strike was akin to suicide by bringing a *fatwa* that mentioned the verse not to kill themselves:

> This was the Pakistani chaplain who watched us get stripped naked and beaten, who watched us get punished for practicing our faith, and as far as we knew had never said a word in protest.
>   'As you know, it is our religion to pray together,' we said. 'Why do you sit by and watch them beat us for practicing our faith?'
>   He had no answer for this. So none of us listened to him.[8]

As we were in the final throes of writing this book, Khader Adnan, the Palestinian rights activist, hunger striker and baker, was killed by the Israeli state after his body succumbed to multiple hunger strikes that took a toll on his body. After years of unjust imprisonment at the hands of a settler-colonial-apartheid force, his refusal to eat became the only line of defence remaining to protect his own sense of dignity and freedom – leading ultimately to his *shahadah* – his martyrdom. For Adnan, he was not considered by those he left behind as someone who had taken his own life, but rather that it was the Israelis who had taken his life through his continued unlawful detention at their hands.

Near the end of his life, and deep into his hunger strike, the Israelis attempted to convince Khader to break it, even giving him access to his family and wheelchair-bound mother to convince him. Misinformation began to filter through the media and back to the family. A journalist reported that his wife Randa had requested

Khader break his strike, but more importantly, that a *fatwa* had been issued by a scholar at Al Azhar University in Cairo, claiming that if Khader were to lose his life, he would be guilty of having committed suicide.

The fact that it allegedly emanated from Egypt is important, because this was a situation developing in Palestine, but Egypt became the site of religious authority on the acceptability of hunger striking. This was for two key reasons: the first was the weight that Al Azhar University carries in relation to the production of scholarly works, but the second was due to Egypt's role as one of the strongest partners in the global War on Terror. The *fatwa* itself thus becomes a site of contestation – a place where the war is produced and continued. They also had their own prison population to contend with – a population that had asserted their right to hunger strike. As evidenced in Chapter 7 on hunger strikes, every effort was extended to try and convince those on hunger strike that what they were doing was *haram* – even as officers and interrogators were willing to contravene Islam in manifold ways.

The spectre of Azhari authority that has permitted great violence against protesters and political prisoners looms large in Egypt's post-coup world. The role played by Ali Gomaa, the Grand Mufti of the institution at that time, is crucial to the religious cover that was needed for the army to kill protesters, and for the carceral state to disappear thousands into its secret system of incommunicado detention. As David H. Warren wrote of Gomaa's religious discourse on the protesters, that by protesting they 'were killing people figuratively (*ma'nawiyyan*), but God would judge them as though they had actually killed people'.[9]

The narrative of Ali Gomaa at the time of Rabaa, however, would not exist in that moment alone, but rather the repercussions of it would be felt throughout the carceral experience, as young Egyptian men and women would be refracted through the lens of terrorism as a way of ensuring that their convictions and death sentences could be secured. The nine men that were sentenced to death in 2019 by the Chief Judge Hassan Farid and through the ratification of the Grand Mufti Shawki Allam, only reinforced the need of the carceral and national security state to rely on a religious discourse to obtain legitimacy for its unlawful actions. The political and religious swim alongside one another – they operate in tandem to enforce the ultimate form of legitimacy for the repressive acts of the state. This duality produces a form of liberal state *takfir* where the prisoner is not only seen as seditious to the state, but pronounced religiously seditious and heretical – only furthering the notion that the state is deified as the ultimate moral force – and to critique it, is to be both religiously and spiritually blasphemous.

The latest permutation of Ali Gomaa's legacy since Rabaa, is through his student and adviser to El-Sisi – Dr Usama Al-Azhari – who was responsible in helping to develop Correction and Rehabilitation centres,[10] very much in the mould of countering-violent extremism operations across the world. In a promotional video for the new centres, Al-Azhari's narrative focuses on changing the mindsets of those who are imprisoned, in particular focusing on the aspect of violence. The video pastiche rings as somewhat ironic, considering the extent of state-sanctioned violence for which he has provided cover.[11] The video also introduces religious figures from the Coptic Church hierarchy, who serve a similar function to the Islamic scholars – placing the sanctity of the state above all else.

In January 2023, Usama Al-Azhari travelled with a group of scholars and Muslim figures on a joint delegation to East Turkestan, while being hosted by the Chinese authorities. They were given a guided tour through the Uyghur regions in a manicured display to show that the Chinese government was not repressing the Uyghur, but rather there was an issue of terrorism and extremism that needed to be addressed. Al-Azhari's public statements came out in favour of the Chinese government, stating that terrorism was an international problem,[12] without questioning the version of the Uyghur experience they had been given. Such state-sponsored visits serve little purpose except to give cover to their own countries that they have analysed an issue, and that their populations should not be concerned over the extent of human rights abuses taking place. As individual and sporadic acts of rioting or violence are considered to be the ultimate evil in the worldview constructed by Al Azhari and others, the settler-colonial violence of the Chinese government in East Turkestan warrants little concern. There is a cyclical argument that is used in order to maintain the status quo of each country – so their collective rights records cannot be undermined due to the overwhelming concern for national security.

There is a pretence that must be maintained by the carceral state, that is, the fictions of its own making. Basma Abdel Aziz captures this perfectly by making the killing of protesters in her novel an act that was erased from public history – thus no one could have been hurt at all during the Disgraceful Event, because no one could have been shot, even if someone had a bullet lodged in their body from security forces firing at them. When Amani – one of the protagonists of the novel – attempts to save her lover from the fate of being killed slowly by a bullet lodged in his body, she is categorically informed by the chief medical security officer, that such a thing is not possible, because 'No one was injured by any bullet that day or the day after or on any other day, do you understand?' Amani still doesn't understand the need for the state to protect this narrative, and when she threatens to go public with the proof, she is interned into the state's secret system of incommunicado detention.[13]

Amani is disappeared into what Abdel Aziz describes as *nothingness* – a void of any sensory deprivation that harms her sense of self so fundamentally, that she cannot do anything other than to call on her own oppressors to save her: 'But everything remained as it was: nothingness.'[14]

The Queue's dystopian vision of solitary confinement is less dystopian, as much as it is a soupçon of the everyday nightmare that plagues solitary confinement across the world – but particularly in the US. Uzair Paracha's time in the solitary confinement cells of the US's Supermax facilities gave him a direct understanding of how dehumanising is the entire edifice of detention: 'About one in ten guards treated us like normal human beings. About one in ten hated us with a passion and harassed us at every opportunity. One of the respectful ones explained the harassment as the others wanting a piece of the action in the war on terror.'[15] Harsher treatment was reserved for the period of pre-trial detention – largely to try and coerce a prisoner into taking a plea deal, due to the daily oppressive conditions serving as a warning against risking a lifetime in the Supermax. As the carceral state par excellence, the United States of America has created a system of warehousing prisoners in giant behemoth structures that have been built in rural areas – so they remain out of view.[16]

Following the militarised and carceral technologies of the global War on Terror, Egypt has followed other Middle Eastern countries such as Saudi Arabia and the United Arab Emirates by building large modern Supermax prison facilities. Since the coup in 2013, Abdel Fattah el-Sisi has constructed 28 new modern prisons, some of which have come to replace the traditional prisons such as the large Tora complex that were used to house political prisoners. Situated northeast of Cairo, the Badr Correctional and Rehabilitation Center has come to replace structures that housed political prisoners in the past, in particular Badr 3. These prisons are dark holes that have been constructed with high levels of surveillance and automation, removing any ability to have meaningful human contact, even between prisoners.[17]

The old Tora complex on the other hand, which had been previously built on a cemetery, has now been turned into high-end apartments for the uber-wealthy of Egyptian society. There are layers of haunting that occupy the land, as the *jinn* that used to occupy the cemetery were disturbed by the construction of the prison, only for that very land to be doubly-haunted by the screams and cries of the prisoners tortured throughout the complex. Erasure of these old prisons only serves one real purpose in the end, which is to eviscerate the memory of violence of the state by destroying the very site of the crime. What does it mean for prisoners in Egypt when the prisons they were tortured in are destroyed, and yet the reality of incarceration remains real every single day of their lives? They live with the knowledge that these carceral states are national security states which are ultimately states of impunity.

Throughout this book, we have sought to provide a snapshot of the confessional lives of Muslim prisoners as they seek to engage with what their faith means within the context of incarceration for political crimes. There is no one clear pathway that they follow, but one thing that does stand out is the extent to which they attempt to find meaning in both their individual relationships with God, and through the maintenance of ritual practice – even if it means to pray within their hearts so their outward practice could not be seen.

There is so much that we would have liked to have written about, particularly in relation to the lives of prisoners once they are released. There is often an assumption that the most difficult part of the detention experience is being inside prison, but freedom brings its own challenges, both materially and spiritually – even some of the most intense crises of faith coming once freedom has been obtained. We want to leave the last words to ensure that readers do not stop thinking about the harm Muslim political prisoners experience in the global War on Terror as a phenomenon that is limited to their period of detention, but rather as a continuity that can last decades after their release. As they sought to make community within prison walls, we too must create new forms of community for them so that they are cocooned from the trauma of release.

Glossary

adhan – the call to prayer
adkhar – remembrances of Allah
adhkar al-sabah – morning litanies
ahsan al-qassas – the best of narrations (Qur'an 12:3)
akhira – the afterlife
amn al-dawla – state security
anasheed – devotional songs
arkaan – the necessary
asbab – fulfilments of Allah's intent
awrah – nakedness, i.e., parts of the body that are not permitted to
  be exposed to others
Ayyub – job
baladiyya – municipal council
ayah – verse in the Qur'an
dalil – proof from the *Sunnah*
din – faith, religion
dhuhr – midday prayer
dhikr – remembrance of Allah and supplications
du'a – supplication to Allah
dunya – the world
fajr – pre-sunrise prayer
fakir – poor person
faraj – relief from hardship
fard – religious obligation
fatiha – the first chapter of the Qur'an – meaning 'opening'
fatwa – Islamic legal opinion; plural *fatawa*
fiqhi – jurisprudential
ghusl – the ritual washing of the whole body, as prescribed by
  Islamic law to be performed in preparation for prayer and
  worship, and after sexual activity, childbirth, menstruation, etc.
gina'i inmates – those incarcerated for criminal offences
hadith – Prophetic tradition

haqq – truth

haram – prohibited according to Islamic law

huffadh – lit., the protectors; those who have memorised the Qur'an

Ibrahim – Abraham

iftar – breaking of the fast, during Ramadan

ijaza – authorisation to transmit knowledge

ijtihadat – making legal decisions by independent interpretation of the scriptural sources

isbaal – recommendation for Muslim men to keep their garments above their ankles

i'tikaf – devotional seclusion

jama'ah – congregational prayer

jihad – struggle

jinn – ethereal being made of smokeless fire imperceptible to the sight of humans

kaamyaab – skilled

khalwa – spiritual solitude

khutba – sermon

lutf – benevolence

madhhab – jurisprudential school

maghrib – post-sunset prayer

mahram – a person with whom marriage is prohibited because of their close blood relationship, because of *radaa'ah* (breastfeeding) by the same mother, or because of being related by marriage

miskeen – a person in an unfortunate circumstance

muhsin – one who has constant awareness of Allah

mu'min – one who believes

muqeem – inhabiting

Musa – Moses

musafir – a traveller

mus'haf – the physical copy of the Qur'an

muslim – one who submits

qada wa qadr – fate and predestination

qibla – direction of prayer towards Mecca

qirat – recitation of the Qur'an

qiyaam, ruku', sujud, and *tashahhud* – stages of prayer – standing, bending, prostrating, sitting

quwwa – power

rahma, maghifra and *afw* – mercy, forgiveness and pardoning (Qur'an 2:286)
rakat – a single unit of prayer
rukhsa – leniency
ruqya – spiritual healing
sadaqah – charity
sabr – forbearance, patience
sahih sitta – the six collections of Prophetic traditions considered to be the most authentic
sahir – a practitioner of black magic
sajjadah – prayer rug
salat – prayer
salat al-gha'ib – absentee funeral prayer
salat al-khawf – prayer during a period of fear
salat-ul-jama'ah – congregational prayer
sarf and *nahu* – forms of Arabic grammar
shafi'i – the Shafi'i jurisprudential school of thought
shahadah – witnessing, in the context of witnessing and ultimately a declaration of faith in one God (Allah) and His messenger, including martyrdom
shari'ah – the corpus of Islamic law and belief
sihr – black magic
Subhan Allah – glory be to Allah
suhoor – pre-*fajr* meal before beginning the fast *suhur*
sujud – prostration
sunnah – the Prophetic tradition
sutra – a barrier for the imam, designating the physical prayer space
ta'dib – disciplining
tafsir – exegesis of the Qur'an
taghriba – a form of punishment where prisoners are relocated to far away and remote prisons
tajwid – science of Qur'anic recitation
takbir – proclaiming Allah is greater than anything
takfiri – a Muslim who claims other Muslims have disassociated themselves from Islam
tarawih – evening prayers during Ramadan, completed alone and in congregation

tashahhud – lit., testimony [of faith]; supplication while sitting in prayer, of Allah's One-ness and the finality of the Prophet Muhammad

tasbih – prayer beads

tashrifa – the 'welcoming party' – the beatings, torture and sexual humiliation prisoners habitually encounter when they are first detained

tawwakkul – reliance on Allah

tayamum – ritual purification with dust, when water is not accessible

thabaat – steadfastness

ummah – the global community of Muslims

usul al-fiqh – the principles of Islamic jurisprudence

wallahi – an oath translated as 'by Allah'

witr – the final unit of supererogatory prayer for the night

wudu – ritual purification before prayer

yaqeen – certainty

Yunus – Jonah

Yusuf – Joseph

zakat al-fitr – the obligatory tax to be paid or distributed before the Eid prayer after Ramadan ends

zaman – time

Notes

INTRODUCTION

1. Adamson, P. & Benevich, F. (2018) The Thought Experimental Method: Avicenna's Flying Man Argument, *Journal of the American Philosophical Association* 4(2), pp. 148–149.
2. Ibid.
3. ElGendy, A. (2020) *Depersonalization-derealization disorder*, Mada Masr.
4. Herman, J. (1997) *Trauma and Recovery: The Aftermath of Violence – From Domestic Abuse to Political Terror*, Basic Books, p. 1.
5. Ibid., p. 47.
6. Ibid., p. 93.
7. Oestergaard, K. (2009) The Process of Becoming Muslim: Ritualisation and Embodiment, *Journal of Ritual Studies* 23(1), p. 3.
8. Ibid., p. 5.
9. Ellis, R. (2023) *In This Place Called Prison: Women's Religious Life in the Shadow of Punishment*, University of California Press, p. 82.
10. Herman, *Trauma and Recovery*, p. 1.
11. Ibid., p. 3.
12. Ibid., p. 79.
13. Ralston, J. (2017) Bearing Witness: Reframing Christian–Muslim Encounter in Light of the Refugee Crisis, *Theology Today* 74(1), p. 31.
14. Ibid., p. 34.
15. Bush, G. W. (20 September 2001) President Bush Addresses the Nation, *Washington Post*.
16. See Al Arian, L., Al Arian, S. and Qureshi, A. (2021) *The Terror Trap: The Impact of the War on Terror on Muslim Communities Since 9/11*, American Educational Trust.
17. Aziz, S. (2022) *The Racial Muslim: When Racism Quashes Religious Freedom*, University of California Press, p. 123.
18. Chan-Malik, S. (2018) *Being Muslim: A Cultural History of Women of Color in American Islam*, New York University Press, p. 22.
19. Ibid., p. 92.

20. Abozaid, A. (2022) *Counterterrorism Strategies in Egypt: Permanent Exceptions in the War on Terror*, Routledge, p. 24.
21. Ibid., p. 8.
22. Ibid., p. 44.
23. Ibid.
24. Ibid., p. 52.
25. Ibid.
26. Youssef, A. (2017) *The Uprising Will Not Be Filmed: Cinematic Representations of the 1977 Bread Riots*, Mada Masr.
27. Abozaid, *Counterterrorism Strategies in Egypt*, p. 56.
28. Ibid., p. 9.
29. Chick, K. (24 July 2013) Egyptian Army Chief Calls for Help to Fight 'Terrorism' of the Muslim Brotherhood, *Christian Science Monitor*.
30. Yee, V. (8 August 2022) 'A Slow Death': Egypt's Political Prisoners Recount Horrific Conditions, *The New York Times*.
31. Fisher, M. (5 February 2013) A Staggering Map of the 54 Countries that Reportedly Participated in the CIA's Rendition Program, *The Washington Post*.
32. Qureshi, A. (2007) *Beyond The Law – The War on Terror's Secret Network of Detention*, CAGE.
33. Ibid.
34. Qureshi, A. (2009) *Rules of the Game: Detention, Deportation, Disappearance*, Hurst, p. 3.
35. Ibid., p. 138.
36. Ibid., p. 27.
37. Ibid., p. 143.
38. Ibid., p. 11.
39. Li. D. (2020) *The Universal Enemy: Jihad, Empire and the Challenge of Solidarity*, Stanford University Press, p. 457.
40. Ibid., p. 460.
41. Ibid., p. 464.
42. Qureshi, *Rules of the Game*, p. 110.
43. Ibid.
44. Ellis, *In This Place Called Prison*, p. 8.
45. Felber, G. (2020) *Those Who Don't Know Say*, University of North Carolina Press, p. 56.
46. Spearlt (2021) 9/11 Impacts on Muslims in Prison, *Michigan Journal of Race and Law* 27(1), p. 238.
47. Ibid.
48. Ibid., p. 239.

49. Rodriguez, I. (8 April 2022) 'Outrageous Outcomes': Please Bargaining and the Justice System, The Crime Report. https://thecrimereport.org/2022/04/08/outrageous-outcomes-plea-bargaining-and-the-justice-system/
50. Human Rights Watch (11 March 2022) *After Israel's Designation of Human Rights Groups as 'Terrorists,' Biden Should Release Palestinian-Americans Imprisoned Over Similar Claims*, Joint Statement by US and International Civil and Human Rights Organizations and Individuals.
51. Stahl, A. (2011) *Too Blunt for Just Outcomes: Why the US Terrorism Enhancement Sentencing Guidelines are Unfair, Unconstitutional and Ineffective in the Fight Against Terrorism*, CAGE.

1 CUSTODY

1. Adayfi, M. (2021) *Don't Forget Us Here*, Hachette Books, p. 4.
2. Musharraf, P. (2006) *In the Line of Fire*, Simon & Schuster, blurb.
3. Alhaj, S. (5 May 2018) Prisoner 345 – My 2330 Days in Guantánamo, *Al Jazeera*, p. 37.
4. Adayfi, *Don't Forget Us Here*, p. 4.
5. The Millennium Bomb plot was a series of alleged attacks that were to be carried out across the world on 1 January 2000, for an Algerian man named Ahmed Ressam was charged and convicted.
6. Slahi, M. O. (2015) *Guantánamo Diary*, Canongate, p. 12.
7. Ibid., p. 12.
8. Ibid., p. 218.
9. Ibid., p. 286.
10. CAGE (25 April 2018) Torture in America: 121 Summaries of Interrogation in compliance with Judge Mihm's order, Unclassified Documents – DOJ/CTS U/FOUO SUM08 – 0008. www.cage.ngo.
11. Ali al-Marri, Segregated Housing Unit Pass Down Log Record, 23 June 2003–1 August 2004, notation, 5 February 2004 – documents leaked to CAGE.

2 THE PRAYERS OF PRISONERS

1. Alhaj, S. (5 May 2018) Prisoner 345 – My 2330 Days in Guantánamo, *Al Jazeera*, p. 62.
2. Errachidi, A. (2013) *The General*, Chatto & Windus, p. 57.
3. Ibid., pp. 58–59.
4. Alhaj, *Prisoner 345*, pp. 48–50.

5. Adayfi, M. (2021) *Don't Forget Us Here*, Hachette Books, p. 67.

6. In this book, the terms 'political prisoner' and 'prisoner incarcerated for criminal offenses' do not seek to replicate, nor does it accept state narratives on criminality. At the outset, these categorizations are enforced constructs fraught with complexities and contradictions. It is often classed as working-class individuals who would face criminal charges for actions like resisting police coercion, for example, refusing to work as informants. At its heart, a political act would carry criminal charges. Sex crime charges – often politically motivated – could also be classified as criminal charges. Moreover, individuals who might not be actively involved in politics may be charged with 'joining a terrorist organization,' which is ostensibly a political charge if they were arrested in the vicinity of a protest (even if they were bystanders).

   This highlights the arbitrary nature of these distinctions, as the larger framework of incarceration is inherently political. Despite these complexities, the distinction serves a functional purpose within the context of the Egyptian security apparatus. The book adopts the same classification: 'gina'i detainees' are those primarily engaged with by regular police forces, while 'political detainees' encounter the National Security Agency. This differentiation extends to their treatment and housing in prison, often with distinct wards and management approaches for each group. Thus, the term 'prisoners incarcerated for criminal offenses' is used not as a label defining their identity, but as a reflection of the state's perception and handling of these individuals.

7. *Fiqh* is the term used for Islamic jurisprudential rules.

8. Begg, M. (2006) *Enemy Combatant*, Simon & Schuster, p. 19.

9. Zaeef, A. S. (2015) *Ambassador POW*, CAGE, p. 66.

10. Boumediene, L., and Ait Idir, M. (2017) *Witnesses of the Unseen*, Redwood Press, p. 87.

11. Adayfi, *Don't Forget Us Here*, pp. 23–24.

12. Slahi, M. O. (2015) *Guantánamo Diary*, Canongate, p. 235.

13. Ahsan, H. (2015) *Exposing Supermax Prisons: What Talha Ahsan and Babar Ahmad Endured*, CAGE.

3   THE UMMAH OF PRISONERS

1. Begg, M. (2006) *Enemy Combatant*, Simon & Schuster, p. 131.

2. Ibid., p. 133.

3. Zaeef, A. S. (2015) *Ambassador POW*, CAGE, p. 68.

4. Errachidi, A. (2013) *The General*, Chatto & Windus, p. 87.
5. Adayfi, M. (2021) *Don't Forget Us Here*, Hachette Books, p. 37.
6. Kurnaz, M. (2007) *Five Years of My Life*, Palgrave Macmillan, p. 152.
7. Zaeef, *Ambassador POW*, p. 91.
8. Shaykh Rabee' al-Madkhali is an Islamic scholar based in Saudi Arabia whose theological positions within the Salafi system of belief is closely associated to his name – Madkhalism. Its feature is a political obedience to ruling elites, regardless if they are systemically oppressive.
9. The Persian story of tragic lovers that dates back as far as the ninth century.

4   BELIEF, CRISIS AND THE QUR'AN

1. Alhaj, S. (5 May 2018) Prisoner 345: My 2330 Days in Guantánamo, *Al Jazeera*, p. 10.
2. Ibid., p. 7.
3. Ibid., p. 62.
4. Ibid., p. 62.
5. Slahi, M. O. (2015) *Guantánamo Diary*, Canongate, p. 147.
6. Zaeef, A. S. (2015) *Ambassador POW*, CAGE, p. 56.
7. Ibid., p. 65.
8. Alhaj, Prisoner 345, pp. 88–89.
9. Qureshi, A. (2009) *Rules of the Game: Detention, Deportation, Disappearance*, Hurst, pp. 93–94.
10. Errachidi, A. (2013) *The General*, Chatto & Windus, p. 91.

5   ETHEREAL BELIEFS

1. Begg, M. (2006) *Enemy Combatant*, Simon & Schuster, pp. xv–xvi.
2. Bukhari, 6499: Muhammad al-Bukhari was the ninth-century Islamic scholar notable known for his compilation and categorisation of Prophetic traditions in *Sahih al-Bukhari*.
3. The *Great Book of Interpretation of Dreams* (Arabic: تفسير الكبير الأحلام, *Tafsir al-Ahlam al-Kabir*) attributed to the seventh-century Muslim scholar Ibn Sirin which was originally compiled in the fifteenth century by al-Dārī under the title *Selection of Statements on the Exegesis of Dreams*.
4. Al-Kandari, F. (2022) *Surviving Jinns & Black Magic in Guantánamo Bay*, Crescent Feed, YouTube. www.youtube.com/watch?v=_AVHeoVgOyo
5. Errachidi, A (2013) *The General*, Chatto & Windus, p. 118.

6. Adayfi, M. (2021) *Don't Forget Us Here*, Hachette Books, pp. 116–117.

6 TORTURE

1. Kurnaz, M. (2007) *Five Years of My Life*, Palgrave Macmillan, p. 56.
2. Begg, M. (2006) *Enemy Combatant*, Simon & Schuster, p. 112.
3. Boumediene, L., and Ait Idir, M. (2017) *Witnesses of the Unseen*, Redwood Press, p. 160.
4. Ibid., pp. 141–142.
5. Federal Bureau of Prisons (2004) *Religious Beliefs and Practices*, Program Statement 5360.09.
6. Slahi, M. O. (2015) *Guantánamo Diary*, Canongate, p. 27.
7. Boumediene and Ait Idir, *Witnesses of the Unseen*, pp. 97–98.
8. Slahi, *Guantánamo Diary*, pp. 225–226.
9. Ibid., p. 231.
10. Dodds, P. (27 January 2005) Gitmo Soldier Details Sexual Tactics, *Salon*. www.salon.com/2005/01/27/gitmo_7/
11. JTF GTMO SERE SOP (2002) *Guidelines for Employing "SERE" Techniques During [sic] Detainee Interrogations*. https://humanrights. ucdavis.edu/projects/the-Guantánamo-testimonials-project/ testimonies/testimonies-of-standard-operating-procedures/ jtf-gtmo-sere-interrogation-standard-operating-procedure
12. These are predominantly second-hand testimonies from human rights organisations.
13. *Al Jazeera Mubashir* (17 June 2017), *Ihalat awraq 31 mutahman li-mufti fi qadiyyat ightiyal al-na'ib al-'am* (Referring to court documents of 31 defendants to the Mufti in the assassination case of the Attorney General).
14. *BBC News* (20 February 2019), Egypt executes nine over 2015 killing of public prosecutor. www.bbc.co.uk/news/world-middle-east-47308541
15. Most of the accounts in this chapter come from the Freedom Initiative 2022 report on sexual violence in Egyptian prisons: *'No one is safe': Sexual Violence Throughout the Life Cycle of Detention in Egypt 2015–2022*, The Freedom Initiative. https://thefreedomi.org/reports/ no-one-is-safe-2/
16. Human Rights Watch (23 March 2020), No One Cared He Was A Child: Egyptian Security Forces' Abuse of Children in Detention. www.hrw.org/report/2020/03/23/no-one-cared-he-was-child/ egyptian-security-forces-abuse-children-detention

17. Radwan, A. (23 January 2007), Egypt's Torture Video Sparks Outrage, *Time Magazine*. https://content.time.com/time/world/article/0,8599,1581608,00.html
18. *Middle East Observer* (27 April 2021), Heinous Sexual Assault of Detainee 'al-Shuwaikh' in Egyptian Prison. www.middleeastobserver.org/2021/04/27/heinous-sexual-assault-of-detainee-al-shuwaikh-in-egyptian-prison/
19. Freedom Initiative, 'No one is safe'.
20. Berger, C. (20 February 2014), Egyptian Detainee Handcuffed to Bed After Having Baby is Released, *The Guardian*. www.theguardian.com/world/2014/feb/20/egyptian-detainee-handcuffed-bed-childbirth-released

7 FAITH AND RESISTANCE

1. Kurnaz, M. (2007) *Five Years of My Life*, Palgrave Macmillan, p. 192.
2. Errachidi, A. (2013) *The General*, Chatto & Windus, p. 130.
3. Ibid., p. 130.
4. Ibid., p. 131.
5. ElGendy, A. (11 February 2022) The Power of a Smile in Prison: How One of Sisi's Prisoners Maintained His Dignity While Jailed, *New Lines Magazine*. https://newlinesmag.com/first-person/the-power-of-a-smile-in-prison/
6. Adayfi, M. (2021) *Don't Forget Us Here*, Hachette Books, pp. 38–39.
7. Ibid., p. 40.
8. Ibid., p. 238.
9. Kurnaz, *Five Years of My Life*, p. 153.
10. Alhaj, S. (5 May 2018) Prisoner 345 – My 2330 Days in Guantánamo, *Al Jazeera*, p. 140.
11. Ibid., pp. 143–145.
12. Human Rights Watch (28 September 2016), 'We are in Tombs': Abuses in Egypt's Scorpion Prison. www.hrw.org/report/2016/09/29/we-are-tombs/abuses-egypts-scorpion-prison

CONCLUSION: RELIGION AND THE DEIFICATION OF THE NATIONAL SECURITY STATE

1. Abdel Aziz, B. (2013) *The Queue*, Melville House, Apple Books e-pub, p. 6.

2. JTF GMO SERE SOP (2002) *Guidelines for Employing 'SERE' Techniques During [sic] Detainee Interrogations.* https://human rights.ucdavis.edu/projects/the-Guantánamo-testimonials-project/testimonies/testimonies-of-standard-operating-procedures/jtf-gtmo-sere-interrogation-standard-operating-procedure
3. Abdel Aziz, *The Queue*, p. 30.
4. Ibid., p. 34.
5. Ibid., p. 50.
6. Mahmood, S. (2006) Secularism, Hermeneutics, and Empire: The Politics of Islamic Reformation, *Public Culture* 18(2), pp. 326–327.
7. Ibid., p. 66.
8. Adayfi, M. (2021) *Don't Forget Us Here*, Hachette Books, p. 40.
9. Warren, D. H. (2017) Cleansing the Nation of the 'Dogs of Hell', *International Journal of Middle East Studies* 49(2017), pp. 457–477.
10. Alsafhatu Alrasmiatu liwizarat Aldakhiliat [The official page of the Ministry of Interior], *Tanzima ihtfalyh lilaalana an badi altashghili altjrybi liadada 3 marakiza aislahi wtahyl jadidahu* [Organizing a celebration to announce the commencement of the trial operation of three new rehabilitation and reform centres]. www.facebook.com/watch/?v=167046279543516
11. Ibid.
12. Xin, L., and Lingzhi, F. (9 January 2023) Islamic Scholars from 14 Countries Visit Xinjiang Region, *Global Times*. www.globaltimes.cn/page/202301/1283507.shtml
13. Abdel Aziz, *The Queue*, p. 56.
14. Ibid.
15. Casella, J. et al. (2016) *Hell is a Very Small Place*, The New Press, p. 48.
16. Alexander, M. (2012) *The New Jim Crow*, The New Press, p. 195.
17. Middle East Eye (1 March 2023) Egypt: Why Inmates are Dying in Sisi's New 'Model' Prison. www.middleeasteye.net/news/egypt-why-inmates-dying-model-prison-badr

References

Abdel Aziz, B. (2013) *The Queue*, Melville House, Apple Books e-pub.

Abozaid, A. (2022) *Counterterrorism Strategies in Egypt: Permanent Exceptions in the War on Terror*, Routledge.

Adamson, P., & Benevich, F. (2018) The Thought Experimental Method: Avicenna's Flying Man Argument, *Journal of the American Philosophical Association* 4(2).

Adayfi, M. (2021) *Don't Forget Us Here*, Hachette Books.

Ahsan, H. (2015) *Exposing Supermax Prisons: What Talha Ahsan and Babar Ahmad Endured*, CAGE.

Al Arian, L., Al Arian, S., and Qureshi, A. (2021) *The Terror Trap: The Impact of the War on Terror on Muslim Communities Since 9/11*, American Educational Trust.

Alexander, M. (2012) *The New Jim Crow*, The New Press.

Alhaj, S. (5 May 2018) Prisoner 345 – My 2330 Days in Guantánamo, *Al Jazeera*.

Al Jazeera Mubashir (17 June 2017) *Ihalat awra 31 mutahman li-mufti fi qadiyyat ightiyal al-na'ib al-'am* (Referring to court documents of 31 defendants to the Mufti in the case assassination of the Attorney General).

Al-Kandari, F. (2022) *Surviving Jinns & Black Magic in Guantánamo Bay*, Crescent Feed, YouTube. www.youtube.com/watch?v=_AVHeoVgOyo

Aziz, S. (2022) *The Racial Muslim: When Racism Quashes Religious Freedom*, University of California Press.

BBC News (20 February 2019) Egypt Executes Nine Over 2015 Killing of Public Prosecutor. www.bbc.co.uk/news/world-middle-east-47308541

Begg, M. (2006) *Enemy Combatant*, Simon & Schuster.

Berger, C. (20 February 2014) Egyptian Detainee Handcuffed to Bed After Having Baby is Released, *The Guardian*. www.theguardian.com/world/2014/feb/20/egyptian-detainee-handcuffed-bed-childbirth-released

Boumediene, L., & Ait Idir, M. (2017) *Witnesses of the Unseen*, Redwood Press.

Bush, G. W. (20 September 2001) President Bush Addresses the Nation, *The Washington Post*.

CAGE (25 April 2018) Torture in America: 121 Summaries of Interrogation in compliance with Judge Mihm's order, Unclassified Documents. www.cage.ngo

Casella, J. et al. (2016) *Hell is a Very Small Place*, The New Press.

Chan-Malik, S. (2018) *Being Muslim: A Cultural History of Women of Color in American Islam*, New York University Press.

Chick, K. (24 July 2013) Egyptian Army Chief Calls for Help to Fight 'Terrorism' of the Muslim Brotherhood, *Christian Science Monitor*.

Dodds, P. (27 January 2005) Gitmo Soldier Details Sexual Tactics, *Salon*. www.salon.com/2005/01/27/gitmo_7/

ElGendy, A. (2020) *Depersonalization-derealization Disorder*, Mada Masr.

ElGendy, A. (11 February 2022) The Power of a Smile in Prison: How One of Sisi's Prisoners Maintained His Dignity While Jailed, *New Lines Magazine*. https://newlinesmag.com/first-person/the-power-of-a-smile-in-prison/

Ellis, R. (2023) *In This Place Called Prison: Women's Religious Life in the Shadow of Punishment*, University of California Press.

Errachidi, A. (2013) *The General*, Chatto & Windus.

Federal Bureau of Prisons (2004) *Religious Beliefs and Practices*, Program Statement 5360.09.

Felber, G. (2020) *Those Who Don't Know Say*, University of North Carolina Press.

Fisher, M. (5 February 2013) A Staggering Map of the 54 Countries That Reportedly Participated in the CIA's Rendition Program, *The Washington Post*. www.washingtonpost.com/news/worldviews/wp/2013/02/05/a-staggering-map-of-the-54-countries-that-reportedly-participated-in-the-cias-rendition-program/

Herman, J. (1997) *Trauma and Recovery: The Aftermath of Violence – From Domestic Abuse to Political Terror*, Basic Books.

Human Rights Watch (28 September 2016), 'We are in Tombs': Abuses in Egypt's Scorpion Prison. www.hrw.org/report/2016/09/29/we-are-tombs/abuses-egypts-scorpion-prison

Human Rights Watch (23 March 2020) No One Cared He Was A Child: Egyptian Security Forces' Abuse of Children in Detention. www.hrw.org/report/2020/03/23/no-one-cared-he-was-child/egyptian-security-forces-abuse-children-detention

Human Rights Watch (11 March 2022) *After Israel's Designation of Human Rights Groups as "Terrorists," Biden Should Release Palestinian-Americans Imprisoned Over Similar Claims*, Joint Statement by US and International Civil and Human Rights Organizations and Individuals.

JTF GTMO SERE SOP (2002) *Guidelines for Employing 'SERE' Techniques During [sic] Detainee Interrogations.* https://humanrights. ucdavis.edu/projects/the-Guantánamo-testimonials-project/ testimonies/testimonies-of-standard-operating-procedures/jtf-gtmo-sere-interrogation-standard-operating-procedure

Kurnaz, M. (2007) *Five Years of My Life*, Palgrave Macmillan.

Li, D. (2020) *The Universal Enemy: Jihad, Empire and the Challenge of Solidarity*, Stanford University Press.

Mahmood, S. (2006) Secularism, Hermeneutics, and Empire: The Politics of Islamic Reformation, *Public Culture* 18(2), pp. 326–327.

Middle East Eye (1 March 2023) Egypt: Why Inmates are Dying in Sisi's New 'Model' Prison. www.middleeasteye.net/news/egypt-why-inmates-dying-model-prison-badr

Middle East Observer (27 April 2021) Heinous Sexual Assault of Detainee 'al-Shuwaikh' in Egyptian Prison. www.middleeastobserver.org/ 2021/04/27/heinous-sexual-assault-of-detainee-al-shuwaikh-in-egyptian-prison/

Musharraf, P. (2006) *In the Line of Fire*, Simon & Schuster.

Oestergaard, K. (2009) The Process of Becoming Muslim: Ritualisation and Embodiment, *Journal of Ritual Studies* 23(1).

Qureshi, A. (2007) *Beyond The Law – The War on Terror's Secret Network of Detention*, CAGE.

Qureshi, A. (2009) *Rules of the Game: Detention, Deportation, Disappearance*, Hurst.

Radwan, A. (23 January 2007) Egypt's Torture Video Sparks Outrage, *Time Magazine*. https://content.time.com/time/world/article/0,8599,15 81608,00.html

Ralston, J. (2017) Bearing Witness: Reframing Christian–Muslim Encounter in Light of the Refugee Crisis, *Theology Today* 74(1).

Rodriguez, I. (8 April 2022) 'Outrageous Outcomes': Plea Bargaining and the Justice System, *The Crime Report*. https://thecrimereport. org/2022/04/08/outrageous-outcomes-plea-bargaining-and-the-justice-system/

Slahi, M. O. (2015) *Guantánamo Diary*, Canongate.

SpearIt (2021) 9/11 Impacts on Muslims in Prison, *Michigan Journal of Race and Law* 27(1).

Stahl, A. (2011) *Too Blunt for Just Outcomes: Why the US Terrorism Enhancement Sentencing Guidelines are Unfair, Unconstitutional and Ineffective in the Fight Against Terrorism*, CAGE.

The Freedom Initiative (2022) 'No one is safe': Sexual Violence Throughout the Life Cycle of Detention in Egypt 2015–2022. https://thefreedomi. org/reports/no-one-is-safe-2/

Warren, D. H. (2017) Cleansing the Nation of the 'Dogs of Hell', International Journal of Middle East Studies 49(2017), pp. 457–477.

Xin, L., and Lingzhi, F. (9 January 2023) Islamic Scholars from 14 Countries Visit Xinjiang Region, Global Times. www.globaltimes.cn/ page/202301/1283507.shtml

Yee, V. (8 August 2022) 'A Slow Death': Egypt's Political Prisoners Recount Horrific Conditions, The New York Times. www.nytimes. com/2022/08/08/world/middleeast/egypts-prisons-conditions.html

Youssef, A. (2017) The Uprising Will Not Be Filmed: Cinematic Representations of the 1977 Bread Riots, Mada Masr.

Zaeef, A. S. (2015) Ambassador POW, CAGE.

Index

Patai, Raphael *The Arab Mind* 159
plea deals 17, 25, 103–5
political prisoners 4, 75–7, 171
prayer 3–4, 24, 54–7, 65–6, 77, 80,
    95–6
    communal prayer 53–4, 62–3,
    157–8
    Friday prayers 63–5
prison chaplains 5, 16, 179, 185, 207
prison officers 16, 96–7, 115
    omnipotence of 163, 203
    see also Muslim prison officers;
    women prison officers
prison-industrial complex (USA)
    205
prisoners *see* criminal prisoners;
    Muslim prisoners; political
    prisoners; student prisoners;
    women prisoners
prisons
    British prisons 87–9
    execution wards in 148
    Islamophobia in 157–8
    strip searching in 162, 163
    transitory cells in 61, 77–8
    see also specific prisons, e.g.
    Bagram; Guantánamo Bay;
    carceral system
prophets 60

Qal'a Prison 72
Qala-i-Jangi Prison 120
Qanater El Khayereya Women's
    Prison 77, 79, 148
Qatar National Bank 33
Qur'an 6, 117–30
    desecration of 68–9, 119
    Sahih Bukhari corpus 91, 94
    Surah al-Ahzab 130
    Surah al-Baqarah 79, 143
    Surah al-Duha 126
    Surah al-Nisa' 8

Surah Ash-shu'ara 124
Surah al-Rahman 122
Surah Maryam 112–3, 149
Surah Yusuf 41, 117, 121, 124,
    126–9
Qur'anists 81

Ra'fat, Shaykh 140
Rabaa Massacre (2013) 12, 26–7,
    109–11, 200
Ralston, Joshua 8–9
Ramadan 84–5, 88–90, 98–9
Rawan (prisoner) 172
Reagan, Ronald 205
Regeni, Giulio 29
religion: role of 4–5, 202, 205–6,
    208–9
rendition 12–13, 52
ruqya (spiritual healing) 150–1

Saar, Sergeant Erik R. 161
Sadat, Anwar 11–12, 24, 150
Sami (prison officer) 181
Samia (prisoner) 170
Saudi Arabia 211
Scorpion Prison 147, 191–2
Segregated Housing Units 34
Sign al-Nisa (soap opera) 99
Slahi, Mohamedou Ould 31–2,
    102, 159, 160
slave trade 18, 162
solitary confinement 17, 60–2, 70
Soltan, Mohamed 37, 61, 76–7,
    96–7, 115–6, 125–6, 136–7,
    150, 192–6, 198
    relations with father 91–3
Soltan, Salah 150
SpearIt 17
Special Administrative Measures
    (SAMs) 34
Standard Operating Procedures
    (SOPs) 35, 162, 203

Thanks to our Patreon subscriber:

Ciaran Kane

Who has shown generosity and
comradeship in support of our publishing.

The Pluto Press Newsletter

Hello friend of Pluto!

Want to stay on top of the best radical books
we publish?

Then sign up to be the first to hear about our
new books, as well as special events,
podcasts and videos.

You'll also get 50% off your first order with us
when you sign up.

Come and join us!

Go to bit.ly/PlutoNewsletter